THE MAN WHO
WALKED BACKWARD

ALSO BY BEN MONTGOMERY:

Grandma Gatewood's Walk
The Leper Spy

THE MAN WHO
WALKED
BACKWARD

AN AMERICAN DREAMER'S
SEARCH FOR MEANING
IN THE GREAT DEPRESSION

BEN MONTGOMERY

Little, Brown Spark
New York Boston London

Little, Brown Spark
Hachette Book Group
1290 Avenue of the Americas, New York, NY 10104
littlebrownspark.com

First Edition: September 2018

Little Brown Spark is an imprint of Little, Brown and Company, a division of Hachette Book Group, Inc. The Little, Brown Spark name and logo are trademarks of Hachette Book Group, Inc.

The publisher is not responsible for websites (or their content) that are not owned by the publisher.

The Hachette Speakers Bureau provides a wide range of authors for speaking events. To find out more, go to hachettespeakersbureau.com or call (866) 376-6591.

ISBN 978-0-316-43806-3
Library of Congress Control Number: 2018948994

10 9 8 7 6 5 4 3 2 1

LSC-C

Printed in the United States of America

For John Burruss

Never mind how far he got.
What it is, is the tilt of the hat.
—Dodie Messer Meeks

CONTENTS

CONTENTS

Dear reader,

Plennie Wingo died in poverty in the fall of 1993. He was buried in Wichita Falls, Texas, about 180 miles from my hometown of Slick, Oklahoma. I first heard of him in 2013 while researching unconventional pedestrians. A few years later, when I could not forget him, I decided to try to write a book. The first thing I did was buy a Clason's Touring Atlas, circa 1931, one of the first ever made, so I could follow in his footsteps to see what he might've seen, and to see how we've changed. One note about change: to avoid littering the text with calculations, I've left it to you, dear reader, to put dollar amounts into familiar context. So, $1 in 1931 is equal to roughly $16 in 2018; $5 then is $80 now; $10 is $160; and so on.

I've tried my best to tell his story true. Nothing in this book is fabricated by me, including the dialogue. If it's in quotes, it comes from a historic document or Plennie Wingo's own humble account of his trip. I've tried to tell the story of that dark period true, as well. For that reason, and because we are occasionally mean to one another, you should be aware that this book depicts quite a bit of violence.

Thank you for reading,
Ben

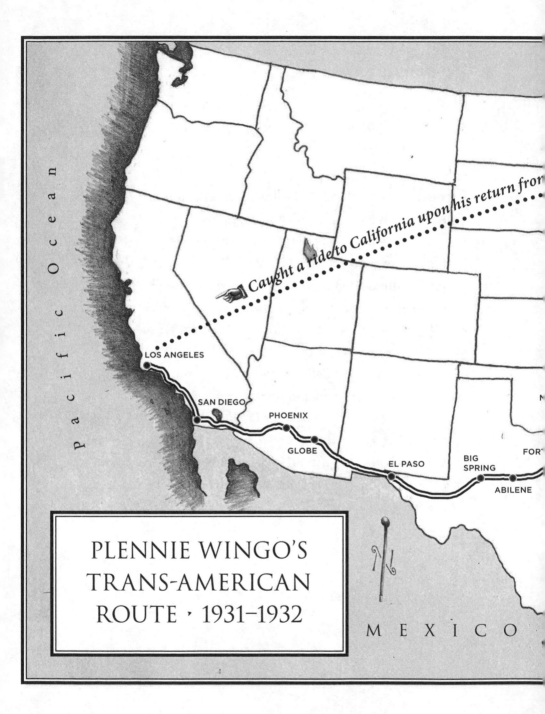

Caught a ride to California upon his return fron

LOS ANGELES

SAN DIEGO

PHOENIX

GLOBE

EL PASO

BIG
SPRING

ABILENE

FOR

Pacific Ocean

MEXICO

PLENNIE WINGO'S
TRANS-AMERICAN
ROUTE · 1931–1932

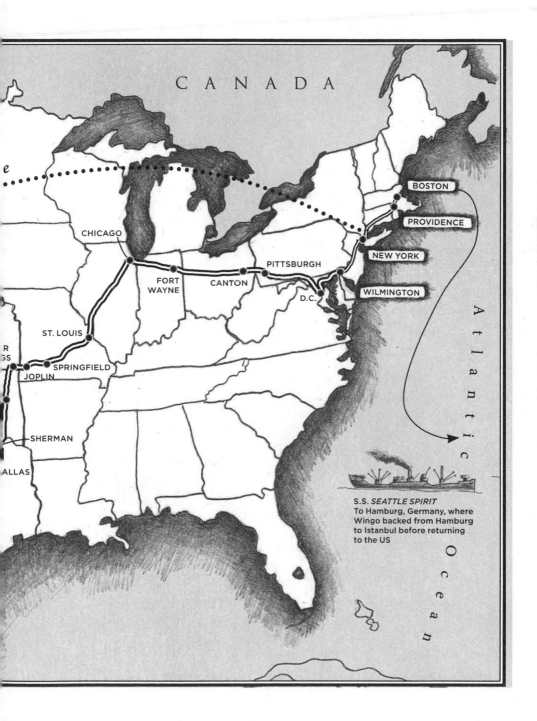

CANADA

CHICAGO

FORT WAYNE

CANTON

PITTSBURGH

D.C.

ST. LOUIS

SPRINGFIELD

JOPLIN

SHERMAN

ALLAS

BOSTON

PROVIDENCE

NEW YORK

WILMINGTON

Atlantic Ocean

S.S. *SEATTLE SPIRIT*
To Hamburg, Germany, where
Wingo backed from Hamburg
to Istanbul before returning
to the US

THE MAN WHO
WALKED BACKWARD

1.

THOSE GOLDEN DAYS

Sunrise, West Texas.

Time of morning when the dead black gives up to the first throws of yellowpink in the east, out beyond Fort Worth and Dallas, past Shreveport and Jackson and Montgomery and Savannah. A man here in Abilene walks this morning, like every morning, down a bone-dry farm-to-market road outside town. He is out before the sun because he walks backward, that is to say, he walks in reverse, and he chooses this time so he may behave in this odd fashion cloaked in darkness lest his neighbors see and cast judgment upon him, make him for crazy. His own mind is fairly certain on the point, but he'll admit there is room for doubt.

He is not a brilliant man. Some would say he does not even encroach on smart. But inside his balding head he has a bold idea, and sometimes when a certain kind of man has a certain kind of idea, one that he considers good, that good idea takes hold of him and it swells up behind his eyeballs and expands, balloonlike, so big that it crowds out all the other thoughts and ideas, and it becomes the one thing he thinks about, the only thing. Such is the case with Plennie Lawrence Wingo, who is nearly penniless but full of ambition just shy of his thirty-sixth birthday and a hair short of what would be one of the worst years in American history.

The idea has become an obsession, though he's not ready to admit that just yet. He thinks of it when he wakes in the morning and it follows him all day long, and when he closes his eyes at night he is wrapped completely in the blanket of his vision.

The idea is why he walks. It is why he walks backward.

Five miles some mornings. Ten, others. Hours alone in the last gasp of night, scooting retrograde across the long shadows drawn on the dawning landscape, the place they called the Great American Desert, *Llano Estacado*, past the roadside tufts of buffalo grass and thickets of honey mesquite, the reaching lechuguilla rods and smoke bush and angry explosions of butterfly weed. Backward across the land from which they pulled oil until that went bust; the land upon which, before the oil, they raised cattle until that too went bust; the land from which, before the oil and the cattle, they harvested buffalo bones, full skulls and skeletons that once gave shape to the great roaming beasts of the Plains, the givers of tools and food and warmth for the natives, and, after them, fertilizer for the white men in sweat-stained cowboy hats who stacked their bones like cordwood, building white hills head-high and as far as you could see. The bones brought twelve to fifteen dollars a ton to any man resourceful enough to pile them high, and they were plentiful in Abilene, the epicenter of this macabre market for three hundred miles in most directions. They took the bones, then the beasts, then the oil beneath, and then it was all gone. What was next for the taking was anyone's guess. What else was left?

Now the town near which he walks holds abundant life, or at least enough to advertise to the outside world. The rising sun in the east outlines its elegant business structures and its beautiful, commodious homes, its apartment houses with up-to-date Frigidaire refrigeration, its magnificent public buildings and institutions like the Abilene State Hospital for Epileptics and Simmons College, its model school buildings, three now, its federal post office and courthouse, its compress, its oil mill, its electric light plant, its ice factory, its impressive fairgrounds, its artificial lake, its parks, its paved boulevards, its railways, and, pitched against the weak sunlight, its Paramount Theatre, built this very year, 1930, its grandeur unrivaled between El Paso and Fort Worth. To think that so much had sprung forth from nothing but dry Texas dirt in just fifty years.

That same dry dirt chalks his teeth and cakes his forehead, and his garments show signs of a man who has put in a full day's work by the time most are beginning to wipe sleep from their eyes, drag on their trousers, and start the percolator. He thinks about them, how they'd whisper if they ever caught sight of him out here, all alone and going backward. How they'd wonder what he was up to, what kind of crazy had gotten hold of him. They would, of course, ask him, *Why?* Over and over again, *Why are you doing this?* Even now, he is formulating his response.

He has not known a full day's work in some time. They'd talk about that, too, for sure. How his lot had soured. How they'd read about his troubles with the police in the paper. Another reason he is here, backpedaling in the dawn.

He hoped they'd remember the good times and his good name. He'd experienced high days, sure, when his future seemed full of promise. He was a man of business for a time, resourceful, straight as a preacher on Sunday.

His professional life in Abilene began six years before, in February 1924, at age twenty-nine, when he struck a lease deal with C. Hall for the north half of the lower story of the Morgan Jones building at 127 Chestnut Street, in Abilene's busiest district, for a monthly payment of $65, and opened a restaurant soon after. He was P. L. Wingo, owner of the Crescent Café. Those golden days.

Then, in March of '27, looking for a bigger slice, he signed a lease with C. C. Tate, renting the basement beneath Tate's Dry Goods store on Lots 1, 2, 3, 4, 5, and 6, at the corner of Chestnut and South First Streets for a sum of $30 a month on the promise that Mr. Tate would build a staircase from the basement to the first floor so customers could use the water closet. He was then P. L. Wingo, owner of the Mobley Café and Dining Room. Glorious days.

He swept floors and bused tables and counted dollar bills. He served meat-and-threes to tenant farmers and ham and eggs to country lawyers and fried squash to the ladies from the Baptist church. The city directory called him proprietor and the humble newspaper advertisements he ran beckoned the hungry, the conservative, the children. *There is no better way to make mother happy than to take her to a nice lunch room for a Sunday dinner.*

Things were good for Plennie Wingo. Things were good for most everybody.

In the blink of the last few breakneck years of that roaring decade, something incredible happened. Something happened that had never happened before and would never be repeated. Books would be written, scores of them, about the era of vision and optimism and boundless hope.

Who knows exactly where it started, but if you back up a bit, you can see the boom taking shape. Archduke Franz Ferdinand fell in 1914. Germany sank the British liner *Lusitania* in 1915. Ten million American men walked to their local polling stations in the summer of 1917 to register for the war Woodrow Wilson had finally decided to enter. Fifteen days later, Newton D. Baker, Wilson's secretary of war, stuck his hand into a goldfish bowl containing 10,500 numbers and drew out a black capsule marked No. 258, drafting into service one man from each precinct across a country that was not at all ready for the First World War.

If this was the sowing of the seeds of hope, maybe its roots took hold in one of those foreign foxholes filled by one of those 24 million American doughboys along the Paris-Metz highway or in Murmansk or Romonofska. Or maybe it was back home, where the women planted victory gardens in public parks and went to work in huge numbers for the first time on assembly lines in factories, building trucks and munitions for shipment overseas. Maybe its first shoots emerged from the soil after 17 million soldiers and civilians had been killed abroad, when the American men came home—some disengaged and disenfranchised, all having passed the first big test of loyalty in a young multicultural nation—to a newfangled communal exaltation conjured by a government trying to dampen nationalism abroad and fuel it at home: the patriotic parade.

They marched stone-eyed down American boulevards and heard tell they were heroes. Some of them believed it.

Whatever the building blocks of the prosperity to come, when Warren Harding was elected president in November 1920 by the smallest turnout of voters in American history, he did something that set the tone for the next decade in a country weary of war and scares and moral rebukes. He gathered his clubs and balls and played a round of golf.

"America's present need," the former small-town newspaperman said, "is not heroics, but healing; not nostrums, but normalcy; not revolution, but restoration; not agitation, but adjustment; not surgery, but serenity; not the dramatic, but the dispassionate; not experiment, but equipoise; not submergence in internationality, but sustainment in triumphant nationality."

What followed was optimism, and mass production, and the mass production of optimism. The city skylines rose and invention burst and productivity soared. Henry Ford turned out a new car every ten seconds and the nation's first network of dealers rose up to sell them, followed quickly by a vast web of paved roads, traffic lights, hot dog stands, repair shops, and filling stations, allowing the weekend adventurer to drive the countryside confident that he wouldn't wind up spending the night stuck in a rut or searching for a spark plug. Almost as quickly rose a nationwide network of antennae and broadcasting stations and hookups to pipe the phenomenon called radio into homes across America. Advertisers immediately lined up to introduce a Happiness Boys song with a quick pitch about insurance or greeting cards, a controversial new offense on family circles called a "commercial."

If you looked at a graph that mapped economic ebbs and flows of the decade, you'd see a jagged but lofty incline starting in 1923 and growing yearly toward a glorious mountain of prosperity. The United States was on its way to manufacturing 43 percent of the entire world's products, and the advertisements in the new glossy national magazines like *TIME* made a man want one of everything.

A pretied bow tie, a pair of fringe-tongued Mayflowa brogues, and a Jordan roadster in the garage. "Somewhere west of Laramie, there's a bronco-busting, steer-roping girl who knows what I'm talking about," smooth-talked the *Vanity Fair* ad for the latter. "She can tell what a sassy pony, that's a cross between greased lightning and the place where it hits, can do with eleven hundred pounds of steel when he's going high, wide and handsome. The truth is, the Playboy was built for her. Built for the lass whose face is brown with the sun when the day is done of revel romp and race. She loves the cross of the wild and the tame...."

And Campbell's, by God! Campbell's was making twenty-one different kinds of canned soup. Not just tomato and beef and pea soup—you could get ox tail soup, turtle soup, mutton soup. Some Plennie Wingo couldn't even pronounce. *Julienne? Printanier? Consommé?*

By 1925, American capitalism churned like a hungry machine. The number of manufacturing facilities in the United States had skyrocketed and the worth of that output sprang up. In just five years, industrial production had nearly doubled. Bellwether radio sales, which accounted for $60 million in American spending in 1922, grew 1,400 percent.

"No Congress of the United States ever assembled...has met with a more pleasing prospect than that which appears at the present time," said President Calvin Coolidge, who had taken over from Harding and whose name would become synonymous with "prosperity," in his last message on the State of the Union to Congress in 1928. "In the domestic field there is tranquility and contentment...and the highest record of years of prosperity."

This wasn't a speculative splurge like in 1637, when Dutch venturers saw wealth in tulip bulbs, or 1720, when Parisians lost their shirts hoping to find gold in Louisiana. It wasn't the real estate bubble of 1814 or untamed speculation in canal investment in 1830 or the railroad boom of 1873. The economy was buoyant, profits endless.

"The main source of these unexampled blessings," the president said, "lies in the integrity and character of the American people."

Business earnings soared. Big corporations ate smaller ones whole. The market gave birth to powerful companies like United States Steel Corporation, International Harvester, and American Tobacco, and gave rise to a wealth of utilities, food retailers, variety stores, motion picture theaters, and chain retail stores like Montgomery Ward, American Stores, and Woolworth, companies built to last.

And men dumped their money into investments and reaped the profits hand over fist. They threw money at the stock market, as much as they could scrape together, and became proud shareholders in companies that were great and some that were phony. They flocked south, with income and access never before available, and bought subdivided land in Florida, sight unseen, both waterfront properties with golden views and worthless mosquito-filled tracts of muck and detritus, and called it all paradise. Then they sold it for a profit. These new playboys and sun worshipers didn't need to be coaxed to buy in. They needed an excuse. And even the swamp had value.

Never before had so many become so stupendously, so pain-lessly, so expeditiously rich.

They were happy. They were credulous.

And there stood Plennie Wingo, whose father died when he was a baby, whose mother married his uncle and bore ten more children, who learned to read and write and saved his money and opened a shop to cash in on the swirling American adventure. He was a self-made man at a time when the business of America was business, as the president said. The businessman, someone else said, was the dictator of destiny, ousting the statesman, the priest, the philosopher. *The Man Nobody Knows*, which cast Jesus of Nazareth as "the world's greatest business executive" and the parable of the prodigal son as the world's greatest advertisement, topped the best seller list, and the optimistic autosuggestion that "Day by day, in every way, I am getting better and better" was on the lips of men everywhere. It was an age of improvement, and Plen-nie was riding shotgun, all angular youth and bootstraps. He had a house in the city and a wife who loved him and a young daugh-ter to whom he could one day leave his fortune. He leaned in the doorway of his café before the crowds trickled in, one hand in his pocket, a smile on his face, his necktie tight, shirt starched stiff, and his spit-shined wing tips planted firm on the productive earth of a country oozing with promise.

That was then. Now he scoots in reverse. The sun creeps up and the shadows shrink as he wipes sweat from his face and picks up his pace. If he could walk backward through time itself, he would. He should've seen the signs. He should've known the men were coming for him, because they came for everybody.

They came on March 17, 1928, first to the dusty town of Pecos, 240 miles west. Fourteen strong-jawed lawmen and two federal prohibition officers seized 610 gallons of mash and whiskey and a 300-gallon still, then captured four ruffians on a ranch just over the New Mexico line and threw them in the Reeves County Jail, charged with supplying the whole damn West with strong drink.

They came again on April 7, 1928. Squinty-eyed border patrol officers down south in desolate Del Rio confiscated 628 quarts of tequila and cognac in one of the largest liquor hauls anyone could remember.

They came to the region time and again that year, doling out enough liquor charges to fill entire columns in the morning newspapers. They popped George Stringer of Abilene for transportation. Arrested Bud Moore of Abilene for possession. Collared Fred Mc-Casland of Abilene for both.

The pace of takedowns was the talk of Abilene, and folks wondered if the harassment was simply the last gasp of the teetotaling arbiters of amusement. They wondered, after nearly a decade of Prohibition, after seeing the illegal booze market boom almost unchecked, whether anyone of import would have the political will to keep up the charade. By 1928 the issue at last found its way into a presidential campaign. New York governor Al Smith, running for the Democrats, didn't like the ban and had big ideas to change it. Herbert Hoover was considered a dry, though he left room for interpretation, calling Prohibition "a great social and economic experiment, noble in motive and far-reaching in purpose," which "must be worked out constructively."

The American people, for their part, abstained or kept good secrets, or read in the local newspaper about those who couldn't do either. In Texas, substantially more than half of all cases brought to court in 1928 revolved around booze: the making, the selling, the carrying, or the drinking.

So ubiquitous was intoxicating liquor and so close behind was the legal trouble in February 1928 that T. H. Millhorn was charged with possession, sale, and transportation. Millhorn was operator of the Southland Hotel, at 917 South First Street. And if a ten-year-old girl stood in front of Plennie Wingo's café, she could throw a bottle of Waterfill and Frazier and hit the Southland Hotel.

He should've seen them coming.

The disappointment was fresh in his mind two years later, and when he closed his eyes he could still feel the click of the handcuffs around his wrists, the shame of his escort to the Taylor County lockup, the sting of the headline in the *Abilene Morning Times*.

Liquor Cases Are Pending Against P.L. Wingo Here

Restaurateur P.L. Wingo, 33, was bound over Tuesday afternoon to await the action of the grand jury on a liquor complaint in which he is charged with selling and possessing intoxicating liquor.

Thus he became one of the 55,729 liquor cases brought to court in the United States that year. The grand jury was cold, and the bond $750, more than two years' rent on the café. It was terrible. Terrible, but not impossible to overcome. A black eye, but not a knockout for a man obliged to do better and better. With enough sweat and traffic, he'd be back in the black in six months, a year tops. People had money to spend and Plennie was ready to trade them for fried chicken.

In early March 1928, the market surged up and stayed there. The tight-lipped Federal Reserve Board met daily in Washington, fifteen hundred miles from Plennie Wingo's limping café in Abilene, and no one knew exactly why. By the end of the month the tension was un-bearable and people began to sell their stock. Favorites like Wright Aero and American Railway Express were dropped like they were hot. Things got worse as a wave of panic swept the market. Folks sold in astonishing volume and prices plummeted.

But the market steadied, then rose, then rose some more, as

though the quick drops had shaken out those who lacked the will to play it for eternity. Up it went, and smart observers noted that there had been a mighty revolution in industry, trade, and finance, and that the stock market was but an indicator of those tremendous changes in progress. People took to calling it a Big Bull Market. Herbert Hoover latched the Republican ticket to the wagon and rode it into the White House, crushing Al Smith in both the popular vote and the Electoral College. And in accepting the presidency, he reflected what many must have felt in their souls in those heady, lofty, optimistic days.

"One of the oldest and perhaps noblest of human aspirations has been the abolition of poverty," he said. "We in America today are nearer to the final triumph over poverty than ever before in the history of any land."

Plennie Wingo was listening.

"The poorhouse," Hoover said, "is vanishing from among us. We have not yet reached the goal, but, given a chance to go forward with the policies of the last eight years, poverty will be banished from this nation."

The audacity. The pomp. The language. It was all absolutely perfect for the moment. It was also very, very wrong. So wrong that Hoover—a Horatio Alger–esque multimillionaire who would later be summoned to service by more presidents than any other American chief executive, who was awarded more honorary degrees than any other American, whose relief efforts are said to have saved more human lives than those of any other individual in all of human history—would be defined by and remembered for how wrong he was.

And what comes next sets the stage for our story.

By the time Hoover was having the very first telephone installed in the Oval Office, the financial system had become so entangled and convoluted, the securities-absorbing investment trusts and branch offices of Wall Street trading firms so numerous, the ticker so over-worked, that few had any real idea what was actually happening. But the massive majority did not care. They expected whatever was going on to keep on going on, and someday they would cash in that American Can stock and think themselves wise. The skies would be full of airplanes, the roads full of shiny new cars, and poverty would be a forgotten social ill of a bygone era.

Then, in early September, the market broke. The drop was short-lived, and by midmonth averages were back up. Then it slipped harder, and by early October most watchers knew something was wrong, though they weren't sure what. They remained optimistic, outwardly at least. The pointy-heads at the Harvard Economic Society said that "despite its severity, we believe that the slump in stock prices will prove an intermediate movement and not the precursor of a business depression." Iron output was slower. Steel production was off. Fewer cars were selling and fewer were coming off the line. Home building was down. Freight-car loadings fell. Nonetheless, "the conditions which result in serious business depressions are not present," said the head of the Cleveland Trust Company. "Unless we are to have a panic—which no one seriously believes—stocks have hit bottom," said the director of McNeel's Financial Service. "The industrial situation in the United States," said the chairman of the National City Bank of New York, "is absolutely sound and our credit situation is in no way critical."

What came next was monumentally bewildering and frightening to anyone paying attention. What came next, on the morning of Thursday, October 24, 1929, was liquidation. Prices dropped. Dropped fast. Dropped hard. Dropped vertically. Dropped with an unprecedented and riveting violence. Dropped so mercilessly that outside the stock exchange, a roar rose into the morning air as a crowd gathered on Broad Street. As the New York City police arrived, a workman appeared atop a building to do some repairs. The hysterical crowd had made him for a suicide and was encouraging him to jump.

The hysteria bled into the next week.

Stocks were selling for nothing. Weren't selling. Rumors spread like wildfire. A suicide wave started, and eleven well-known speculators killed themselves. Two men with a joint account jumped hand in hand out a window in the Ritz. An investment firm ran an ad in the *Wall Street Journal* that read: "S-T-E-A-D-Y Everybody! Calm thinking is in order." Police fished the body of a commission merchant out of the Hudson River—his pockets contained $9.40 and some margin calls. Desk clerks in New York hotels, it was said, were asking guests if they would be using the room for sleeping or jumping.

The market fell and fell until the news at last, slowly but surely, reached the rest of the puzzled nation around the time the market finally stopped its monthlong slide in the middle of November.

In Abilene, there were no runs on banks in those early days. They were paving a new stretch of Highway 30 and playing host to a conference of Methodists, and the Majestic was showing *The Saturday Night Kid*, a talkie starring Clara Bow, James Hall, and Jean Arthur. But Plennie Wingo read the bleak and foreboding reports.

Midwestern livestock was selling slow in Kansas City, with the chief influence cited as a "sluggish, depressing beef trade." Fort Worth livestock wasn't even selling. Cotton was down. Grain was haunted by reports that Europe was overloaded with breadstuff supplies, and the Chicago wheat market suffered material setbacks in prices, which "bumped into a stone wall," as a reporter put it.

The seams had come apart.

In the first three months of 1930, as scientists settled on naming a newly discovered planet after the Roman god of the underworld and judge of the dead, the stock market looked as though it were making a recovery. But in April it lost momentum, and it dropped hard again in June, and continued to drop, week after week and month after month.

Before, the fundamentals were simple. A man needed to eat in order to work and he worked in order to eat. But the house of cards had collapsed for reasons Plennie could not fully understand, and on October 29, 1929—the worst day of all, the newspapers said—some 16 million shares of stock changed hands and the *New York Times* industrial average plunged almost forty points. What Plennie *could* understand was what he could see, that work was drying up in West Texas, and with it, the essential sustenance on which a profitable café is run: a man with money enough to afford a meal in a restaurant. Business was down. Way down.

Plennie tried advertising for $2.50 in the *Abilene Daily Reporter*, and for less in the student newspapers at Abilene Christian College and McMurry College. But traffic slowed and bills came due and he held on as long as he could. He scaled back by laying off employees, the hardest thing he'd ever had to do. Their names flitted through his mind like flies through the holes in a screen door. Anderson Webb, helper; Marcellus Hughes, helper; Frank Lawson (wife Parthenia), dishwasher; Plummer McKinney, waiter; Margaret Neighbors, waitress; Calvin Smith (wife Lula), cook; Hugh Knight, waiter; Grover Howe (wife Marie), cook; Davis Nordyke (wife Pearla), cook; Rollie O. Cloud (wife Myrtle, and daughter Ruth), waiter.

And finally, when the bank came to take the café for good: Plennie Lawrence Wingo, proprietor.

But he is unlike them in one way: he has a plan. His toes are pointed west in the new light as he reverses down First Street and rounds the bend onto Chestnut. If at first it was difficult to manage a mile or two backward without tiring, he can now finish ten without difficulty. He feels now, after months of training, as though he has been walking backward his entire life. He turns around as he nears his house, the sun higher now, the birds awake, the 'poorwills and wrens and flycatchers. He walks normal now, facing forward, up the sidewalk toward a home he stands to lose if nothing is done to make money, a home where his loyal wife and loving daughter are sleeping, a home where the plan first struck him like a rattlesnake, seized him cold, and began to swell in his mind, his singular hope against hope: to gain fame and fortune by walking backward around the great world.

2.

DOING SOMETHING

In early 1931 it wasn't like you could step outside and see the Depression hanging in the air like fog on an April morning. But maybe you could hear it, if you were in the right place at the right time. You could hear your neighbor joking about the farmer who broke his back trying to lift twenty-five cents' worth of wheat. You could hear the governor-elect of Texas saying that the "Depression clouds had all but blacked out the sun of optimism." You could hear it standing in England, Arkansas, when five hundred farmers stormed the business district, demanding food and threatening to take it, until a hurried call was placed to the Red Cross. You could hear one of the farmers, crying and halfheartedly waving a pickaxe, saying, "We are not going to let our children starve." You could hear it in Oklahoma City, as a mob of a thousand jobless men and women coalesced and marched on City Hall, looting stores on the way, until police dispersed the crowd with tear gas and fire hoses and arrested twenty-six people. The whole damn country was rioting: Los Angeles, San Francisco, Amarillo, Austin. You could hear it riding in a train car from town to town, dodging the bulls, listening to the stories of honest men who yearned for work of any kind; some two million were now living as nomads, crisscrossing the country, looking for any employment.

On certain days in certain places, you could hear the gunshots or see the bodies falling, as each bank failure led to more unemployment and less credit and less cash.

They would later say it was a myth, an urban legend, that men offed themselves after the market crashed. And maybe they'd be right: the official mortality numbers show no immediate uptick in suicides. But the evidence of a macabre trend piled up in the papers. Alongside articles about plummeting wages for those blue-collar workers lucky enough to have kept their jobs, and the eight million unemployed Americans desperate for a paycheck, they told of Lee A. Gamble, thirty-five, of 950 Park Avenue, a graduate of Phillips Exeter who schooled in the Ivy League and fell or jumped from a window at the Yale Club, opposite Grand Central Station, at 4 p.m. on New Year's Eve, 1930. He'd bought his seat on the stock exchange just a year before, and when he landed nine stories below, witnesses were horrified. They told how in March 1930, Dr. Benjamin F. Battin, fifty-five, a former Swarthmore College professor and vice-president of the National Surety Company, used a rope to hang himself in his hotel room on Eighth Avenue, leaving a note that expressed fear he would soon lose his job. Bellboys found his body when he didn't answer calls. And on the same day in April 1931, John W. Marshall, vice-president of Safe Deposit & Trust Company, shot himself in Baltimore, and Frederick Holdsworth, a real estate agent, leaped from a bank building in Boston.

Closer to home, A. A. Glover, the mayor of San Angelo, Texas, eighty miles southeast of Abilene, leaped to his death from the sixth floor of a bank building downtown. He was a husband and father of two, Methodist, a Royal Arch Mason, founding member of the Kiwanis Club, and a member of the Knights of Pythias, like Plennie. He was also general manager of Martin Glover Wholesale Company, and friends said he had been worried the past few weeks about "reverses in finances." No one saw him jump, but they found his hat on the fire escape and his coat folded neatly on the windowsill.

On and on it went. Men handled the worst of the hard times in different ways.

On April 15, 1931, the sun skimming up on Fort Worth, Plennie Wingo pulled on his best pair of pinstripe pants, one leg at a time. He buttoned his white Oxford over his lean Texan frame, tied his best necktie snug, slipped into his shiny black Sunday shoes, and slid into a suit coat that matched his trousers. He finally pulled a white Stetson down on his ears, a good-guy hat for a guy trying.

If a man aimed to walk backward around the world, best to leave no doubt in the minds of passersby that he was doing so with purpose.

This mission was no lark.

Though his means of traverse was unusual, let there be no doubt that Plennie Lawrence Wingo was a businessman on a business trip. The letters he carried on his person—official letters, mind you, from half a dozen Texas dignitaries—spoke to his resolve and the serious nature of what might have been interpreted as an act of folly. He hoped they'd help grease his path through the bureaucracy of municipalities that might frown on a man engaged in such peculiar behavior at such a serious and trying time. He had received letters of introduction and character references from Mr. Carswell, president of the Abilene Chamber of Commerce; Mr. W. R. "Ruck" Sibley, chief of the Abilene Police Department; Dr. L. W. Hollis, who had received Plennie Wingo into the world thirty-six years before and testified truly that he had known the young man his entire life; and the Honorable Thomas E. Hayden Jr., mayor of Abilene, Texas.

Notably missing from the bundle of good tidings was a letter from William Bryce, mayor of Fort Worth. That was something of a sore spot for Plennie, who had sought out the mayor's endorsement the previous afternoon. He asked specifically if Mayor Bryce could address a letter to James John Walker, known to the world as Jimmy Walker, the flamboyant playboy mayor of New York City, currently on holiday in Palm Springs, California, while officially under investigation for allegations of misfeasance, incompetence, inefficiency, neglect of public duties, and bringing the city administration "into disrepute."

"I don't believe so," Mayor Bryce had told Plennie, seeming embarrassed.

Plennie had thanked him and exited City Hall with yet another name on the list of people who had backed out or were otherwise unwilling to fully support his bold idea. That list included his original publicity man, who had a car, his backup publicity man, who had an even better car, and, sadly, Plennie's wife, Idella, who had never really warmed to the idea of her husband leaving on a trip around the world while she scratched to survive the greatest economic depression the world had ever known, alone.

The defections solidified his determination. The naysayers were all now fuel for the fire that raged inside his belly.

He had let fly his frustration the day before during a meeting with officials at the Fort Worth Chamber of Commerce, whom he tried to convince to fund his trip in exchange for advertising Fort Worth to the whole wide world. He was certain clerks and secretaries could overhear his complaints, but he couldn't keep his disappointment inside any longer.

"I know times are bad and most everybody is grabbing at straws to survive, and so am I," he ranted to the Chamber, after his second publicity man reneged. "But I think my two defecting managers are just plain sissies and afraid to take a chance."

He didn't have much money to begin with, but he told the businessmen he was going to wire all he had to his wife and start his trip without a penny in his pocket, just to prove he could.

"And I promise I will not beg, borrow, or steal," he said. Barring sickness or accidents or objections, or maybe laws that would prohibit him from walking backward across certain states or countries, he was going to do it, or die trying.

THE MAN WHO WALKED BACKWARD

"I firmly believe I can complete the tour around the world on my own and alone," he said.

One of the men piped up.

"Mr. Wingo, I admire your spunk," he said. "I believe you will go far."

With that, Mr. Charles G. Cotten, manager of the Trade Extension Department for the Fort Worth Chamber of Commerce, penned a letter and handed it to Plennie.

To whom it may concern:

This will introduce Mr. Plennie L. Wingo of Abilene, Texas. Mr. Wingo begins a backward walking tour of the world from Fort Worth on Wednesday, April 15th. Upon his arrival at the various cities scheduled on his itinerary, he will report to the office of Western Union and it will be appreciated if you will be kind enough to indicate the time of arrival in your city and the time of departure with our thanks.

Mr. Wingo comes to us very highly recommended from Abilene, Texas, a nearby prosperous West Texas city. Just recently, Mr. Wingo conducted quite a great deal of backward walking stunts, lending publicity to the Southwestern Exposition and Fat Stock Show March 5th to 15th.

We certainly wish Mr. Wingo the very best of luck on his tour of the world walking as he will the entire distance facing the world backwards.

Any courtesy shown him will be appreciated and possibly serve to speed him on his way happily anticipating what he might face next, even though he would be getting a rear vision of the world.

Very truly yours,
Charles G. Cotten

It was tucked into the black notebook Plennie had bought from the variety store, along with a cheap ballpoint pen. He also carried a new Holy Bible, a gift from a street preacher named Paul Clifton from the Open Bible Mission whom he'd met the day before. Clifton had recognized Plennie from the newspapers and approached him on the street.

"My prayer will be with you all the way," he had said, and it had made Plennie wonder about things.

Now Plennie dragged his suitcase into the Greyhound bus station.

Now he showed Mr. Cotten's letter to the man behind the counter.

Now the man looked Plennie over, then studied the letter, then agreed to carry Plennie's luggage free of charge all the way to New York City, in the spirit of goodwill.

Plennie walked from the Greyhound station to the Western Union and showed his letter to the clerk, A. C. Farmer, who, upon reading the letter, stamped it in the bottom left-hand corner:

9:03 a.m., April 15th, 1931

"Which way are you going around the world?" Farmer asked.

"Going east," Plennie said. "You keep watching west and I'll be back."

His friends had clustered outside. So had some strangers wondering what the commotion was about. Plennie greeted them all, shook their hands, and thanked them. He turned to face the west, waved, took his first step backward, then tore out like a page from the Bible.

And so it began, a man walking east toward Dallas, down Main Street to Highway 1, on his way somewhere, doing something. He was backing smooth and easy now, like he had been born to go backward. He watched automobiles appear like ants at the end of a long, unspooled ribbon of highway, the land as flat as a table-top, and they grew larger as they drew closer, closer, closer...then zoomed by in a gust of dust. The dirt devils danced at his feet as he hugged the shoulder, as close to the edge of the road as possible, for 6,230 people had already been killed by automobiles in the first three months of 1931, an astonishing number of newfangled deaths. He nodded or waved or smiled as drivers and wives and backseated children bent their necks and puzzled over the odd man on the highway. And then they were gone as quickly as they came. He was tickled by the looks on their faces. It was him they were trying to see.

One hundred twenty-five million Americans on the planet, and only one walking around it backward.

* * *

Once he reached the country outside town, slipping out of the Grand Prairie, through the Eastern Cross Timbers, and into the Northern Blackland Prairie, Plennie had a chance to reflect on the chaotic whirlwind of events that had brought him to this shoulder of barren Texas highway. He would tell his own origin story hundreds of times in hundreds of places, to anyone who cared to listen, until it became something like a hymn. He would skip the part about going to jail.

He was born on his mother's twentieth birthday, January 24, 1895, the second son of John Newton Wingo and Willie Drucilla Warren Wingo, and his parents never would tell him or anybody else why they named their squirmy baby boy Plennie. John Newton's people came from Alabama to help settle East Texas in the mid-1800s, and that's where he was born, in Red River County. John fell ill in his early twenties and was killed by pneumonia five and a half months after Plennie was born. Willie, originally from Union City, Tennessee, buried her young husband under a handsome column in the municipal cemetery in Abilene and, soon after, married his younger brother, Thomas. She would bear him ten more children, one every two or three years for the next twenty years: Elias, Pearce, Lula Mae, Aubrey, Vera, Thomas, Bruce, Achel, Dee, and Lena.

Plennie was enterprising from the outset. When he was a boy he learned to catch rattlesnakes, plentiful in West Texas. He'd use a long stick with a forked end to pin the rattler's head down, then carefully grab the tail beneath the rattles and use the stick to guide the snake into an open burlap sack. They went for a few cents each, depending on the size, for meat or fashion, and the ones he caught weighed anywhere between two and six pounds. He sold them for spending money, and he was never afraid.

Plennie Wingo (back row, fifth from right) is pictured with his schoolmates in Tye, Texas, west of Abilene. (Courtesy of Pat Lefors Dawson)

He started waiting tables as a teenager, working for a man named Jim Thurmond in a café in Abilene when he wasn't in school. He was a decent student, but he always had a restless and entrepreneurial spirit. "Mama," he would tell his mother, "I want to go around this whole world."

Plennie Wingo (back row, center) with his family, sometime between 1911 and 1914. (Courtesy of Pat Lefors Dawson)

Plennie met and married Idella Richards, a hard-faced woman from Hays County, Texas, down around Austin, and she delivered their first and only child, Vivian, in 1915, when Plennie was twenty years old. In the early 1920s, a chunk of the Wingos—including Plennie, Idella, and Vivian—left the Caprock region in a wagon brigade and made their way back east to Clay County, near Wichita Falls and the Oklahoma line. Within a few months, Plennie and Idella opened a restaurant in nearby Dundee, which had been carved out of the T Fork Ranch and swelled in population after the Wichita Valley Railway Corporation ran a line through town and built a three-story hotel there as a stopping-point station. Besides the restaurant and hotel, the new town featured two livestock dealers, a clothier, a general store, a hardware store, and an organ shop. After a few years, the Wingos moved to the boomtown of Abilene, which saw its population grow 600 percent from 3,400 in 1900 to more than 23,000 in 1930.

Plennie Wingo with wife Della and daughter, Vivian, taken around 1919. (Courtesy of Pat Lefors Dawson)

Plennie's daughter, Vivian, was celebrating her fifteenth birthday with a party at their house when Plennie first bumped into his big idea. This was two and a half months after the stock market crashed, and Plennie had already begun to worry about his financial security. They'd had cake and opened gifts and Vivian and her friends were talking in the parlor, mostly about nonsense, like kids do. Plennie was reading the paper and minding his own business as they went on and on about how every physical feat had been accomplished...and wasn't it true?

If the boom years of the 1920s had illustrated anything, it was that the country could be shaken coast to coast by a trifle, and there seemed to be something new every day. There were fewer newspapers than ever before, and those had larger circulations than ever before, and now some 55 newspaper chains controlled some 230 daily papers with a combined circulation of more than 13 million. Overall newspaper readership had soared from 28 million to 36 million in a little more than a decade, 1920 to 1930. The papers were also relying more on syndicated wire services like the Associated Press and Newspaper Enterprise Association, so articles that might once have stayed local were now being read in papers across the country. On top of that, the sudden ubiquity of broadcast radio made it possible for more people to hear the same show at the same time. So the latest news felt made for the masses, and the United States had become a nation of fad-loving gossips, prone to being swept up on waves of excitement generated by whatever was new or odd or dramatic.

Little attention was given to issues of import that might have dominated the day, like political scandals or Prohibition or the rise of the Ku Klux Klan, lighting their crosses on the public squares. In the year 1919, after the Great War—which lasted 1,563 days, destroyed empires, killed some 10 million soldiers, and cost more than $300 billion—more than 4 million Americans participated in roughly three thousand strikes over labor, communism, socialism, and anarchy. But a mere two years later the Era of Wonderful Nonsense was in full swing, and with a chicken in every pot and a car in every garage, Americans had withdrawn into an orgy of self-indulgence.

Bring on the fickle.

This was the era in which a young man named Richard Simon, who was launching a publishing house with his friend Schuster, took a clue from a relative who was addicted to the crossword puzzles that had for years appeared in the Sunday *New York World*. Within a month of publication, Simon & Schuster's crossword puzzle book had become a best seller. It went on to sell hundreds of thousands of copies and started a puzzle craze that swept the nation. Women whose husbands devoured the puzzles referred to themselves as "crossword widows," and practically everyone knew the two-letter name of the Egyptian sun god.

The public's appetite for all things trivial could not be quenched. Americans wanted to read about the marriage of Hollywood starlet Gloria Swanson to the French aristocrat Marquis de la Falaise de la Coudray. They wanted the details of the Scopes Monkey Trial in Dayton, Tennessee, and the daily unfolding drama of Floyd Collins, a Kentucky explorer who got trapped in a cave and could only be reached by a small reporter for the *Louisville Courier-Journal*. They wanted Jack Dempsey and Red Grange and Babe Ruth and Paavo "Flying Finn" Nurmi. They wanted a cartoon panel of fascinating facts called *Ripley's Believe It or Not!*, which was at the peak of its popularity, syndicated internationally and read by some 80 million people.

They wanted to see men and women dancing marathons and swimming the English Channel and walking upon the wings of airplanes. They wanted to be the first, the strongest, the best, the fastest—or to at least read about those who were.

They read daily about William Williams, a Texan who embarked in 1929 on an odd physical challenge in Colorado that exemplifies the era. Zebulon Pike had first spotted Pikes Peak in 1806 while exploring land acquired by the United States in the Louisiana Purchase and concluded, after a failed attempt to summit, that "no human being could have ascended to its pinnacle." But fourteen years later, an explorer named Edwin James reached the top of the 14,115-foot mountain. Then in 1858, Julia Archibald Holmes became the first white woman to ascend to the pinnacle. In 1901, two men from Denver drove a steam-powered car to the top. Then came Williams at the end of the Incredible Era, a man of his time, pushing a peanut up the mountain with his nose. He blew through several pairs of shoes and gloves and more than a hundred peanuts, and he wore an advertisement for a Georgia peanut company. He finished in twenty-two days and offered the press a quote as odd as his stunt: "It doesn't require pull for one to get ahead in life—it just takes push."

The American people wanted entertainment. They wanted hullabaloo and ballyhoo.

And, oh, how they wanted Charles Lindbergh.

The handsome young pilot wasn't the first to cross the Atlantic by air, but he captured the country's attention like no one else had or, arguably, ever would again. After a New York hotel owner offered up a prize of $25,000 for the first nonstop flight from there to Paris, most everyone gave favorable odds to one of two well-known planes and crews: Clarence Chamberlin and Lloyd Bertaud flying the *Columbia*, or North Pole explorer Richard Byrd and crew flying the *America*. But Lindbergh, flying the *Spirit of St. Louis*, hopped off first and alone on the morning of May 20, 1927, and the entire country fixed its hopes and common exaltation on the pilot.

Soon after being mobbed by Frenchmen upon arrival at Le Bourget aviation field, "Lucky Lindy" was bigger than life. It helped that he was modest and charmingly thankful and eschewed the offers to appear in movies or to charge for his autograph. ACCLAIMED BY WORLD AS GREATEST HERO IN HISTORY OF AVIATION, read the headlines in several Texas newspapers, which devoted hundreds of column inches to the airman.

A navy ship dispatched by President Coolidge fetched the ace and his plane and delivered him to a country in need of a man to save it from its media diet of novelty and guilty pleasures. The street cleaners in New York swept up 1,800 tons of scraps of paper that had been thrown out of windows onto Lindbergh's parade through the streets. He received the Distinguished Flying Cross and Congressional Medal of Honor. He heard Coolidge deliver a presidential speech as long as his State of the Union address to Congress. Towns, schools, and streets wanted to share the distinction of his name. His reception, historians would note, took on the aspects of a vast religious revival.

Plennie Wingo had witnessed such a scene himself when Lindbergh came to West Texas in September of 1927, just four months after his epic flight.

Oh, the excitement. The Hilton Hotel hosted the Lindbergh Hop featuring the Bob Dean orchestra. Downtown businesses competed for prize money by decorating Lindbergh-themed window displays, with model airplanes suspended over construction-paper Atlantic Oceans and replica Eiffel Towers and Statues of Liberty. The event was so big that the *Abilene Morning Reporter-News* published its largest ever paper at 102 pages, heralding "Lindbergh Day" with a special section devoted to the colonel, and bragged that the paper used to print it, unspooled, would stretch all the way to San Antonio, 250 miles away. It was a chance for ambitious Abilene to put itself on the map, and the effort included verbatim testimonials from dozens of citizens about why their parched West Texas town was the greatest in America, and a feature story boasting of the city's modern infrastructure, like gas, electric, paving, and a sewer system.

The Lindbergh welcome committee alone included seventy-one regional mayors, ninety-five newspaper editors, twenty-eight chamber of commerce officials, and seventy-three of the most beautiful young ladies in West Texas, called "The Spirits." Reporters estimated that all 30,000 Abilene residents, plus 40,000 out-of-towners, turned out to watch the dapper barnstormer ride in a seventy-four-car parade from the airfield to downtown Abilene. Seated next to Lindbergh in an open-topped sedan was the First Lady of Texas, an Abilene girl whose father ran Citizens Bank in town. The National Guard and the Boy Scouts saluted as the cavalcade traveled west to Oak, north to South Fourth, then on to Chestnut, gliding in all its glory right past the front door of Plennie Wingo's café.

And seeing all that, bearing witness to the outpouring of pomp and solemn communal exaltation, changes a man, makes him want to be something more than he already is. How could it not?

So maybe that set the stage for Plennie's idea, when Lindbergh came to Abilene.

But then a few months later, in January of 1928, a man named Henry "Dare Devil" Roland scaled the walls of the nine-story Mims Building and scattered the *Abilene Morning Times* from his perch as an advertising stunt. And then another "human fly" by the name of Al Willoughby climbed to the top of the Grace Hotel wearing a cape advertising a local business and dropped two boxes of free pencils embossed with the business's name to the crowd watching below. Not to be outdone, a third, Babe White, climbed the Hilton and hung from a ledge, clinging to a stylish silk dress that was for sale at nearby Minter's.

The madness would not stop. In 1929, a man named Harm Bates Williams rolled a steel hoop 2,400 miles, from City Hall in

Texas City to New York City. Two apparently sane men, a tailor and a barber from Rule, Texas, announced plans to play a running game of croquet all the way to Manhattan but were broke by Dallas. "We can't eat croquet balls, you know?" one of them told reporters. And a San Benito cowboy named Ralph Sanders began training a bull named Jerry, with plans to ride the beast from the Rio Grande all the way to New York.

"Has a wave of mild insanity swept over the American people," asked the *Shamrock Texan*, "or are all these things merely the result of an inordinate craving for publicity?"

Then, in the summer of 1929, just days after President Hoover signed the Kellogg-Briand Pact to forever outlaw war, and days before Babe Ruth hit his 500th home run, a stunt man named Benny Fox began training to sit for 100 hours on a flagpole atop Abilene's high-rise Hilton Hotel. Ten thousand people were expected to watch, like little ants below, and the stimulation surrounding the sedentary stunt was superlative.

Fox-related advertisements filled the newspapers front to back. He would be treated before and after the stunt by Dr. Nisbet, chiropractor, the ads said. He would be driven to and from the stunt in a Lincoln, "BENNY FOX'S OFFICIAL CAR." He would tell time on a watch from Joe Ellis Jewelry Co. He would eat frozen custard from Polar Bear Products, milk and butter from Pangburn's Milk and Butter, and "pure, clean wholesome bread" from Mead's while "enduring the pangs of 100 hours." He would quench his thirst with Weber's Root Beer, "Benny Fox's favorite drink," and also Nehi, "his chief refreshment."

For days and days the advertisements ran.

Benny Fox says "the water's fine" at Johnston's Swimming Pool, on Fort Worth Pike.

Radio music from Majestic will help Benny Fox endure his

100 hour sit on the Hilton flag pole. Benny says, "I'm way up where the tone quality means a lot."

Will Mrs. Fox worry-worry-worry with Benny's Laundry? NO! She will call 8866, the Abilene Laundry. We will keep Benny's clothes clean during his 100 hour sit.

Up goes Benny Fox... Down go the prices at Barrow Furniture Co., Inc.

When he came down, Benny Fox went to sleep in a bed in the Barrow showroom window and didn't wake up for eleven hours, three minutes. Nearly three thousand people gambled on guesses at how long he would slumber, but Mrs. Ben H. Gray won a free mattress for being astonishingly close with a guess of eleven hours, two minutes. Before Benny skipped town to start training for his next stunt, crossing the Atlantic on a flagpole above the rigging on the steamship *Leviathan*, the Hilton hosted a dance in his honor, and long was the line of Texas girls wanting a spin with Benny. One lovely lady, Pearl Pilkington, had been gazing at the Fox all week from an office window, and wrote him a peachy poem:

Stark against the lucid sky
  You sit, an ominous bird, and survey the town,
  Like a huge insect—a fly—
  Impaled upon a pin
  Under the shimmering waves of heat
  You seem to float at noon;
  Or drenched by the lurid sunset
  Thankful for the coming gloom
  Gloating, at midnight line and black,
  Jutted sharply
  Between me and the puzzled moon,
  Stubbornly you defy the hours,

Stringing them slowly, as beads upon a string,
Greedily—one by one.

A man reads something like that, sees Benny Fox twirling the ladies and riding up front in a parade, sees how a show of endurance and good salesmanship makes people gush and practically *hand* over their money, well, it impacts him, gets him to thinking. Makes him wonder if he might have a stunt or two up his own sleeve. How long would his parade be? Would it stretch from Fort Worth all the way to Dallas?

And when the stock market crashes in New York, and the cash register falls silent in a café in Abilene, and the owner begins to wonder how he'll pay his own bills and keep his family fed, thoughts that once seemed crazy don't seem so crazy anymore.

And so at a birthday party the following year, as the boys and girls were in the parlor talking nonsense about how everything under the sun had been done and how there were no more stunts to pull, how a man had pushed a peanut up Pikes Peak with his nose and how a man had flown from New York to Paris alone and how you couldn't even find an empty flagpole anymore, Plennie Wingo looked over the top of his newspaper and came right out and said something he could not put back in the bottle.

"Well," he said. "Not everything has been done."

3.

DIRT DEVILS AND DETAILS

He could see the Dallas skyline growing larger in his rearview mirrors when a man pulled onto the shoulder and climbed out of his car.

"What are you doing?" the fella asked Plennie. "Where are you going?"

"Fort Worth," Plennie said.

"But you are going *from* Fort Worth," the man said.

Plennie explained that, yes, he was backing away from Fort Worth, but eventually he would circle the globe and, thus, come *to* Fort Worth, his absolute certainty such that it made perfect sense to him. The sun beat down on them both on the dry and dusty shoulder. The man shook his head.

"How are you going to make a living?" the man asked.

That was a fine question.

* * *

He'd certainly thought through the economics of his plan, but the math remained a little fuzzy.

After the bank took the Mobley Café, Plennie took a job at the K.C. Waffle House on Pine Street. He was working ten hours a day, seven days a week, and his take-home pay was a measly twelve bucks. Seventeen cents an hour. It was something, but he had to draw money from his savings every week to feed his family, maintain the house, and keep Vivian in school. And little by little his stash dwindled away. But that's what made the stunt seem even more appealing. If you're working seventy hours a week for scraps, is it really that big a gamble to try to make money by walking backward around the world?

He had tried his best to sell Idella on the idea long ago, backing into it gently at first, talking about folks like Benny Fox and Babe White. He'd show her articles in the newspaper and comment upon how much money other people were making off stunts. He was so persistent that she cut him off one day.

"You've got something foolish on your mind," she said. "If so, out with it."

He felt the courage slip up into his throat. He spilled.

"Is it so bad to appear foolish if you're well paid for it?" he said. "Suppose it pays off. Look at Lindbergh. Everybody called him crazy too."

He kept it up, trying to wear his practical wife down, eroding the edges of her resistance.

What about Vivian? Idella asked one day. *She wouldn't like the idea of her daddy doing such a thing.*

The girl came along easier. He suggested to her that someone could make a boatload of money by reversing around the globe. He told her that he was going to pass his good idea along to a friend. Somebody should give it a shot, he said.

"Why give it to someone else?" Vivian replied. "Why don't you do it for yourself?"

One down, one to go.

He kept plying Idella while he made preparations. He knew a chiropractic doctor, a Scotsman, who had advertised that he could train a human being to overcome any physical challenge whatsoever. Plennie walked to his office one morning, waited until he had a free minute, then described his idea. He asked the doctor what he thought of it.

"Mr. Wingo," the doc said, "if you want to try it, I'll be glad to give it some thought and work out some exercises to develop the muscles you'll need."

Part of Plennie had been hoping the good doctor would talk him out of it.

"But it will take work on your part to get ready," the doctor said.

"Well, it won't hurt to train, will it?" Plennie said.

"Not at all," the doctor said. "It will help you physically, even if you eventually give up the trip."

The doctor thought about it for a week, then devised an exercise routine that would work the set of leg muscles Plennie would need to walk twenty or thirty miles a day, backward. He gave Plennie the instructions, then insisted he would take no payment for his help. He said he wanted to help prove that a human could do whatever he set his mind to. He said he'd be repaid with satisfaction when Plennie returned.

He also predicted a challenge Plennie hadn't really thought about. So far, Plennie had been holding a mirror in his extended arm and using the reflection to guide his walking. Alas, that didn't seem practical if Plennie intended to put in serious mileage, or traverse highways, crowded city boulevards, stairs, hills, dales. Who knew how many mountain ranges there were out there? This posed a problem, both men agreed.

The answer appeared a few days later, almost like magic, in the back of a magazine. An advertisement featured a pair of sunglasses with small mirrors affixed to each side, meant for motorcyclists and sports car drivers for extra safety. Plennie couldn't believe it, took it as a sign that this was meant to be. He pulled more from his savings and sent money along with his order. When the glasses arrived, he'd been at his exercises for several weeks. He'd lost weight. Gained confidence. Felt great. He practiced by wearing the glasses around the house, then ventured out in the daylight, making sure he turned around and walked forward when a car slagged by so no one thought him a fool or tried to steal his idea.

When the plan began to feel real, he started corresponding with shoe companies, but didn't let on in the letters what he planned to do, just that it would be big and would involve shoes and that they'd want a piece of it, definitely. He received several kind replies, but no takers, not until they learned what it was he had in store. He kept the letters anyway, and waved them in front of a few close friends, passing them off as propositions for sponsorship contracts. He was surprised by how suddenly they went out of their way to do him favors.

He convinced one of them, a young friend who was about twenty, to join his endeavor and work as an advance publicity man. Basically, Plennie told him, your job will be to drive ahead to the next town of size, where you'll contact the city officials, newspaper types, businesses that might need the advertising, and get them all interested and ready for Plennie L. Wingo, the Backward Walking Champion of the World. Whatever ventures you line up, Plennie said, we'll split fifty-fifty. Sounded to the boy like a good deal.

The two hit up the Abilene Chamber of Commerce first, with a grand offer: Plennie would talk up the beautiful city of Abilene everywhere he went if the chamber would offer a purse at the end of the journey, some sizable amount of money that would make it all worthwhile. The chamber folks seemed deeply interested but admitted they were broke. The Depression had wiped out the budget for ambitious...world advertising. But, they said, try a larger city.

The next day, Plennie and his new partner climbed in the car and headed east 150 miles on State Highway 1 to Fort Worth. They tried the chamber of commerce first, but again, no luck. An official there directed the pair to the Southwestern Exposition and Fat Stock Show, which was opening in a few days. Plennie let his partner do the talking as he watched the faces of the stock-show men change from curious to jaded. Before they had a chance to say no thanks, Plennie jumped in and turned on his Texas charm.

"Mr. President," he said, "suppose we travel through towns within a hundred-mile radius of here, I will get out at the city limits and walk into town backwards, while my partner gets publicity for your show's opening date?"

The president consulted with his men and came back with a question.

Would they work for ten days, carrying signs advertising the stock show in towns like Plennie said, for $250?

Two hundred fifty dollars. It would've taken Plennie fifteen weeks to earn that at the K.C. Waffle House. Yes, he said. And he signed a contract immediately.

He made his first nervous appearance on March 3, the same day President Herbert Hoover signed a law making "The Star-Spangled Banner" the official national anthem of the United States, and maybe that was fitting. Plennie wore cowboy clothes, cowboy boots, and a ten-gallon hat. He backed timidly at first, but his training took over and before long he was crossing busy streets and climbing easily over curbs. A crowd gathered to stare at the fella scooting around like an upright crab for no apparent reason. They had a thousand questions. Was it natural for him to walk backward? Where did he learn it? How long had he been practicing? What would he do when he came to the ocean?

The publicity man told the people to read about it in the papers the next day, and they did.

REVERSE WALKER IN CORSICANA TUESDAY ADVERTISING SHOW, read the headline in the *Corsicana Daily Sun*, eighty miles southeast of Fort Worth.

Plennie Wingo, claiming to be the first reverse walker of the world, was in Corsicana Tuesday boosting the Southwestern Exposition and Fat Stock Show which opens at Fort Worth Friday night, March 6, and which will continue through Sunday, March 15.

Wingo is beginning a world tour. He says he will walk backwards around the world. He climbs stairs, dodges pedestrians or automobiles and otherwise walks backwards and apparently about as good as the average person does normally. His only aid is eye glasses which he wears and which have tiny mirrors at the side of each eye.

Wingo has been in training for months for his world tour and decided to open it by boosting the Southwestern Exposition. While walking around here he bore signs which read: "Walking Back to the Rodeo, Fort Worth, March 7 to 15."

Six months ago Wingo decided that to walk backwards would be novel. He went into constant training because he says that if a person walks backwards even for a short distance he becomes fatigued and suffers discomfort. He did not want any other person to get on to his idea so he trained at night at his Abilene home, walking 15 to 20 minutes each night.

Many stared at Wingo as he walked backwards here.

They drove across God's country for the next six days, stopping in any town with enough people to form a crowd. Waco, Hillsboro, Burleson, Cleburne, Weatherford, Decatur, Denton. The newspapers in every city printed favorable stories, usually accompanied by photographs. Plennie spent the last four days of the contract walking around the showgrounds wearing the advertising and silly cowboy getup.

The turnout for the show broke every record, and the officials were well pleased.

Plennie was exhilarated. Felt like he was made for this moment.

He had expected public reaction, but nothing on the level he'd witnessed. If only he had more money—or the promise of money—he could get started. His advance man drove home to Abilene to tie up loose ends and Plennie again approached the chamber of commerce, this time with two items of collateral: proof that he could and would walk backward, and that doing so would get results. The chamber board agreed that if he mentioned Fort Worth everywhere he went, the publicity alone would be worth about $5,000. But they couldn't afford to offer that as things were.

Plennie was disappointed, but he soon had another idea. If no purse was promised and no sponsor materialized, he could sell postcards to the curious featuring an image of the Backward Walking Champion himself.

Postcards.

* * *

"How are you going to make a living?" the man asked.

"I'm not sure yet," Plennie said. "But I have plans to sell my pictures on postcards."

Without missing a beat, the man replied: "We'll take one."

Plennie pulled out his black notebook and his new ballpoint pen as he explained that he didn't quite have them made, not yet, but they'd be ready soon.

"If you'll give me your name and address I will be glad to mail you one from Dallas," Plennie said. An investment, so to speak.

There at the top of the first page he had typed and pasted the following:

Starting without a single pinney depending on selling postal cards with my picture and details of the trip around the world walking backwards.

Your name and address will be placed below for cards to be mailed to you later the price is what you feel like paying. I am doing this stunt to raise money to educated my sixteen year old daughter, Thanks very much.

He took down the man's name and said nothing else. He just stood there in awkward silence until the man realized what he was waiting for and went for his wallet.

"How much?" he asked.

"However much you want to pay," Plennie said. Again, he hadn't fully thought it through, but the names and home addresses of travelers who stopped him on the highway began to add up.

CC Pierce, 804 W 3rd St, Fort Worth, Texas
Carl Hendren, 11 16th, Houston
Dick Hamblin, 407 N 58th, Dallas

He let folks try out his glasses and handle his walking cane. They looked foolish, but he decided he would oblige anyone who asked.

Steen Service Station, Arlington
Miss Flassie Watson, Arlington, Tex
Jack Gilstrap (city hall) Fort Worth

He soon realized he had to keep the visits short if he wanted to get anywhere. He'd chat awhile and then finally say, "Well, it has been nice talking to you, but I had better be going. It's a long way around the world."

H. P. Hoffman, Route 6, Arlington
Eleanor Truelove, 907½, Throckmorton, Tex
Arcadia Garage, Route 8, Box 438, Dallas

A few gave a dollar. A few gave a dime. Some didn't pay at all. Plennie hassled no one. He kept sliding back until he reached Arlington, a full sixteen miles from where he'd begun, and checked in at the Western Union, where the man behind the counter stamped his book with the time and date. A large crowd had gathered outside and Plennie did brisk business when he emerged. They were especially interested in his walking cane, which he graciously displayed and permitted them to touch. The coffeewood cane with a polished buffalo-horn handle was a gift from a friend in Abilene. Plennie had no idea what the mystic symbols carved into it meant, but he thought it was beautiful and mysterious. He didn't *need* it, but carrying the cane made him appear dapper, and it gave him something to do with his hands. It would come in useful. He lent out his glasses, too, and put new names in his book, orders for postcards he didn't yet have.

He stayed the night in Arlington with a friend from high school, then put in a few more miles the following day, but found himself quickly exhausted. All the training had helped, but twenty miles backward was a struggle. He slept the night at a tourist court outside the big city, compliments of the Richardson family, who thought he was curious.

By the time he set off in the morning, he had fifty-nine names in his notebook and $23.50 in his pocket. He was hoping that when he reached Dallas he wouldn't wind up getting hassled by the police. That had happened before, when he was advertising the stock show.

4.

POSTCARDS AND PUBLICITY

Plennie Wingo stood still in the hot lights, a curtain painted with a rural scene of tall trees and a winding river behind him, as the photographer made adjustments to his camera. Plennie assumed the posture of a man walking in reverse, though in the image that would be frozen in time, he could just as well have been walking forward, or sideways for that matter. His feet were inside shiny black shoes and he wore a light patterned necktie and a dapper homespun suit one size too large for his small frame. His brown hair was neatly trimmed around his ears and he wore on his face driving goggles with small, rectangular mirrors fixed to the rims. In his left hand he held an impressive carved coffeewood cane with a polished buffalo-horn handle. Missing from that hand was his wedding ring.

He stood just five feet, five inches tall but wore the shifty smile of a man twice his size, revealing a gap near his upper left bicuspid, the tooth behind the canine. He had been professionally photographed once before, sometime around 1911, his sixteenth year, with eight siblings and his mother and stepfather, but he was grown and independent now, twenty years later. A man, alone in the big city of Dallas, making a go of it. If his mother could see him, see how he eased with confidence backward across the busy big-city boulevards, how he'd already made more than a regular week's pay in just two days...

Plennie Wingo, April 1931, Dallas, Texas. (Courtesy of Pat Lefors Dawson)

He had expected trouble in Dallas and was apprehensive upon arrival. While advertising for the stock show, he had been hassled by the Dallas police, who informed him that the city had implemented an ordinance prohibiting the carrying of signs of any type. So he stopped at a filling station on the edge of town to phone the mayor. Plennie explained that a policeman had nearly arrested him the last time he passed through, just a few weeks ago.

"Yes, but what's your problem now?" the mayor asked.

Plennie explained what he was doing and that he planned to walk through Dallas in reverse. "May I ask your permission to pass through your city like that?" he asked.

"Well," the mayor said, "we don't have laws against the way you walk." But he hesitated when Plennie told him he might soon be carrying a sign that said something like AROUND THE WORLD BACK-WARDS.

After some hemming and hawing, the mayor said: "Oh, well, you come on through. If any of the boys stop you, just refer them to me."

"Thank you, Mr. Mayor," Plennie said, "and look out Dallas."

A police officer seemed to be waiting for him when he reached the Trinity River, the Dallas skyline jutting into the air behind him. He thought the mayor had double-crossed him, but the cop was just as curious as everyone else. Plennie explained himself.

"Buddy," the officer said, waving him through, "the town is yours."

Before long a crowd formed and began following Plennie through the streets, between the impressive high-rise buildings, toward the Western Union. Dallas had grown leaps, and construction remained strong even then. The year before, a wildcatter had struck oil about a hundred miles east, and the city fast became the hub for black-gold affairs across Texas and Oklahoma. While other industry failed, oil development remained strong. In the first few months of 1931, nearly thirty petroleum-related business ventures had sprung up or moved to Dallas, and banks were providing loans to develop fields as far away as the Texas Panhandle and the Permian Basin out west.

When Plennie emerged facing forward from the Western Union with his book stamped, the crowd began to boo. It took him a second to realize why. He explained that his stunt was to walk every step backward between cities, but once he got the stamp he could walk forward about town until he was ready to leave, whereupon he'd return to the Western Union and start again backward. Folks seemed to understand, and Plennie thanked them and checked into a nearby hotel, where he cleaned up a bit and set out to take care of a few chores. He met a man who agreed to paint a sign on a piece of sheet metal—AROUND THE WORLD BACKWARDS—for no cost. He gave an interview to a reporter for the *Dallas Morning News*, and a short item ran in the April 19 paper under the headline WALK AROUND WORLD BACKWARDS IS GOAL OF VISITOR FROM ABILENE:

There may be nothing new under the sun, but Plennie L. Wingo, 36, of Abilene is trying for something he has never heard of being accomplished. He left Fort Worth Wednesday on a backward walking journey around the world and arrived here Friday. He will leave Monday, planning to visit McKinney, Sherman and Denison, Texas; Joplin and St. Louis, Mo., and Chicago, Ill., en route to New York, where he hopes to arrive by Christmas, 1931. He will take a boat for England and there will resume his walking campaign. He wears sun glasses equipped with mirror attachments, making it possible to see behind him. He hopes to walk around the world in three years. He was born and reared at Abilene, where he has been in the café business. He is married and has a 16-year-old daughter.

Then he ducked into the first photo studio he saw, Hugh D. Tucker's studio at 2012½ Elm Street, which offered copying, enlarging, portraits, Kodak finishing, and postcards. Tucker told Plennie his rate was twenty dollars for a thousand cards, which sounded like a deal, but after the hotel rent Plennie didn't have enough for a thousand. They hashed it out, decided that he'd pay for half now to take with him, then Tucker would ship the other half somewhere along his route and Plennie would pay cash on delivery. Deal.

When the flashbulb popped there in H. D. Tucker's studio, freezing in sepia for all time a man on the front end of a very important thing, Plennie was smiling like he could hear a cash register ringing. He determined then that he would sell each postcard for twenty-five cents, versus the way he had been doing it—"Just whatever you wish to pay"—which seemed less like he was asking for charity.

Before printing, he adorned the cards with a simple explanation along the sides and bottom portion of his portrait, an open-ended launch that answered four of the five Ws: who, what, when, where. The why would take some explaining.

WALKING
BACKWARD'S
AROUND
THE
WORLD.
STARTED
4/15–31
IN
FT. WORTH
EAST
TO
N.Y. CITY
PLENNIE. L. WINGO
OF ABILENE TEXAS

He spent the rest of the evening and into the late night addressing postcards to the folks who had paid and, for good luck, to the ones who had not, to Gene Humphreys of McCamey and the folks at the Dallas Oak lunchroom, to Jack Nelson on South Erving and G. W. Seago on First Avenue. He also took a few minutes to update his journal in passable cursive (with slightly less passable spelling): "I spent the knight with Mr. + Mrs. Hoffman in their Tourist Camp at Arlington, Tex. The Courtesy shown me by them will be remembered through out my trip. As well as lots of other good people that I met in Arlington."

He was, even then, beginning to think about turning his adventure into a clothbound book. If all went well, the postcards would support his day-to-day needs, but liquidating his epic journey by way of book sales could potentially make him a wealthy man for life. If he could accomplish the enormous task of walking backward around the world—no small feat!—he could certainly capture the experience with words. What was so hard about it? If Pearl S. Buck and Edna Ferber could do it, so could Plennie Wingo. And who wouldn't want to read that? The audience had taken shape already, in the crowds of looky-loos following him through the streets. All he had to do was put the words on the page and convince them to part with their money. And he'd only just begun.

5.

WHERE THE GRASS GREW THE
THICKEST

When he woke early the next morning, on Monday, April 20, 1931, it was to a vision. The only father he'd ever known, storming into the room he shared with six brothers, all sound asleep. "Get up, boys," Plennie heard the old man holler. "It is Monday morning and we have work to do."

Family was on Plennie's mind as he shot out of bed, stuffed clothes in his trunk, and tugged on his suit. Things had been growing steadily worse back home, and the downturn was hurting a quarter of all Americans, since nearly one in four at the last decade's end lived on a farm. Same for his people. While the stock market crash of 1929 made only ripples in much of rural America, the following year brought a terrible reality to the Great Plains, that massive swath of fertile land that jutted down into Texas like a thumb: they'd farmed too much.

Plennie could see it on the roadsides as he backed out of Dallas and pushed north up State Highway 6 toward Denison, Texas, and Oklahoma beyond that. His bag was aboard a bus headed the same direction and the driver slowed outside of town long enough to holler—"Come on, buddy!"—and then he was gone, leaving Plennie alone with his thoughts.

He was a pilgrim on a peculiar journey through a gallery of the consequences of conquest. The land on both sides of the highway had been overworked, yes, but it was more than that. He was bearing witness to the side effects of generations of shortsighted subjugation.

What had once been the magical and diverse bequest of the New World was now in many places pathetic, dry, tortured earth. The Great Plains had once been bountiful grasslands covering a full contiguous fifth of the United States and Canada, the largest single ecosystem in North America outside the boreal forest, stretching some three thousand miles from the Mackenzie River at the Arctic Ocean in the north to the Rio Grande down south, and hundreds of miles from the interior lowland and Canadian Shield in the east to the great Rocky Mountains out west. The Plains covered more than a million square miles and ten American states and, before European settlement, was home to vast herds of grazing buffalo and pronghorns, as well as other smaller, familial animals like coyotes, prairie dogs, prairie chickens, and rattlesnakes. The first Europeans to gaze upon the big flat country were Spanish colonists from Mexico in the sixteenth century, and they brought with them cattle and horses. The introduction of the horse gave rise to a thriving nomadic Plains Indian culture, and tribes like the Arapaho, Blackfoot, Cheyenne, Comanche, Crow, Apache, Sioux, Tonkawa, Iowa, Kanza, Mandan, Omaha, Osage, Pawnee, Ponca, Quapaw, Santee, and Wichita flourished. Before the Spaniards brought the horse, hunting buffalo was difficult. Hunters would surround the beasts and force them off cliffs or into corrals made from downed trees for easier slaughter. But horses gave hunters the ability to cover great distances and strike with speed and precision. The Comanche were among the first of the tribes to adopt a mounted nomadic lifestyle, in the early eighteenth century, and they were extraordinary horsemen. They became known as the Lords of the Plains and numbered about twenty thousand by the mid-1700s. They lived off the buffalo, using every part of the beast.

The meat was stew or jerky. The hide was clothing or shelter or shields. The bones were ladles or tools. The sinew made bowstrings or moccasins. Dried dung was fuel.

The Comanche were persistently hostile to the Spanish invaders, then the Mexican invaders after them, then the Texan invaders after them. They fiercely protected their territory, known as the *Comanchería*, from lighter-skinned men trying to claim land in North Texas. The land—like a river, or a bird—belonged to no one and everyone; ownership and property rights were concepts of imperialists or "settlers," as the white men thought of themselves. So when Texas became a republic and organized a militia called the Texas Rangers to combat the natives in the 1840s, the Comanche struck back hot and hard, displaying time and again their skill and courage in raid after raid.

Near the small town of Plano, about twenty miles northeast of Dallas, Plennie walked past the site of a slaughter that would live on in Texas lore, despite the lack of white witnesses. There on the bank of Rowlett Creek were buried the bodies of two of Plano's first settlers, Jeremiah Muncey and McBain Jamison, who had tried to lay claim in the 1840s to more than six hundred acres given them by the Republic of Texas. Ninety years before Plennie passed by, Muncey and Jamison had built a lean-to and were working on a log house when a hunting party stumbled across the two men dead on the floor. They found the mutilated bodies of a woman and child nearby. Two other boys had gone missing, and their remains were found in the nearby woods a year later. They blamed the Indians.

So went the surge and heave of bloody settlement, the constant taking and resisting, the steady stream of immigrants staking out turf in a world that was not theirs. By 1867, the federal government had decided to try to negotiate with the tribes who had successfully resisted white encroachment into the Great Plains. The government dispatched a Congressional Peace Commission to broker the deal. The Medicine Lodge Treaty of 1867 granted the Sioux a reservation in the Northern Plains, and the Fort Laramie Treaty the next year gave a reservation in Indian Territory to the Cheyenne, Kiowa, Arapaho, Kiowa-Apache, and Comanche.

The decision whether to cooperate and relocate fell to Ten Bears, the elderly leader of the Comanche. The terrible dichotomy of his predicament—to resist or retreat—gurgled through his address to the commission.

"It was you who sent out the first soldier, and it was we who sent out the second," he told the men. "Two years ago, I came upon this road, following the buffalo, that my wives and children might have their cheeks plump, and their bodies warm. But the soldiers fired on us, and since that time there has been a noise, like that of a thunderstorm, and we have not known which way to go. The Comanches are not weak and blind, like the pups of a dog when seven sleeps old. They are strong and farsighted, like grown horses. We took their road and we went on it. The white women cried, and our women laughed.... You said that you wanted to put us upon a reservation, to build us houses and to make us Medicine lodges. I do not want them."

Ten Bears had been born upon the prairie, where the wind blew free, where there was nothing to break the light of the sun. There were no enclosures. Everything drew a free breath. And he wanted to die there, not within walls.

"I know every stream and every wood between the Rio Grande and the Arkansas," he said. "I have hunted and lived over the country. I lived like my fathers before me, and like them, I lived happily. When I was at Washington, the Great Father told me that all the Comanche land was ours, and that no one should hinder us living upon it. So why do you ask us to leave the rivers, and the sun, and the wind, and live in houses? Do not ask us to give up the buffalo for the sheep."

He expressed hate for the Texans, who'd reneged time and again on their treaties, and felt that the land was not the federal government's to offer up.

"The Texans have taken away the places where the grass grew the thickest and the timber was best," Ten Bears said. "Had we kept that, we might have done the thing you ask. But it is too late. The white man has the country which we loved and we only wish to wander on the prairie until we die."

So the invading US Army began to destroy the homes and livestock of the Indians, raiding villages with wagon guns and modern rifles and using women and children as human shields. They began to cut off the food supply of the natives. In the Plains, this meant killing the buffalo that had roamed the grasslands since the last ice age, ten thousand years before. Within a few years of the Medicine Lodge Treaty, whites were killing buffalo by the millions. Railroads advertised excursions wherein passengers fired .50-caliber rifles into the herds from the windows of trains for sport. One man named Orlando Brown claimed to have killed six thousand bison himself and lost his hearing from the constant shooting. When it looked like the population was decimated, the Texas Legislature considered passing a bill to protect the surviving herds, but US Army general Philip Sheridan opposed it.

"These men have done more in the last two years, and will do more in the next year, to settle the vexed Indian question, than the entire regular army has done in the last forty years. They are destroying the Indians' commissary," he said. "And it is a well-known fact that an army losing its base of supplies is placed at a great disadvantage. Send them powder and lead, if you will; but for a lasting peace, let them kill, skin and sell until the buffaloes are exterminated. Then your prairies can be covered with speckled cattle and the festive cowboy...forerunner of an advanced civilization."

In a two-year period in the 1870s, one government agent estimated the bison slaughter at 25 million. The beasts were stripped of hide and horn for trading back east, and their rotting carcasses were left strewn across the great grassland. The Indians looked on in horror. The white-hot sun bleached the buffalo bones as men laid railroad ties through open lands, and the man who financed it all said, "Immigration will soon pour into these valleys," and, "Ten millions of emigrants will settle in this golden land in twenty years," and, "This is the grandest enterprise under God!" The last spike was driven in the Pacific Railroad in 1869, and a mere three hundred buffalo remained. Sixty million buffalo to three hundred buffalo in a hundred years. That's what civilization looked like.

The Indians submitted and the buffalo rotted and the Plains sat empty. No one was sure what to do with them next. They turned to the plow. The land once described as unalluring and uninhabitable and worthless was pitched as bountiful and prosperous in brochures that made it all the way to Europe. The farm was the way forward. Turn the land, the boosters said. Rain would follow the plow. And it did, for a time.

The railroad came to Plano, Texas, in 1872. The town incorporated in 1873. Barbed wire was invented in 1874. By 1888, when the St. Louis, Arkansas, and Texas Railway Company ran lines intersecting the Houston and Texas Central, Plano was a bursting outlet for productive blackland-prairie farmers. The Indians and bison were gone and the land was fertile. The telephone line came, then the public school and the fire department and the Palace Theater and City Hall.

To make money in an unsustainable market, speculative farmers turned millions upon millions of acres of flourishing prairie in the High Plains states of Texas, Oklahoma, Kansas, Nebraska, Colorado, and New Mexico into wheat fields. In the early twentieth century, when one million immigrants a year flowed into the

United States, some stayed put and made homes in the great cities of the East. But thousands of others set out for the Plains, lured by the temptation to work their own tracts of prairie and get rich off dry-land farming. In good times they busted the sod, turned it with machines, and made profits ten times over the cost of production. Word spread that a woman had made a profit of $75,000 on two thousand acres of Kansas, more than the president of the United States earned. Two hundred million acres of land on the Great Plains was homesteaded between 1880 and 1925. In the next five years, five million acres of native sod was plowed in the Southern Plains. So much food was produced that by 1929 there was a surplus in the United States. Farmers stacked unsold wheat in giant towers or left it to rot in the fields rather than pay to harvest what would not be returned in profit. Early the next year, 1930, while Plennie was hatching his backward idea, wheat was selling for an eighth of what it had sold for ten years before. Suitcase farmers who had flocked west to cash in ghosted their homesteads. The grass was gone. The land was now exposed soil. Those who remained plowed more with the idea that to break even, they had to expand even farther. The harvest in 1930 would break every known national record for wheat grown.

But amid the big run-up, the prices crashed. Then the rains disappeared and a hard, years-long drought set in.

They all but ignored the coming hard times in Texas. "As a matter of fact, in America, we dont know what hard times are," a 1930 Star-Telegram editorial said. The daily newspapers in Fort Worth pointed to increased construction, railroad traffic, oil production, and cattle and poultry sales as stabilizing influences.

But something else began to happen.

When the land was covered with grass, the prairie winds could blow strong all day and all night and you wouldn't know unless you stood outside and felt the rush of breeze, strong and steady. But now, with the grass gone and the tilled earth exposed over so many acres, the wind began to lift the dirt. The black storms were coming.

They were small at first. On March 7, 1930, the *Mt. Pleasant Daily Times*, twenty miles east of Plano, noted an unusual occurrence with a short front-page story, headlined DUST STORM THURSDAY: "A dust storm blowing from the west visited this section Thursday. The dust was largely high in the air and caused no inconvenience except to dim the sun considerably. The atmosphere was much colder Friday, following the blow."

No cause for concern.

Two months later, a Simmons College student noticed that the dark sky outside seemed to be moving. Scared as she was, she felt a sense of peace that she was studying the Bible inside while hell seemed to be coming outside. "Dean says it isn't right to trust the lord too far, though," she wrote in her journal.

A few days later a savage storm hit Coleman, fifty-two miles southeast of Plennie Wingo's house in Abilene, and the paper called it "the worst wind and dust storm Coleman has had in more than a decade." A gust of thirty miles per hour could lift dirt. Anything higher made a monster, and this storm was both strong wind and microbursts of tornadoes, or "roof-busters," as they were called. The "smiles that spread over the faces of the people after the big Sunday rain were converted into frowns," reported the *Coleman Democrat-Voice*. "Every hour brings additional reports of damage done in various parts of the county and an accurate estimate of the storm's toll cannot be made."

The following month, on June 26, 1930, the *Sweetwater Daily Reporter*, forty miles west of Abilene, reported that yet another odd dust storm had dumped additional sand in Sweetwater homes the previous evening. Temperatures had broken records every day that week, no rain in sight, with the Wednesday high at 102 degrees. Also breaking records was the water consumption to keep the crops growing through the heat wave. Farmers had sucked 1,533,700 gallons of water from the Watts Well and Lake Trammell in a single day.

The news by then had taken a decidedly dour turn. The same front page that reported the dust storm in Sweetwater shared news that Brownwood State Bank, eighty miles southeast, had failed and would never again open, and that the US House had confirmed Hoover's veto of the bill that would have provided relief to the thousands of unemployed war veterans massing in Washington, DC, refusing to leave, building haphazard shanties on government grass that would come to be called Hoovervilles.

The largest storm came in September 1930, when a strong wind from the west lifted earth from Kansas and pushed it into Oklahoma and Texas, a massive black cloud rolling across the land, carrying dirt and static electricity and scratching skin like steel wool. No one knew exactly what to make of it. Many called the government offices to ask what was happening, ignorant that the bullheaded rape of the land in which they were engaged had anything to do with the dirt clouds blowing in the air.

Some knew, though.

"Of all the countries in the world, we Americans have been the greatest destroyers of land of any race of people barbaric or civilized," said Hugh Bennett, who had studied the earth, when the dust had started to blow and the government kept pitching the soil to entrepreneurial farmers as the one resource that could not be exhausted. Bennett called it a symptom of "our stupendous ignorance."

In February 1931, with drought gripping the Plains and crops shriveling in the fields, the government finally stepped in to help. President Hoover, who'd become so despised that Texans had dubbed armadillos "Hoover hogs," approved a bill that would add $20 million to a $45-million drought loan relief package for farmers.

The blood had long since disappeared from the Muncey-Jamison massacre site near Highway 5 and Rowlett Creek when Plennie Wingo backpedaled through Plano in April 1931, walking along the eastern edge of what had once been a bountiful grasslands, home to some 470 native species. The new century's promise had vanished. The crops and livestock that had replaced the Indians and buffalo over the course of a few short decades had become a curse to the six million farmers who now called Texas home, and the landscape looked completely different from the way it had appeared even five years before.

What Plennie saw instead were scorched fields and weary people. They seemed to wear tension on their sagging shoulders like overalls. Their farms had seen better days. The wind was carrying the earth. They bore the posture of the doomed.

As Plennie made his way through Plano, he sold postcards to anyone who would stop, and business was pretty good. It was too early to turn in for the night, so he pushed on. About two miles north of town, the skies broke open. Glorious rain fell, the last for a while. He wished his cane were an umbrella. He was soon sopping wet, but with no options for shelter, kept walking until he saw a lit farmhouse on Route 2 appear in his tiny mirrors. He backed onto the porch. A man answered the door and Plennie did his best to explain the circumstances.

"Sure, come on in," the man said.

The Robbinses were farmers, and one of their two sons, whom they called Little Bill, was shy at first but soon warmed up when Plennie started telling stories. The boy leaned in close to his mother.

"What kind of man is he?" Little Bill asked.

Before long the boy was friendly. He wanted Plennie to autograph a postcard so he could show his friends. When Plennie handed him a signed card, Little Bill's face lit up like he had a million dollars. Plennie promised to write Little Bill when he got to Europe. He made a note that night in his journal, a reminder, such was his confidence. He had not really thought about it until then, but he wondered now how far it really was around the world.

6.

ROUND, SPINNING

On December 30, 1930, a noisy crowd of scientists packed a hall in Cleveland, Ohio. The members of the American Association for the Advancement of Science had gathered for their eighty-seventh annual convention, along with some folks from Sigma Xi, a research honor society. The crowd quieted as Dr. C. E. K. Mees, director of research for the Eastman Kodak Co., took the stage. Mees projected a photograph on a large screen, and the scientists weren't certain what they were looking at. He explained that the picture had been taken recently from an airplane in South America, by Captain A. W. Stevens, a professional aerial photographer, who had pointed his camera in the direction of the mountains he knew were there but could not see. One snap of the camera shutter, at one fiftieth of a second, recorded a panorama of an area larger in size than many states in the country. The scientists could see that the distant horizon line of the pampas bent slightly downward at one end, kind of like a photograph of the curving edge of the moon. Mees traced the barely distinguishable curve with his finger, and pointed out the level pampas stretching ahead for nearly 300 miles, ending in a long range of the Andes Mountains, and behind them, 320 miles from the Stevens airplane, the peak of the volcano Aconcagua.

Was the earth round? Eratosthenes, the father of geography, had noted 250 years before Christ that on the longest day of summer, the sun cast no shadow at noon at Syene, while at Alexandria, farther north, the shadow gave an angle of seven degrees and fifteen minutes, and that this amounted to about one fiftieth of the 360 degrees in a circle. If the earth was round, that meant the distance between Alexandria and Syene was one fiftieth of the distance around the earth in a north-and-south direction, and that, after one measured the distance between the two places, the circumference of the earth could be calculated at about 24,500 miles—which would prove to be very, very close to the facts. But it was theory.

Mees told the scientists that the photo was made possible by the development of photographic plates sensitive to rays of light that were invisible to the human eye. Stevens could not see the shape of the mountains on the horizon, but they were there, and the camera saw them, or rather, saw the light behind them.

The scientists were beholding, Mees said, the very first photographic evidence that the earth was round.

Two short weeks after the Mees presentation, scientists with the Argentine Astronomical Society gathered beneath the dome inside the congressional palace in Buenos Aires. From the vertex of the dome they had hung a 200-foot cable, and attached to the end of the cable a 56-pound ball of lead. A pin attached to the bottom of the ball touched a layer of sand, which was spread on the floor below, so that the movement of the pendulum was traced in sand by the pin. It was the exact experiment first conducted eighty years before, in 1851, at the Panthéon in Paris by the French scientist Foucault. At that time, the idea of a rotating earth was accepted among intellectuals, but still many had doubts. The revolutionary work of Copernicus in the sixteenth century and many observations made possible by the invention of telescopes had made an unmoving earth improbable, but it wasn't until Foucault's experiment that anyone was able to show that the earth spins on its axis.

Now, in 1931, the scientists were attempting to re-create the Foucault trial to verify his findings. The scientists held the pendulum stationary using a cotton string, making certain the sphere was absolutely still; then they burned the string. The observers watched as the ball began to move back and forth; the pin cut the sand in a slightly different line with each swing, rather than drawing just one line, as would have happened were the earth not rotating. Foucault was right.

Thus in two weeks on the front end of 1931, scientists proved beyond a doubt that the great world was not only round, it was spinning.

* * *

Upon the crust of the spinning sphere reversed Plennie Lawrence Wingo, in late April 1931, up Highway 6, in the northern portion of the American state of Texas. He noticed how the underfed animals regarded him as he came into view. The cows behind the barbed wire would lift their heads and chew their cuds and watch him reverse past. Chickens scratching and pecking on the dusty roadsides would flap and flutter away in a flurry of feathers when they saw him coming, as though a hawk were swooping down. Once, a mule stopped eating, raised his head, and watched Plennie. The mule stood still as a mouse, but his head followed Plennie as he passed by, staring until his neck was bowed and his ears leaned forward, like he knew something was odd. Plennie was a good ways down the road before the mule broke eye contact, shook his head, and went back to eating.

Dogs were especially funny. Even the most vicious farm dog would turn tail and run when the backward-walking human lifted his cane. It was as though the canines were surprised the man could see them coming.

When he arrived in Allen, a small railroad town built by Irish and German immigrants, he backed into the general store to say hello and perhaps sell a few postcards. The proprietor saw him coming and grimaced, not knowing Plennie could see him. Plennie straightened his tie, approached a couple of customers, and introduced himself, telling them what he was doing. He was asking if they wanted to see his postcards when the owner shouted.

"Stop that nonsense and get out of here!" he said.

The hostility was palpable. It was the first such meanness Plennie encountered, though it would not be the last. He didn't want to cause trouble, so he backed out of the store and stepped down off the porch, the proprietor trailing behind, or in front, as the case was.

"See you when I get back from around the world," Plennie said, smiling, his heels already kicking up dust.

"Not if I see you first!" the man shot back.

The rejection was a jolt, but he was on his way. No more than a hundred yards up the road, he saw two or three people dart out of the store, the proprietor with them. They shouted for him to come back. He turned and backed toward them, and when he got close he could see their tiny smiles in his mirrors.

"You must be the man I read about," a woman said. She explained to the shopkeeper that this was the guy walking backward around the world. The man began apologizing, grunting about the number of drifters and ne'er-do-wells lately. He was the first one to buy one of Plennie's postcards.

7.

RUBBLE AND RACE

There wasn't much left of the Negro quarters of Sherman, Texas, in the spring of 1931. Three whole blocks of black businesses and homes had been reduced to heaps of charred rubble, broken brick, and shattered glass. As Plennie walked down Houston Street he noticed that the courthouse, too, was just a gaping and burned husk of a building. It had been glorious when built in 1876, a two-story white stone edifice with long windows, and on top sat a tower that held a clock and a bell. Now, though, it was gutted, its burned contents spilling out of cavities like big black tongues.

Plennie stuck to the sidewalk. He had plans to scoot right on through to make Denison by nightfall. But a man walked past Plennie, then turned around, stopped, and introduced himself as Mr. McDonald, proprietor of the McDonald Hotel and Dining Room, situated catty-cornered from the used-to-be courthouse on Houston Street. The man handed Plennie a business card with a paragraph of text on its face:

All My Life

I have been bawled out, balled up, held up and held down,
bull-dozed, black-jacked, walked on, cheated, squeezed and
mooched; stuck up for war tax, dog tax and syntax, liberty

*bonds, baby bonds and matrimony, Red Cross, green cross and
double cross, asked to help the society of John the Baptist,
G.A.R., Woman's Relief Corps, men's relief and stomach relief.
I have worked like hell; I have been drunk and have gotten others drunk, lost all I had and part of my furniture; and because I
won't spend or lend all of the little I earn, and go beg, borrow
or steal, I have been cussed and discussed, boycotted, talked to
and talked about, lied to and lied about, held up, hung up,
robbed and damned near ruined, and the only reason I am alive
today is because I eat at the . . . (Over)*

McDonald Dining Room
115 East Houston St.
SHERMAN, TEXAS
"Where You Get Those Home Cooked Meals."

Mr. McDonald had read about Plennie in the newspaper, figured he'd be coming through Sherman, and invited him in as a
guest. The news of Plennie's walk was novel and needed in a
time of trouble in Sherman, the seat of Grayson County, a black-
dirt farming region on the south bank of the Red River with a
population of about sixty-five thousand. The State of Texas was
preparing to bring its case against J. B. McCasland, a nineteen-
year-old who stood accused of setting fire to the courthouse across
the street. Prosecutors had readied their witnesses and diligently
sorted through the compounding evidence. All that was left was
proving to a jury that McCasland was responsible for stepping out
of a mob of thousands and hurling a five-gallon canister of gasoline
through a courthouse window to set fire to the black man being
held inside.

Sherman had made national news before, like when the worst
tornado in Texas history spun through in 1896, killing some sev-

enty people and destroying dozens of homes and businesses, or when Teddy Roosevelt visited the courthouse square in 1905. Neither of those events brought shame on the town, though, not like what had happened eleven months before.

In early May 1930, a forty-one-year-old black farmhand named George Hughes had gone to the home of his employer, five miles southeast of Sherman, to collect his pay of six dollars. What happened next, according to those in the white community, was awful: Hughes raped his employer's wife and mutilated her throat and breasts. The story that spread through the black community was that the employer, a rent farmer, didn't have the money to pay Hughes and prodded his wife to invent the assault. A deputy tracked Hughes down quickly, obtained an alleged confession, then hustled him to the county jail, two blocks west of the courthouse, to face what seemed like an open-and-shut case.

That was May 3. On May 9, George Hughes stood trial, and the wild whites showed up from all directions. Rain had fallen for the past few days and the fields were too wet to work. They came by car and wagon and on foot, and reporters smelled corn liquor on the breath of more than a few. They were described variously as men, men and women, hard-bitten men, a small group of boys in their teens, mostly boys, mostly teens, boys surrounded by quite a sprinkling of young girls, a few mothers cradling babies in their arms, women and children, an orgy of madness, a dangerous disturbance, and, mostly, an angry mob. Some said there were several hundred, some said twenty thousand.

Sherman didn't seem like a ripe locale for mob violence. Situated on the extreme edge of what folks called the cotton kingdom, it was known as "the Athens of Texas," on account of the five colleges and twenty churches within its limits. People liked to talk about "the better element" in Sherman, the Rotarians, Kiwanis, and Lions Club types—businessmen, churchgoing, patriotic, hardly redneck. As far back as anyone could remember, there had been but one lynching in Grayson County, thirty years before, in 1901. True, the Ku Klux Klan had risen again in the last ten years, after going dormant in the 1870s and hibernating for fifty years. The racists had been revived by a failed Georgia preacher named William Joseph Simmons, who was inspired by a 1915 film considered a cinematic masterpiece. Made by the once-poor Kentuckian D. W. Griffith, *The Birth of a Nation* glorified the secret fraternity of the KKK as protectors of decency against carpetbaggers and freed slaves during Reconstruction. Woodrow Wilson even screened the film in the White House.

While recovering from a car accident, Simmons dusted off the old Klan's manual and wrote his own prospectus for a reincarnation of the organization. He and some buddies burned a cross atop Stone Mountain on Thanksgiving 1915, a ritual taken straight from the movie, and the *Atlanta Constitution* made small note. The group puttered along, almost lifeless, until Simmons hired a public relations man named Edward Clarke, who ran the Southern Publicity Association, the same firm that had successfully represented the Salvation Army and the Anti-Saloon League.

Clarke established a system wherein a Klan recruiter got to keep a percentage of the initiation fee for each new member. Soon, the hierarchy stretched long, each rung keeping a chunk of the fee for each new recruit. And to get new recruits to sign on, the "Kleagles" were encouraged to appeal to whatever racist predilection was at play on the local level. Simmons broadened the targets of Klan hatred to include Jews, Catholics, leftists, Mexicans, immigrants, bootleggers, and adulterers. Everyone was fair game, so long as Klan members' actions shielded the "sanctity of home and the chastity of womanhood" and maintained "forever white supremacy," per the Konstitution. The Klan had become a sort of perverse pyramid scheme, making its leaders incredibly wealthy. And once a man became a member, he was encouraged to buy from the Klan all sorts of things, like robes, life insurance, robe dry-cleaning services, helmets, Bibles, and even Klan candy.

A congressional investigation in 1921, prompted by a report of the Klan's secrets in the *New York World*, brought down founder Simmons and his ad man, Clarke. A Texas dentist named Hiram Evans took over. He appealed to the lower-brows and yokels, describing himself as "the most average man in America" and saying the Klan was proud they were "hicks, and rubes, and drivers of second-hand Fords." Membership grew fast.

By its peak in 1924, the membership had grown to some 4.5 million men, or about 15 percent of the eligible population in the US. The new numbers earned the Klan political power. The group claimed to have helped elect governors in Oregon, Arkansas, Indiana, Ohio, California, Oklahoma, and Texas. And those governors often did nothing to prevent mob violence. Sometimes they did the opposite, stoking racial anger with supremacist language. Upon becoming president of the Oklahoma constitutional convention, soon-to-be governor William H. "Alfalfa Bill" Murray explained that blacks were "failures as lawyers, doctors and in other professions" and called it "an entirely false notion that the Negro can rise to the equal of a white man in the professions or become an equal citizen." He said, in the same speech, "I appreciate the old-time ex slave, the old darky, and they are the salt of their race—who comes to me talking softly in that humble spirit which should characterize their actions and dealings with white men."

It's impossible to say whether the rising Klan rolls produced more racial violence, or whether their swelling was a symptom of something deeper, some dastardly social movement afoot on the front end of very hard times. In the photographs taken at many lynch scenes, the bystanders wear no hoods or robes, but jackets and neckties and floppy sun hats. The emotions of nationalism and group loyalty that rose up during the First World War lingered long after the intended enemy retreated, and it seemed to be finding new targets. Even though more than two million African-Americans were drafted into the war—with very few claiming exemptions—some of the seventy lynched in the first year after the war were still in uniform.

Between 1889 and 1930, 59 whites and 290 blacks were lynched in Texas, a number exceeded only by Georgia and Mississippi. Lynchings generally were on the decline, though. In 1929, according to the record department at the Tuskegee Institute, ten people were lynched nationally—three whites and seven blacks—the fewest in any year since Reconstruction.

But in May of 1930, the trend didn't seem to be holding steady. In the two weeks preceding the arrest of George Hughes of Sherman, there had been three separate lynchings in the South. And what was widely known in Sherman was that after Hughes's arrest a man named Slim Jones rode through the rural outskirts of town telling people about the case and the time of the trial. Whether Jones was an agent for a Klan organization trying to demonstrate its bloodlust is lost to history.

On May 9, inside the building across the street from the McDonald Dining Room, where, eleven months later, Plennie Wingo would be digging into a lunch on the house, the hallways and staircases leading to the courtroom filled as George Hughes pleaded guilty to assaulting his employer's wife. The crowd surged, then surged again. Then the judge suspended the trial, and it surged once more. Someone fired tear gas to disperse the mob, but the fumes made everyone gag and run to the windows for air. The fire department helped evacuate jurors and witnesses and clerks by ladders from second-story windows. The Texas Rangers on hand to quell the mob escorted Hughes to the district clerk's office, a giant two-story vault of steel and concrete in the gut of the courthouse.

Outside, the mob wanted blood. Reporters heard them chanting, "We want nigger meat!" During another surge, a Texas Ranger fired buckshot into the crowd, sending three to the hospital and the rest running. But soon they clawed back, one with a gas canister, and he heaved it through a courthouse window. Someone else lit a torch and touched off an inferno. When the fire department dragged hoses in to try to save the $60,000 courthouse, the mob slashed them. The Rangers would later claim they gave George Hughes the option of running for it or staying in the vault. He stayed. The last man to see him alive reported that Hughes was sitting in a chair in the vault, his head bowed upon his folded arms. According to a reporter, one old man "shook in his tracks with excitement and screamed: 'Let 'er wilt like a cucumber in the sun! Let 'er burn till the last hobnail in the nigger's boots is melted.'"

The governor dispatched National Guardsmen from Dallas. The mob hurled bricks and pop bottles at the white soldiers. The Rangers retreated. One officer held the mob away from the county jail with pistols, a Thompson submachine gun, and a sawed-off shotgun. The mob used dynamite and acetylene torches to blast and cut open the courthouse vault. A man crawled inside and shouted, "Here he is." Hughes was dead with a hole in his head, most likely killed by the dynamite blast. It appeared he'd been pacing the floor, attempting to cool himself with water from a two-gallon bucket.

They heaved the body out of the vault and it fell to the ground and the women screamed and clapped and a great cheer rose over the Texas town. "Glory be!" one woman said. Someone else hitched the torso by a chain to a car, which started down Travis Street and turned on Mulberry, toward North Sherman, slowly, on account of the crowd packing the streets. "On to nigger town," the mob leaders shouted.

They found a cottonwood tree in front of the Smith Hotel and a two-story drugstore owned by a black man. They used a rope to hang the lifeless body from a limb, then piled wood and sticks and looted furniture beneath it and set them alight. They burned the Odd Fellows Hall, a building that housed a beauty parlor, a dance hall, two dentists' offices, and a lawyer's office. They burned two undertaking establishments, a hotel, a movie house, and a life insurance office. They burned three blocks of black-owned homes and businesses. The black people of Sherman fled, hiding in brush thickets and storm drains. The only black resident anyone reported seeing was a single respected doctor, sitting still on his porch, a shotgun in his lap.

By 2 a.m., when a correspondent for the *Baltimore Sun* arrived, the mob had been wilding for fifteen hours and seemed to have run out of rage. The fire under the body had dwindled and the reporter watched as a redheaded man who had rushed from Mesquite, seventy miles away, shamed what was left of the mob.

The driver pushed through the throng, reached the tree and kicked away the wood that burned under what was once a man, albeit a black one. With one hand he grabbed the rope from which the body was suspended and with the other, which held a knife, he slashed through the strands. Then he lowered the body to the ground away from the scattered fire.

"Anybody claim this yere?" he asked of the mob.

Nobody replied.

"Well, then leave it lay," he continued and having issued his orders, pushed through to his car, climbed in and thundered back to Mesquite.

The reporter identified the redheaded man as Schuyler Marshall, former sheriff of Dallas County who had five years before single-handedly repelled a mob bent on kidnapping two black prisoners under his watch. "Sherman goes in heavily for culture," the reporter wrote.

The nation woke to banner headlines like MOB MADNESS TAKES NEGRO and BODY DRAGGED THROUGH TOWN. The local daily paper, the *Sherman Democrat*, decried the violence. "It does not seem reasonable that the people of the civilized community should burn down their courthouse, their temple of justice, where the law is supreme, and where every citizen, no matter how rich or how poor, should be able to go and be given a trial on any charge before twelve of his fellow citizens," read the paper's day-after editorial. "The mob is never right. It is always wrong, and unreasonable, and dangerous, and no half dozen Texas rangers are able to cope with that number of men gone mad. Sherman's name has been dishonored by the people of her own county. It will take a generation to outlive the stain on her honor, if it can ever be done."

The governor declared martial law in Sherman, and for several weeks machine guns were mounted around the square to keep the peace. The black neighborhoods remained empty for quite some time. Hughes was buried in an unmarked grave. A breath-stealing photograph survived, depicting Hughes's charred corpse hanging from a tree, legs bent up froglike and odd at the knees, four white men on the ground behind him, quizzical looks on their faces. Fourteen suspected leaders were indicted, but the trial would take a year.

They lynched another black man on May 17, fifty miles away, at Honey Grove, where two thousand or more dragged the body of Sam Johnson behind a truck for several miles, then hung his corpse upside down from a bois d'arc tree in front of a black church. And another on May 31, 160 miles away, at Chickasha, Oklahoma, when Henry Argo was murdered in his jail cell as a mob gathered outside. They lynched a total of twenty-one that year, more than double the number in 1929.

And then they moved on. Years later, a historical marker would be erected in front of a new courthouse and fail to say anything about why the old one burned down. Plenty of Sherman children would grow up in the years after the lynching having never heard tell of that dark night.

When Plennie finished his lunch, he stood facing the courthouse where George Hughes was cooked inside a locked vault, where women and children watched and men cut fire hoses and threw rocks at Rangers. In a few weeks, the state would make its case against J. B. McCasland, the nineteen-year-old who had hurled the gas can through the window, and the *Sherman Democrat* would proclaim the judgment "the first conviction in Texas in a case growing out of mob violence against a Negro attacker of a white woman." McCasland would be sentenced to two years in prison for arson and rioting. A few months later, charges against all but three of the other men were dropped. Then those charges too would disappear, leaving McCasland the sole convicted culprit of the madness that would soon be swept away from the collective memories of the whites of Sherman, Texas. A mother in Sherman would write a letter to her absent son saying she was thankful he wasn't there to witness the town's "terrible disgrace," like "a circus day crowd looking on a pageant," and that, "Indeed, I'm glad I had no son to blush for in the midst of a spineless population. Were I a man I'd hang my head in shame. As it is, I feel polluted by the contact."

Plennie had made up his mind to respect all races, creeds, and nationalities on his walk, and he hoped they'd respect him. He'd be the stranger on the far side of the Atlantic, the pale man who stood out in a crowd. He said goodbye to Mr. McDonald, pointed his toes to the southeast, and backed down Houston Street and on out of town.

8.

STANDOFF AT THE RED RIVER

Plennie got his shoes resoled and spent two nights at the Hotel Denison, charging his twenty-five-cent meals to his room, like a traveling salesman would do, and that made him feel classy. He was a big hit in the hotel lobby and spent no small amount of time looking to introduce himself to anyone who might happen to be curious about his journey heretofore and who might want to help fund his trip through Indian Territory by purchasing a postcard. Sales were rather brisk, and when it came time to leave he was surprised to learn that his entire stay would be complimentary.

"It has been our pleasure to have you as our guest," the manager told him, "and we wish you the best of success on your journey around the world."

He'd come 109 miles in his first week and was none the worse for wear, and finding success with postcard sales gave him a level of self-assurance he had not yet felt. He was about to leave Texas for the first time in his thirty-six years and could use all the confidence he could find. He had clipped an item from the newspaper and pasted it into his journal, a four-word mantra to help him along: DON'T WORRY. DO SOMETHING.

The first part was growing more difficult by the day. He had not yet sent word on his progress to his kin in Abilene, wanting to put considerable time and distance in before dropping them a letter, but he worried how they were getting along. A cold wave over the weekend had brought freezing temperatures to North Texas, destroying crops before harvest. Dry air and strong winds had decimated the spring wheat belt. The men at the weather bureau said topsoil was blowing away and many farmers were forced to reseed. They called the wind "very detrimental" and said it was wreaking havoc from the western Ohio River Valley all the way across the Plains, and the outlook for spring crops was not good. The cotton crop in Texas was late and said to be in only fair condition.

And the news about finance was getting worse. The Huntsville State Bank down near Houston closed its doors to avoid a run, which caused, according to the papers, "considerable excitement among citizens." The American National Bank in Paris, in East Texas, closed with assets and deposits totaling $1,631,000. The Athens National Bank, southeast of Dallas, locked its doors and posted a notice in the window that it would be voluntarily liquidated. The Miller County Bank and Trust in Texarkana failed. The Garfield National Bank in Enid, Oklahoma, failed. A little pile of pennies—forty of them—was the totality of the cash resources that remained in the vault of the People's Exchange Bank in Archer City when it, too, locked its doors. It wasn't just Texas. On the same single day in Nebraska, sixty-six banks closed, most due to the drought and farming crisis.

And where was the president? Why had he not thrown out any lifelines?

Hoover was fast making enemies, political and otherwise, by telling the American public that everything would be okay. Andrew Mellon, Hoover's secretary of the treasury, had put the hands-off approach of the government bluntly in a statement representing those who thought the market would fix itself without government intervention. "Liquidate labor, liquidate stocks, liquidate the farmers, liquidate real estate," he'd said. Some people might suffer, sure. But if they could just hold on it would be good for them in the long term.

Plenty of farmers and factory men wanted to drag Mellon and Hoover by their belt loops to stand on the breadline in Oklahoma City or eat at Al Capone's free soup kitchen in Chicago or talk to the apple vendors in Manhattan. Or even closer, to the Welfare Restaurant in Harrisburg, Pennsylvania, a short drive north of Washington, DC, where the tragedy of human existence played out at breakfast and supper every day. The joint opened January 12, 1931, with thirty-seven people at the first meal. The next day, as word spread, more than a hundred men showed up. From the third free supper on, the restaurant served its maximum of three hundred plates at every single meal, oatmeal and coffee in the morning, and beef stew or pork and sauerkraut or potpie for supper. If only Hoover could've heard the people talk.

"Me and my boy here haven't had work for months and we are unable to get anything but odd jobs now and then," one man told a reporter for the local paper. "We walk up here from Steelton every day for these breakfasts and suppers. If we didn't, we would have nothing to eat most days. And what little money we are able to earn wouldn't allow us to eat anyway."

"I just got in from Reading," another man chimed in. "I have been clean across the country and haven't found a job. I heard there was work in the East but I ain't been able to find it. Before I was in Reading I was in Lancaster and before that in Washington. I was two weeks in them towns and there ain't a thing doing. It's terrible. This feed is certainly swell, though."

"Butcha can't get it more'n three days," warned another. "You gotta either get a job or move on. This town ain't feeding the whole United States."

"I had to come over here from Enola," a man said.

"I'm from Hummelstown," said another.

"Well, pal," said another. "I would have had to sell what little furniture I have in my home to get enough to eat if it weren't for this Welfare Restaurant, and I live right here in this city. Harrisburg is represented here same as your towns."

There was a family, too, a man and woman and child.

"Here and there it seemed as though a job would be worth more money than Henry Ford owns," said the man. "We moved from town to town. If either of us did get work, it is only for a day. And there weren't many of those days."

By and large, the country was tired of hearing the empty promise that relief was coming. One of Hoover's biggest critics had made that brand of disdain his platform for what would turn into a run at the presidency.

"You can't bring back prosperity by psychology," said Oklahoma governor "Alfalfa Bill" Murray. "Saying that better times are just around the corner won't bring them. If the doctrine of telling the people that good times are just around the corner continues for another decade with the same policy of laws, this republic will go into the revolution with bloodshed unprecedented in the history of the human race."

Plennie found it hard not to worry about his mother and dad, and about Della and Vivian. He also found it hard not to feel terrible that he was sleeping on hotel linens and eating free chicken and biscuits while they were presumably scratching by, facing the storm of a chaotic and unknown future without him. For every story about a bank closing there was one about some robber sticking up a clerk, scaring the hell out of the customers and making off with a few thousand dollars. Heavy guns and affordable automobiles had given rise to gangsters and getaways and cops fiddling for their pistols in clouds of red dust. Made you wonder what was happening in the world. The Kimes brothers had left a trail of bloodshed all over Oklahoma and Texas and the last of them had just been rounded up. No jail could hold William Underhill, the man they called the Tri-State Terror. The Barker-Karpis gang was knocking over banks in Plains and stashing cash in every cranny they could find. Two troubled and tattooed Texas kids named Clyde Barrow and Bonnie Parker had just fallen in love.

But if there was ever any evidence of the irritableness spawned by these hard times, Plennie was coming up on it at the Red River, that 1,300-mile rust-colored *rio rojo* that ran like a rattlesnake from the redbed lands of the *Llano Estacado* to meet the Atchafalaya and the Mississippi River at Louisiana. The Red was the second river he would cross after the Trinity.

Long since ended was the Red River War of 1874, when the US Army removed the Comanche, Kiowa, Southern Cheyenne, and Arapaho Indians from the Southern Plains, forcing them onto reservations in Indian Territory. And it was sheer coincidence that Plennie approached the Red River on April 22, the exact day on which, forty-two years before, the US government opened for white settlement the Indian Territory—land promised for eternity to the tribes who had agreed, albeit at gunpoint, to relocate. It was also sheer coincidence that the motion picture making box offices ring in the spring of 1931 was *Cimarron*, which would win the Oscar for Best Production for offering the splendid white man's perspective of events surrounding the Oklahoma Land Rush of 1889. Its opening slide sets the stage for what amounts to a celebration of genocide, the social degradation of indigenous people, and capitalistic environmental destruction: A NATION RISING TO GREATNESS THROUGH THE WORK OF MEN AND WOMEN . . . NEW COUNTRY OPENING . . . RAW LAND BLOSSOMING . . . CRUDE TOWNS GROWING INTO CITIES . . . TERRITORIES BECOMING RICH STATES. The Indians in the film kowtow. The whites rape the land for oil and shoot one another and get rich. The critics loved it.

Now, in the real world, the white man was about to fight the white man over a bridge.

For decades, thousands of immigrants from the East looking to settle in Texas took their wagons across Indian lands using the Texas Road, which ran from Joplin, Missouri, southward across the territory to the waters of the Red. There they paid a toll to get across the river via Colbert's Ferry. Frank Colbert was half Chickasaw and had the Chickasaw Nation's trust, and he operated first the ferry, then a toll bridge, peacefully for a number of years, then formed the Red River Bridge Company with Denison businessmen to oversee operations. By the age of the automobile, the private two-lane toll bridge connecting Texas and Oklahoma put towns along the road north and south in the running for one of the cross-country car routes every city was after. By 1930, the year before Plennie arrived by foot, more than half a million travelers would follow the King of Trails Highway to the Red River bridge, where they'd pay a toll of seventy-five cents to cross.

Meanwhile, working under the idea that crossing a river should be free and that business interests on both sides would benefit, Texas and Oklahoma worked amiably to sidestep the Indians and build a public bridge, paid for with tax dollars.

When the new bridge was all but complete, the Red River Bridge Company sued, claiming Texas had agreed to pay the company some $60,000 when the new free bridge put the old toll bridge out of service. As a result of the lawsuit, the Texas governor ordered the free bridge barricaded and closed until the legal issues were resolved. This pissed off the governor of Oklahoma to no end. He pointed to Louisiana Purchase documents from 1803 that showed that both sides of the water belonged to Oklahoma, and he ordered men from the highway department to destroy the barricades on the Texas end. When the Texas governor made three Texas Rangers rebuild the barricades and enforce the federal injunction, the Oklahoma governor deployed his National Guard, destroyed the approach to the toll bridge, declared martial law, and came to the site with a pistol on his hip.

The standoff made national news. The *New York Times* and the *Washington Post* treated readers to daily updates on each side's political maneuvers while armed militiamen patrolled both banks and locals brought their picnic lunches to the muddy river to watch the fireworks. The news spread like prairie fire and was said to have reached the eyeballs of Adolf Hitler, a rising German politician, who pointed to the trouble as proof of a weak American capitalist union. A headline in the *Bakersfield Californian* ran across eight columns: OKLAHOMA, TEXAS NEAR CIVIL WAR. "Fiery governor of Western state carries out his own ideas and makes others like it," wrote the *Rochester Times-Union* in New York.

"The free bridge is open," Alfalfa Bill Murray told reporters. "If people are fools enough to want to pay seventy-five cents to cross here, let 'em do it."

No shots were fired in the Red River Bridge War, but Oklahoma sort of won. A federal judge dismissed the toll bridge company's suit, declaring Texas's contract with the bridge company illegal. Oklahoma's squirrelly, big-eared, cigar-chomping governor would ride the attention during a presidential run the following year, and at times he would seem to have the Democratic nomination in hand. He would draw ten thousand in Weatherford a few months after the bridge war, and fifteen thousand in Dallas, where the *Dallas Morning News* would remark, "He is a master of the appeal to the masses." Texas governor Ross Sterling would lose his next election and all but disappear. "He may be a good man," the *New York Times* would declare of the millionaire Texas governor, "but not for public office during these times."

But the three-month dispute had only just begun when Plennie Wingo, bundled against the frigid prairie winds, crossed the Red

River on April 22, 1931. There were no militiamen or looky-loos pacing the banks, just a man walking over water dividing two states. He strode backward alone across the cold span and wondered how many more rivers he would cross. He thought about how he had learned to get along with people, and how folks reacted to him when they first saw him. He thought about how friendly most people were, even if they were up against the wall. "It seemed to make me feel assured of success," he would later write.

He crossed his 110th mile as the stage for the Red River Bridge War faded before him.

9.

JUST HUMAN, SAME AS YOU

He was on a backward tear through the eastern Oklahoma ragweed when the "gypsies" caught him.

Plennie had spent his first night in the Sooner State at Hotel Main in Durant, Oklahoma, for fifty cents, drank a cup at the Bryan Coffee House with a new friend named Ollie James, then backed up Highway 75 through Caddo and Caney, and up the new Jefferson Highway, nearer every day to the geographical center of America, past sparse forests of black dalea, shortlobe oak, and Ashe juniper, through Stringtown and Chockie and Kiowa and other little towns destined to dry up and fall off the map.

It was easy for a man to feel small and insignificant here. To the east lay the Cookson Hills and the Boston Mountains and the Ozark Plateau and then the Mississippi River Valley, all regions where families were packing their belongings to head west toward possibility. While the dust storms in the Plains had already begun uprooting farmers out there, southeastern Oklahoma, through which Plennie now walked, would produce the majority of western wanderers—Okies, they were derisively called. They'd been struggling to grow crops on marginal land, and the depressed market made profitable agriculture nearly impossible. In the next two years, 10 percent of all Oklahoma farmers would lose their land to foreclosure. When the government began paying them to not raise crops, landowners took their tenants' plots out of production. Tenant farmers, who made up 60 percent of the state's growers, had no reason to work difficult land and endure terrible prices when they could head someplace better. Besides, they had a migratory habit and they hadn't been here long enough to grow roots themselves. They'd come for opportunity, and when reality set in, they loaded what they owned on flivvers and navigated gravel roads until they intersected with a new highway called Route 66, which would deliver them all the way to the promised land, Santa Monica, California.

No small number would've wondered about the skinny Texan walking backward down the shoulder of the highway.

When Plennie made it to McAlester, where the big penitentiary held some of the meanest outlaws alive behind barbed wire and concrete, a reporter got his story and took several photographs. Another man wanted to make a sketch of Plennie, so he obliged. Plennie sold a few postcards, but this part of Oklahoma was mostly sandstone hills and Indian grass and oil derricks.

Somewhere south of Checotah, he noticed a colorful roadside camp coming into view in his mirrors, like a sunlit prism. He couldn't make out what it was until he backed up on the camp and saw the wagons and dangling lanterns and smoldering bonfires. Before he could scoot on past, two women set upon him, hustling across the road and asking for matches. Plennie didn't smoke and had no matches. He told the women as much. Alas, they offered to help him search, and before he could object they had their hands in his pants and were feeling around inside his pockets. It dawned on him that they were trying to lift his wallet.

He'd started in Fort Worth with no money, but the postcard sales had worked and he happened to be carrying a healthy chunk of cash. When the jig was up, he began to object and slap at their hands, and he tried hard to back away, but the women wouldn't let him leave. Soon two men rushed out and they, too, wanted to know if he had any matches, and they, too, began feeling around on his person, eight foreign hands now touching him without permission or decency. The whole time, he tried to assure them he had no matches and worked to break free. He felt anger rising up in his chest. He demanded they unleash him immediately. He realized if something didn't give soon things were going to get ugly.

As if on cue, an automobile came burning up the Jefferson Highway and Plennie threw his hands in the air to get the driver's attention. The car barked to a stop and the four slunk toward the weeds, back into the shadows of their colorful caravan.

Plennie ran a quick inventory of personal effects and found nothing missing. He chatted with the driver long enough to catch his breath, thanked him, then hustled north again.

Down the road a stretch, he told an old man about the "gypsies" and the frisking. The man, J. C. Dabbs, owned the most beautiful home Plennie had seen so far in Oklahoma and graciously invited him to stay the night. He told Plennie his family was visiting Tulsa and he'd enjoy some company. The sun had set, besides.

Dabbs was a fine cook and asked a hundred questions about Plennie's walk so far and his plans for the rest. How did he propose to get across the Atlantic? Wasn't he afraid of getting lost? That sort of thing. The old-timer also spun his own yarns about growing up in the Cookson Hills, about the Indians and wild animals and outlaws, about Hanging Judge Parker and the capture of Cherokee Ned Christie at Rabbit Trap, about the bandit Ford Bradshaw and Belle Starr, the sharpest sidesaddle shooter who ever lived. She was buried nearby, God rest her soul, and after dark you can still hear her mare pawing the ground at her grave.

This little spot on earth was curious, a microcosm of the tensions of American expansion, a windswept cauldron boiling with the unholy broth of progress. It was the end of the Trail of Tears, yes, a place where the last of the faith was broken and the land was soaked in blood and oil. It was inhabited by men quick with their Bibles and breechloaders, and they fought over polygamy and slavery and whatever else.

It was the birthplace of the Federal Bureau of Investigation, when the government men came a decade before Plennie did to investigate the murders of Osage Indians, who had wisely held on to mineral rights for the land they owned atop the largest oil deposits in the United States. They had become the richest people per capita in the world, and then they had become dead. It was in many ways the end of the frontier, the last gasp of manifest destiny, having been settled long after the West.

It had filled with people, and the people had built homes and filled those homes with goods purchased on credit, and now those bills were due, and they were either on the move again or staying put and joining the wretched revolution, like Pretty Boy Floyd or the Kimes brothers or the Barker boys. These Cookson Hills seemed almost like a hive of bank robbers and outcasts. Even as Dabbs and Plennie traded stories, sheriff's deputies were transporting outlaws Ed Davis and Paul Martin to Dallas for questioning about their alleged involvement in the murders of two constables in Marlow and the police chief in Beggs, and the robbery of the Lincoln Bank & Trust Company in Nebraska, where bandits made off with $1 million, the largest heist on record in the West.

The state's favorite son, Will Rogers, born just north of here, put it right in a newspaper column welcoming 1931. "The man talked so nice when he sold it to us, we had no idea he would ever want it back," he wrote. "You see in the old days there was mighty few things bought on credit, your taste had to be in harmony with your income, for it had never been any other way. I think buying autos on credit has driven more folks to seek the revolver as a regular means of lively-hood than any other one contributing cause. All you need to make a deferred payment on anything now is an old rusty gun."

While the killing was objectionable, the concept itself—the getting, the survival—wasn't completely foreign, nor unthinkable. The floor had dropped out of the market; did anyone expect it to hold firm under ethics and decency? How thick was the moral membrane between pulling a pistol on a bank clerk and leaving your family to walk backward around the world?

As they finished their meal, J. C. Dabbs told Plennie he was lucky that car pulled up when it did. *Who knows what might've happened? These hills have always been wild and dangerous.*

"Now there are gypsies," the old man said, "and people coming through walking backwards."

They both laughed at the thought of it.

* * *

While Plennie slept in J. C. Dabbs's spare room, newspapers across the United States and Europe received via the ACME Newspictures agency a series of photographs showing Mr. Plennie L. Wingo of Abilene, Texas, in various stages of backward walking. There were close-ups of his grinning face, hat removed for a better view of his glasses, and wider shots of his full body navigating a highway shoulder, his little sign hanging from a string that ran over his shoulders and crossed at his sternum. The photos and accompanying paragraphs would be printed the next morning and evening in newspapers across the country, in places like Dixon, Illinois, and Oakland, California, and Ogden City, Utah. It was his first massive wave of publicity, run alongside stories about the bootlegger Jack "Legs" Diamond dying in a Catskills hospital and New York governor Franklin D. Roosevelt dismissing misfeasance charges against New York City mayor Jimmy Walker.

In the *Daily News Standard* of Uniontown, Pennsylvania, the photos and caption ran adjacent to a story that spoke, perhaps, to the trying era, one headlined MANIAC BINDS TWO BOYS TO TRACKS. The Spoutz brothers, the story said, had been gathering clovers for their pet rabbit when an armed madman abducted them and tied them to railroad tracks. They told police he mumbled the entire time, saying, "There is no reason for you living while I am starving." They were freed by their sister, thankfully, as police searched the area for the assailant. Then there was the retrograde wayfarer.

McALESTER, Okla., April 28. (UP)—Plennie L. Wingo walked backward out of McAlester today bent on circling the globe in that manner.

He wore a periscopic device which enabled him to see the direction in which he was going to avoid automobiles.

Wingo backed into town late yesterday after several days of backing from his home in Abilene, Texas, where he started his tour. He "headed" north for Joplin, Mo., from where he will turn eastward toward New York.

Papers as far away as London and Paris introduced the world to the backward-walking champion. France's *Le Matin* ran a story about Plennie above the fold on the front page, headlined UN AMÉRICAIN VEUT FAIRE LE TOUR DU MONDE À RECULONS.

Go around the world backward, this is the ambition of Mr. Plennie Wingo, a resident of Abilene (Texas), says a dispatch of this city. Equipped with a kind of periscope that lets him see what's going on behind his back, this globetrotter of a new genre has already covered distance between Abilene and McAlester (Oklohama). He's gone again today, all days backwards, to New York, via Missouri.

This ACME photo, taken outside McAlester, Oklahoma, on April 23, 1931,
ran in newspapers across the country. (Courtesy of Acme News Photos)

Even back home in Abilene, Plennie's people read the news. His little sister clipped the story from the newspaper and took it to school the next day for show-and-tell, proud as could be.

* * *

On his way into Checotah, Plennie flagged down the sheriff and told him about the gypsies. The lawman informed Plennie he'd already received several complaints and was on his way to chase them out of the county. Plennie told him about his resolution, to respect all nationalities on his walk, but he didn't know what to make of the handsy gypsies. The sheriff warned him to beware of them.

When Plennie reached Muskogee, it seemed like the whole town knew his name, like they'd been expecting him. He was pleased to learn that the *McIntosh County Democrat* had run a story about his visit to Checotah, and the *Miami Daily News-Record* ran two photographs and a few lines saying he was headed in the direction of that city. "Crabs walk backwards, but Plennie L. Wingo of Abilene, Texas, is not a crab although he does walk backwards," the odd news nugget read. The Muskogee paper, too, published a story in advance of his arrival.

When he hit downtown, a handful of businessmen hustled out to meet him, squeezing his hand and offering up invitations to hotel accommodations and dinner that evening. He met Frank Jamison, secretary of the Muskogee Automobile Club, and L. F. Scroggins, who sold road machinery, and A. H. Craig, who had eaten at Plennie's Mobley Café several years ago, on a trip to Abilene when times were good. Plennie ate for free in a private booth at Pete's Quick Lunch on West Okmulgee and then popped into the American Shoe Shop a few doors down so J. G. Cooper could replace his soles after twenty-two days dragging down gravel roads. A customer in the shoe shop got curious and asked Plennie what brand of shoe he wore.

"It's a good brand," Plennie said, "but until some shoe company decides to sponsor me, no one will ever know what kind of shoes I wear."

"I don't blame you," the fella said.

* * *

North of town he came upon a gas station, the sun high and the sky partly cloudy, the mercury a tad above seventy degrees. A handful of country boys were sitting around in the shade of the overhang, swapping stories. They perked up when Plennie approached. The station boss lifted the hose and motioned with the nozzle toward Plennie.

"Need refueling?" he asked good-naturedly.

"Sure," Plennie said, "but with water and soda pop."

The country boys looked him over, read his sign, then started asking a variety of silly questions.

"You ever stop to sleep?" one said, and the others laughed.

"You eat like other people, or backward, like you walk?" asked another.

Plennie took the ribbing with a smile.

"I'm just human, same as you," he said.

He downed a soda, told the boys to take good care, then began backing north up Highway 73. He wasn't gone long before he heard the whine of an automobile on the Oklahoma wind. When the dust-covered car overtook him, he noticed it was the same old boys from the filling station, slowing down now, stopping. The passenger in the front seat stuck his head out the window and asked if Plennie needed a ride. He politely declined.

"I'm walking all the way," Plennie said.

"Oh, come on," the kid said. "We won't tell anyone."

Plennie kept walking. It would've been nice to take a little ride. He'd already put in more than two hundred miles going backward. His legs were tired and his feet were sore.

"We'll drop you out just this side of town and no one will know about it," the boy pleaded.

"Yes," Plennie replied, "but I will."

Still, they insisted, almost like they had a bet going among them. The boys in the back wanted to know why he refused.

"Let's put it this way," Plennie said. "If I took a ride with you, wouldn't it be nice if I got a story in the paper that I was cheating?"

He looked hard at the boys.

"Just me knowing that I cheated would spoil the rest of my trip around the world," he said.

The car crept along beside him. One of the boys turned to another.

"I guess you owe me a dollar," he said.

Sure enough.

The stretch of road shimmered before them under the high sun. Gusts of prairie wind made the Indian grass dance on the shoulders and out in the fields, where little clumps of sawtooth oaks offered the only shade between them and the tree line. To the east rose the foothills of the Boston Mountains. And to the west, 237 flat miles away, at the bottom of a deep gully, there lay buried in the red dirt, undiscovered, the skull of a bison.

This skull was much larger than the familiar animals and had massive straight horns protruding from the sides of the cranium. It was also quite different in that a jagged, zigzagging line, like a lightning bolt, was painted on the forehead. The substance from which the brick-red paint was made was hematite, an ore of iron, common on the Earth's crust and mined from rock. The hematite itself had begun to form about two and a half billion years earlier, when oceans were rich in dissolved iron but void of free oxygen, and cyanobacteria somehow became capable of photosynthesis. The blue-green wormlike bacteria began using sunlight as energy to convert carbon dioxide into the first free-floating oxygen in the oceans. The oxygen combined with iron in the water to form hematite, which sank to the bottom and became rock. The deposits grew over hundreds of millions of years, layering rock upon rock upon rock, and when the oceans pulled back many years later they revealed mountains made of the stuff.

Much more time passed before an aboriginal hunter or shaman or medicine man mined the rock for ore to make paint, carried it some great distance along one of the innumerable ancient trails crossing the great continent, and drew upon the sun-bleached bison bone a jagged line, a symbol of power, a sign of his skill at killing. It would be another sixty-three years after Plennie took his trip before a university archaeologist would find the skull, painstakingly remove it from the earth, and declare the art to be more than ten thousand years old—the oldest painted object ever found in North America, made by a people who followed no calendar, for whom the seasons and the rising and setting sun ordered life.

The boys in the car watched Plennie.

"This walking backwards is no trick," one of them shouted. "Anybody can do it."

The boy's buddies started questioning his manhood, suggesting he couldn't keep up with old Pennie Wingo for a mile. They'd put money on it.

Plennie was a good sport. He agreed to pace the boy, and out of the car came the kid, shuffling to an imaginary starting line. And they were off. Plennie didn't try to make it hard on the boy, but by that time he was quite skillful at reversing, and people who saw his legs said that his calves had already started to move around to the front, like ripe grapefruit on his shins. The boy stayed with him for a while and then began to fall behind, the kids in the car razzing him as he gave up distance of Oklahoma road to the older man. Plennie watched him and could see the boy puffing hard. Soon he was weaving like a cowboy full of whiskey. By a half mile the boy had tuckered out and plopped down in the middle of the highway.

"I quit," he told his friends. "You can have all the backward walking. I don't want it."

* * *

Plennie stayed for free at the New Majestic Hotel in Wagoner, and the Butler Hotel in Pryor, and the Cobb Hotel in Vinita, and the Palmer Hotel in Afton. Somewhere along the way a man slipped him a business card, which Plennie tucked into his notebook. The card offered a profound paragraph of text explaining what it called the "Theory of Reincarnation":

When a man dies he is buried and his body is turned to fertilizer, which makes the grass grow green. A horse come along and eats the grass. Which after it has been digested, becomes a horse turd. Never kick a horse turd—it may be your uncle.

He spent his last Oklahoma evening in the beautiful Hotel Miami, seven stories tall, 180 rooms and "fireproof," on May 13, 1931. It had risen just a few years before and would service visitors to Picher, Oklahoma, a few miles north, where in 1913 men had discovered the richest lead and zinc mines in the world. Picher sprang up quick after the discovery, and the metal fields went on to produce twenty billion dollars' worth of ore in thirty years and half the lead and zinc used during World War I. The population skyrocketed to nearly fifteen thousand residents in 1926. When Plennie backed through on May 14, 1931, the town was at its apex.

But greed and ignorance have consequences in time, though not always for those who deserve them. The coming decades of unrestricted subsurface excavation would undermine the entire town and raise mountains of toxic, contaminated rock fragments heaped across the region, like the pocked crust of a moonscape. The groundwater would be poisoned. The people would fall ill and die in undignified ways. The government would declare the region ruined and pay people good money to move away and never come back. The homes and businesses would sit vacant, collecting graffiti and broken beer bottles. The city's pharmacist, a man who

swore he wouldn't leave until no one else needed him, who became known as the "last man standing," would die at age sixty of a
sudden illness. Residents of Picher and several other nearby ghost
towns would be mostly gone by the time a historical marker was
planted, nearly a century after man found value in the minerals. It
would stand as a relic among toxic mountains, and a reminder of
the toll of the taking.

10.

THE INTENT IS SUBLIME

Her name was Irene. He would always remember. She was the first sight that appeared in his rearview mirrors as he backed into the lobby of the first hotel he saw in the Kansas town of Baxter Springs. And what a sight she was.

Irene was talking to the landlady when Plennie walked in, but she looked up and fixed her eyes on this regressive but dapper gentleman making his way across the hardwood floor. Then he turned around, gave her a nod, and asked about getting a room for the night.

Before long they were sitting together at a table in the lounge, at her invitation, and Plennie was waxing about the first month of his inverted epic, about the gypsies and whatnot. He wore no wedding ring, and it's unknown whether Irene asked any questions that might have brought Della and Vivian to mind, but Plennie was happy to be in the company of anyone who was interested in his tales. As they talked and laughed, two little girls—pretty, neat, well-mannered—came down the stairs and hurried across the floor to join their mother.

Irene told Plennie that her husband was an interior decorator and he had been working a job in a nearby department store. As she spoke, he noticed that she kept glancing at the lobby door, and through the windows toward the street. Suddenly, she apologized and excused herself, then hustled the little girls up the stairs from whence they came. A few seconds later a man walked into the lobby, just in time to see them headed upstairs. He scanned the lounge, empty but for Plennie. The man gave him a hard look, then hurried up the stairs after his family.

Plennie exchanged glances with the landlady, still behind the counter. When the coast was clear, she walked over and, watching the stairs, told Plennie that the man was Irene's husband, and that he had a proclivity toward jealousy. Irene was so fearful of his covetousness that she didn't dare let him see her speaking with another man. In fact, the landlady said in a whisper, he had threatened to kill any man he caught talking to Irene.

This was a new one for Plennie.

Baxter Springs was a hopping little town, and the new Route 66, opened just five years before, had clearly been good for business. Three drugstores stood like soldiers along the main drag, Military Road, and automobiles lined the curbs. The place had gained notoriety as one of the bulliest cow towns in Kansas, a stopover where pokes could take a bath, tie one on, and get laid all under the same roof. Some thirty ladies of the night worked the crowds of cowboys and miners, prostitution the oldest capitalist by-product of men with time and money. It was a town bathed in blood, too, going all the way back to 1863, when a pro-Confederate band of guerrilla bushwhackers called Quantrill's Raiders slaughtered an unwitting Union detachment in the process of moving command headquarters from Kansas to Arkansas. The death toll totaled 103 men, including the marching band and an artist-correspondent for a news magazine. In 1872, the mayor of Baxter Springs shot dead a marshal trying to serve him with a warrant. In 1876, the outlaw Jesse James held up the Crowell Bank and made off with $2,900, headed for Indian Territory. A posse caught up to him and an accomplice about seven miles south, but the pursuers were waylaid, disarmed, and sent back to town empty-handed. There weren't many spots in Baxter Springs, in fact, that hadn't been the scene of bloodshed or thievery.

Plennie tried hard to keep to himself, wasting the day in the hotel, which sat on the same drag as a business called Harvey Undertaking and Furniture.

That Thursday evening, Plennie carried his pen and notebook and a few sheets of loose paper downstairs to the lobby to write a few letters to the folks back home. He wanted to check in on his mother and on Della and Vivian, to update them all and see how they were getting along. He had just about finished the first letter when Irene came down the stairs. He quickly began to fold the paper so he could proceed to his room and finish in privacy, but Irene stopped him with her eyes. He noticed again how attractive she was.

"Mr. Wingo," she said, "I'm terribly sorry about my husband."

She wore concern on her face. He was silent.

"But he is on this job now and won't get through until two a.m.," she said. "I'm terribly interested in your adventures, and there is no reason why we can't sit and talk, is there?"

Plennie, between a rock and a hard place, sat back down.

"Well," he said, "perhaps we can talk for a little while."

He began to tell of his journeys and the people he had met, but before long the beautiful woman began to pour her heart out there on the polished hotel table. She had marital troubles, she told him in confidence, and her husband was the root of much strife. He was so jealous, she said. She lived in constant fear of him flying off the handle and doing something he'd regret. Plennie couldn't keep his eyes off the front door. Sensing his unease, Irene kept assuring him that her husband would be working well past midnight and Plennie need not worry. They were, after all, just two human beings having a conversation, and what was wrong with that? The minutes ticked by, and Plennie couldn't remember ever being so acutely aware of time passing.

He was a man weighing choices and consequences, and as soon as he decently could, he said good night to Irene, excused himself, and made his way to his room, where he prepared for bed, tucked in, and lay there, wide awake.

At about two o'clock in the morning, the best he could figure, he heard a man's voice. It seemed to be coming from a nearby room, but he wasn't sure which. Then he heard cursing. Then he heard yelling. Then he heard hard-soled shoes on hardwood floors. Then, like a cry in the night, he heard his own name, clear as a bell.

He lay still, his thoughts slamming around inside his head, his heart beating in his ears. Irene and Irene's husband were talking about Plennie L. Wingo.

He would've escaped forward or backward or sideways if he could've, but then he heard Irene's husband say something unmistakable. The man said he was going to beat Plennie's door down and pound the backward-walking son of a bitch to death. He heard Irene's voice, higher, more frightened now, begging her husband to leave Plennie Wingo out of it. He had done nothing wrong. Nothing.

Fate visits Kansas just like it visits anywhere. It had done so a good number of times before, and it would again. Bonnie Parker and Clyde Barrow would rob Eden's Grocery Store down the street twice in the same week. A man would shoot himself and his son, eight years old and named after the god of thunder. Another would douse a grandmother and two police officers with gasoline and set them alight.

That night, Plennie heard pounding on the door. Then he heard a loud voice that did not belong to Irene's husband, but to the hotel manager, who told Irene's husband that if he caused any more trouble the police would be here in no time. Silence followed the shouting, and you could almost cut the stillness.

Plennie eventually found a little sleep and slipped out unnoticed the next morning around sunup, a Friday, as good a day as he could ever remember.

He was long gone, crossing northbound on the Rainbow Curve Bridge over Marsh Creek on Route 66, when the next issue of the *Baxter Springs Citizen and Herald* hit doorsteps. The edition included a column bemoaning what seemed to be a spike in killings. "It is utterly astounding and amazing the way in which wholesale murder exists and thrives in this country," the editor wrote. "Pick up almost any newspaper and read where someone somewhere was shot down on the street or in a café or other public place. As a general rule the news story will close with 'the assailants ran to a car and quickly escaped.' And this is the year of our Lord 1931 when we are supposed to be enjoying the greatest civilization this old world has ever known."

In the column adjacent was an account of the strange, unnamed man who had come backward through town just a few days before. He was held up as an object lesson on how to thrive when your back is against the wall.

WHEN a man passed through Baxter Springs one day this week, walking backward, he was set down by many as just another nut but, like the inebriate who believes all of his fellow men are drunk and himself entirely sober, they are wrong.

This young caterer, who is out of a job, conceived the idea of wearing a pair of spectacles with adjustable reflecting lenses that would allow him to see ahead while walking backward and is willing to punish himself for a period of three years to support his little family down there in Texas. His judgement may be poor but the intent is sublime, while a lot of the fellows who call him a nut are, figuratively, walking backward and looking ahead through reflective spectacles, hoping for good times they are sure they will not experience.

The truth of the matter is that the country is just as rich as it ever was. There is just as much money in the United States as we ever had and there is no over production. The people would eat up and wear out everything that has been accumulated if they could get the work to earn the money with which to purchase it, and it is the back-walkers who are preventing them from getting it.

"There is no business; the country is shot," groans the business back-walker, and he refuses to advertise. "You couldn't get a job for love or money," sighs the working man and he sits down to await the return of prosperity. The aggressive man and the hustling worker cut their overhead and wear out their shoes instead of their trousers, taking what they can get as profits, considering a rapid turnover rather than big profits, and never starve.

When this professional back-walker was in Baxter Springs he took off his reflective goggles and turned around and walked like other men and he looked a lot better. It's that way with the speculative back-walker. They would not only look better but the town would be a lot better off if all of them would remove their goggles and go to walking like normal human beings.

11.

AMERICAN DREAM

Joplin, Missouri, was the most high-and-mighty city Plennie'd seen since Dallas. It stuck out like a bow tie in the Ozark Mountains, stately and polished, trying hard to be noticed.

The "biggest little city in the world," as the boosters called it, was the product of conflict. The first mines were sunk around 1870, when Missouri had become the fifth-largest state by population in the Union, and St. Louis, just shy of three hundred miles east, was third in size of all American cities. Joplin rose up between two prior settlements that fought like angry siblings. It now boasted a streetcar dinging down Main Street, ten parks, six banks, two daily newspapers, 7,468 telephones, eighteen hotels, 450 retailers, eight theaters, two hospitals, twenty-four schools, six railroads, 56,708 volumes in the library, forty-two churches, and one police department made up of twenty-one officers, not counting the chief, Bert Blizzard, who had died from tuberculosis the year before.

It was getting late when Plennie walked into town, so he ducked into a nice café on Murphy Avenue for dinner. The place was clean and the food was delicious, but he ate practically alone. He was surprised it wasn't better patronized. Knowing a thing or two about how to run a café, Plennie asked the proprietor where the customers were.

Leslie Van Cleave said his shop was a new venture aiming to capitalize on the recent growth in Joplin. The city's population had been on the upswing for quite a few years and now numbered more than thirty-three thousand. A nine-story hotel complex had just opened down the street, in fact. But Van Cleave wasn't sure how to get the word out about his café and drugstore.

"What about advertising?" Plennie asked.

"What do you have in mind?" Van Cleave replied.

"Me," Plennie said.

He explained himself, highlighting how much attention is lent to a man going the wrong way. Van Cleave thought it was a great idea. He told Plennie he'd pay ten dollars if Plennie would walk backward around Joplin the next day carrying a sign advertising the café. Plennie was happy to have the work and the promise of extra money.

Plennie woke early the next day in the Roosevelt Hotel on Main Street and went to work, tooling in reverse along a significant chunk of Joplin's seventy miles of paved road, telling everyone he met about Van Cleave's café and drugstore, about the food and BILDUP, the quick tonic, and Caples No. 7 for paralysis, and all the Famous Caples Remedies. He walked and talked all day and was down to his last block when one of Joplin's finest grabbed his collar.

"What do you think you're doing?" the officer asked in a rough tone. "Don't you know there's a city ordinance against wearing signs on the street?"

Plennie said he did not, that he'd been in town less than a day.

"Well, there sure is," the cop said, "and you'd better strip off that sign before I run you in."

Plennie told the officer he was just a block from the café. He asked if he could hustle down the street and take the sign off there.

"No," the officer said. "I mean take it off now, or I'll throw you in the clink."

They'd banned dancing in Galena, Missouri, forbade lawn weeds in Sedalia, Missouri, and prohibited female teachers from smoking cigarettes in Moberly, Missouri, and Plennie wasn't in the mood to upset the cart. He removed Mr. Van Cleave's advertisement, nodded to the officer, and made his merry way down the block to collect his ten dollars and get on out of town.

Dealing with the agents of conformity was trying, no matter how much respect and deference Plennie could muster. It would happen again and again during his walk. So many police seemed to be on edge. The era had been incredibly bloody for men with badges.

Across the country, 307 law enforcement officers had been killed in the line of duty the year before, 1930. In no year since the signing of the Declaration of Independence had the toll of officers killed on duty come even close to that number, nor would it come close in the future, even as the population skyrocketed. The country had reached a sort of lawless crescendo, represented by the number of killed officers each decade since the Civil War: 21 in 1870, 33 in 1880, 58 in 1890, 70 in 1900, 105 in 1910, 202 in 1920, and 307 in 1930.

And 1931 was destined to be comparatively bloody. Shooting police seemed to be *en vogue* in the great cities, where criminal bootlegging enterprises took root after the Eighteenth Amendment was passed in 1919, banning the manufacture, sale, and transport of alcohol. The newspapers, fast becoming uniform, mass-produced rags aimed at the lowest common denominator, lapped up the bloodshed and brutality. So did Hollywood, where a new film called *Scarface*, which glorified the lifestyles of hit men and hoods, was in production and set for release in 1932.

The liquidation haunted even smaller police departments, like Joplin's. Three years before, in 1928, Detective Alex Brown was shot dead with his own gun while trying to apprehend a twenty-six-year-old ex-convict named William Claude Miller, accused of forging checks. Miller was caught a month later in Texas, driving a stolen car. They hung Officer Brown's photograph in the basement of Joplin's City Hall, alongside nine other portraits of policemen killed in the line of duty.

Before month's end, with Plennie still scooting backward through Missouri, Joplin police captain Alex Lachman would be slaughtered in a shootout with a prisoner, Harry Spencer, twenty-six, a former professional baseball player for the Joplin team whom Lachman had arrested for stealing a car.

The killers had a few commonalities, by and large. They were young and lawless and lacked formal education. They came of age at a time of collapse, saw no end to the ruin, and no geyser of upward economic mobility besides taking money and things from people who had both. They had access to weapons for killing and cars for fast getaways. They were *desperados*, and some with blood on their hands would be celebrated long after their deaths. The next Joplin officer to have his portrait hung in the City Hall basement was Detective Harry McGinnis, who was killed trying to arrest a young couple called Bonnie and Clyde in April of 1933.

* * *

An odd thing happened on Plennie's way to St. Louis.

He was nearing Springfield, Missouri, when a car pulled onto the shoulder and two men climbed out, wanting to chat. They made pleasant small talk for a while, mostly listening to Plennie's stories about his trip, and then the driver spoke up. He asked Plennie if it would be okay to carry him a short distance. He said he wanted to prove a point. The question came out of the blue Missouri sky.

"I don't know what your point is," Plennie said, "but if you promise not to harm me, I guess it will be okay."

"Oh, no," the man said. "By all means, no."

Plennie sort of leaned back and the man bent and scooped him into his arms. The stranger carried him like a husband would a bride on their honeymoon, about fifteen paces down the shoulder of Route 66, turned around, then walked back. He set young Plennie down gently, then straightened his posture. Then the man pinched the material of his pants at his thighs and lifted, revealing, to Plennie's astonishment, two artificial legs.

"Well," Plennic said, "I would never have believed it."

The man said he was a representative of a prosthetics company, and if Plennie should lose a leg on the trip, well, he'd be glad to help find a new one.

"Good to know," Plennie said.

* * *

As Plennie backed past his 500th mile on a lonely, littered stretch of Route 66 between Springfield and St. Louis in May of 1931, a writer and historian named James Truslow Adams was putting the finishing touches on a book he'd audaciously titled *The Epic of America*, to be published in the fall by Little, Brown. Adams wanted to plant in the annals of American letters a sweeping one-volume history of the United States, running chronologically from time immemorial to the 1930s, the first years of what was shaping up to be the Great Depression.

What Adams set out to do, more than anything else, was capture a feeling. He wrote that he had grown increasingly conscious of how different modern Americans were from the men and women of any other nation. Americans had been shaped by unique heritage and cultural experience.

He wanted to explore the beginning "of that American dream of a better, richer, and happier life...which is the greatest contribution we have as yet made to the thought and welfare of the world."

That phrase—"American dream"—wasn't in widespread use until Adams wrote that combination of words more than thirty times in his book. He coined it. He defined it.

"Ever since we became an independent nation," he wrote, "each generation has seen an uprising of ordinary Americans to save that dream from the forces which appeared to be overwhelming it."

Adams chronicled the rise of a nation, from a handful of starving immigrants to 120 million industrious individuals made up of all the races of the world, from a country with a guard barely big enough to defend the stockade at Jamestown from Indians, to a nation with 25 million men of military age from whom we could draw a massive army to send across the ocean to fight a world war, all in only nine generations. He chronicled the movement of settlement from east to west, like the sun, to the last frontier, until there was no more land to tame. He pointed out that the pursuit of the frontier, by the perfect concoction of peoples and creeds, is what gave us the American dream. And in 1931, since the frontier no longer existed to absorb our energies, he called for Americans to pour themselves into establishing civilized contentment in the youngest nation.

Adams staked out the ethos of the American dream, for the first time, for everyone to come after him, and the simple phrase would plant itself so firmly in the American psyche that its definition would forever be simply inherited. The American dream was not about owning a plantation in the South or claiming 160 acres in Indian Territory or riding the rails west for unknown opportunity. It was now about settling in.

History had always been on the march from east to west, and explorers had found another West, in North America, to make the sunfall last just a little longer. Then came the Revolution in 1775 and Jefferson's Northwest Ordinance in 1787 and the Louisiana Purchase in 1803 and Lincoln's Homestead Act in 1862 and Horace Greeley saying "Go west, young man" in 1865 and, in 1890, the superintendent of the US Census announced that rapid western settlement meant that "there can hardly be said to be a frontier line," meaning the frontier had been settled, closed. And three years later, in 1893, to mark the 400th anniversary of Columbus's discovery of the New World, historian Frederick Jackson Turner in a big speech floated the idea that the entire conquest of the frontier had been the nation's most formative experience. Manifest destiny had imparted to us as a whole rugged individualism, ingenuity, optimism. Conquest made America great. Turner said the West had been a safety valve for social danger, a bank account on which Americans might continually draw to meet losses. "No grave social problem could exist while the wilderness at the edge of civilization opened wide its portals to all who were oppressed, to all who with strong arms and stout heart desired to hew a home and a career for themselves."

"And now," Turner wrote, "four centuries from the discovery of America, at the end of a hundred years of life under the Constitution, the frontier has gone, and with its going has closed the first period in American history." The Indian gave way to the explorer, who gave way to the trader, who gave way to the rancher, who gave way to the farmer, who built his home. Game trail to footpath to country road to highway, where a man walked backward now, representing his time and place.

When Plennie Wingo's great-grandfather was born, the United States extended only to the Mississippi River. The year his grandfather was born, gold was discovered in California, and as a young man, Benjamin Duncan Wingo moved his family from Alabama to Hale County, Texas, the Caprock region, in what was then called No Man's Land. Plennie's father turned twenty years old the year

THE MAN WHO WALKED BACKWARD

North Dakota, South Dakota, Montana, Washington, and Idaho were admitted to the United States.

Where did that leave Plennie Wingo? His ancestors were concerned with getting there, and they had, and the maps were complete. They closed the frontier five years before Plennie was born. What's a man to do when there is nothing left to be done? When his spirit stirs, when there is no geographical void to receive the fruit of all his energy, what then? Maybe it made perfect sense to turn around and walk backward rather than to simply settle in. Maybe it made sense to re-create in reverse the migration of mankind, from the grave to the cradle, the wellspring of life.

It's funny what a fella thinks about when he's alone.

12.

BONE DRY FOREVER

Rumor of Plennie's walk preceded him to St. Louis, so when he neared the outskirts of the city there were two journalists from the *St. Louis Post-Dispatch* waiting beside the road. That Wednesday was hot and humid, but he was glad to stop for the attention, and for the human contact. He'd walked nearly all the way across the Show Me State having had only one decent conversation, with two men and their wives at a roadside park. They were touring the country on vacation, and they'd read about Plennie and invited him to join them for a picnic lunch so they could ask him about his travels. Before they parted, they told Plennie that if he ever made it to Pittsburgh he should look them up. He put their names in his journal, George W. Trumond and Harry G. Walker, and wives, Pittsburgh.

"Had lunch together," he wrote in the margin. "Colored."

The St. Louis journalists wanted his story and some photos for the evening paper, and before he could really get to telling them about his trip they were hustling off toward the office at Twelfth Boulevard and Olive Street to meet their deadline. That afternoon, as the buildings of the old French outpost on the Mississippi River grew taller in his mirrors, the evening papers went out and readers were treated to news about a black man from Boston who repaired baby carriages for $12 a week winning $150,000 in the Irish Hospital Derby at Epsom

Downs, a wounded bank robber admitting to four local holdups, and the poor Vanderbilt couple over on Locust Street, who were found with their throats slit. Mrs. Vanderbilt had written her cousin, ending her letter with a Sunday school chorus, "O how sweet it will be in that beautiful land, So free from all sorrow and pain." Mr. Vanderbilt had not been able to find work and was fast with the razor.

Elsewhere, the Italian fascists and Mussolini were arresting Catholic youth leaders on political warrants, and Mayor Victor Miller of St. Louis was visiting Paris to lay a wreath on the tomb of the Unknown Soldier at the Arc de Triomphe, and, hey: MAN WALKING BACKWARD AROUND WORLD REACHES CITY.

Plennie L. Wingo, a former restaurant keeper of Abilene, Tex., backed through St. Louis today on a reverse walking trip around the world. He left Fort Worth, Tex., on April 15, expects to be in New York next fall and hopes to return home by way of California within three years. He is 36 years old.

Equipped with rear-vision mirrors on his dark goggles, Plennie backed briskly along Manchester Avenue toward the Free Bridge, pausing occasionally to sell photographs of himself to defray expenses.

"I hadn't heard of anybody backing around the world," he said, "so I just thought I'd try it. I trained for six months before starting out. It's great for the health, all right. I was nearly bald when I started and now look at my hair.

"I've lost 22 pounds and am in fine physical fettle. I average three miles an hour, but stop whenever I feel like it. I haven't any important engagement until I see my wife and baby again three years from now."

So by the time he was in the thick of St. Louis, folks were looking out for him. The manager of the colossal Mayfair Hotel,

Raymond Calt, stopped Plennie on the sidewalk and invited him to spend his stay as a guest of the hotel. Another man interrupted his walk. "My name is Pete Mazza," he said, "and I'd sure like you to spend your time here in my home in University City." Plennie told him about the Mayfair's offer. "Oh, well," Mazza said, "how about coming to my place after a day or two at the Mayfair." Plennie thought that sounded swell and agreed. He sold Mazza six postcards to boot, and pocketed a dollar fifty.

As he was moving on, a man vaulted out of a bar and grabbed Plennie's hand, shaking it and pressing a five-dollar bill into his palm, enough to buy a new pair of suit pants or two new felt hats. "I've been waiting all day for you," the charitable drunk slobbered. Plennie could smell the booze on the man's breath and saw in his unfocused eyes excitement and intoxication. Just as the man was turning Plennie loose, a police car screeched to a stop at the curb and an officer jumped out. The man's expression changed as the cop walked toward him, reaching for his handcuffs. Plennie couldn't help but watch, slack-jawed. Welcome to Mound City.

* * *

Pilgrims brought more beer than water to the New World on the *Mayflower* in 1620, it's true. And it's true that the first cobblestone road in New Amsterdam, later called New York, was laid so a Dutch brewer near Wall Street could have a smooth path from his brewery to the taverns. And it's also true that George Washington was an amateur brewer and Thomas Jefferson fancied himself one, and that the signers of the Declaration of Independence were good and lit much of the time.

But no American city had sprouted up around beer quite like St. Louis. To understand why is to understand the city. As the nineteenth century dawned and the vast area between the Mississippi and the Rocky Mountains opened to settlement with the 1803 Louisiana Purchase, St. Louis was a hopping trading post on the western bank of the Mississippi River, and fresh drinking water wasn't readily available. To partake from the Mighty Mississippi, citizens of St. Louis had to let water stand for a while. And when all the sediment had finally settled, it would fill a full quarter of the container. So they collected rainwater in cisterns, but frequent droughts meant long spells without enough clean water to drink. The alternatives were cider, distilled spirits, and beer. The colonists had always swilled, drinking some thirty-four gallons of beer and cider, five gallons of distilled spirits, and one gallon of wine per person in 1790.

In the beginning, everyone drank local beer because the only beer was local. In St. Louis, as early as 1810, brewers began beckoning trappers, traders, and transplants in the *Louisiana Gazette*, the newspaper that covered the new territory:

> *Those who wish to be supplied with table beer and porter will please direct their orders to the Brewery, or to Edward Hempstead, Esq. St. Louis who will always have a quantity in his cellar ready for sale.*

The opening of canals and railroads gave brewers shipping options, but transporting beer any distance was a problem because of the style of beer settlers preferred. Ale, stout, and porter were all made with a strain of yeast that rose during fermentation, making it prone to bad bacteria and spoiling if the beer wasn't consumed almost immediately. There was an exception, and this is where St. Louis came into the picture. Bavarians had long been brewing beer with a yeast that sank, making a clear and lighter beer, called *lagerbier*. And in the middle of the nineteenth century, waves of thirsty German immigrants had begun to come ashore and head west in search of opportunity in the unsettled lands on the other side of the Mississippi River. Many of them stopped in the French city of St. Louis, and wrote home telling kinfolk of the grand life in the Midwestern United States.

The German Emigrant Aid Society of St. Louis was there to welcome them. The city exploded, by 1850 swelling to four times its population in 1840, the year *lagerbier* debuted. Breweries sprang up in German neighborhoods all over the city, and by 1853 there were thirty-six in operation, making 216,000 barrels of beer a year. Half were lager.

In 1852, as Franklin Pierce and Winfield Scott duked it out for the presidency and Americans debated the controversy of slavery, a German brewer named George Schneider opened a small brewery on a little hill in St. Louis between Lynch and Dorcas Streets. Schneider found such success with his lager that he expanded by building the Bavarian Brewery nearby. But loans came due and bills went unpaid, so he sold his brewery to the Hammer brothers, who tried to make a go of it but wound up in bankruptcy.

The fellow who had a significant lien on the bankrupt brewery happened to be a successful soap and candle maker named Eberhard Anheuser. He took over the brewery and soon partnered with his new son-in-law, Adolphus Busch, who had arrived in St. Louis in 1857 and showed a knack for business working as a mud clerk with the steamboats along Commission Row.

Looking to expand, Busch, who by then had taken over operations, fixed his father-in-law's brew, which one magazine had described as "so inferior [that] St. Louis rowdies were known to project mouthfuls of it back over the bar." He began employing new techniques developed in the 1870s by the French scientist Louis Pasteur, who had figured out that applying heat killed bacteria and extended shelf life. Busch also started to brew a pilsner from a recipe he'd found in a Bohemian town called Budweis.

He called his production Budweiser. In the 1880s, the Anheuser-Busch Brewing Association went from being the thirty-second-largest brewery in the country to the second-largest, behind only the Pabst Brewing Co. of Milwaukee. As Busch's reach grew, he planted new mechanical refrigeration machines in branches in Brooklyn, Kansas City, Dallas, and Sherman, Texas. The invention of the crown bottle cap in 1892 allowed Busch to think even bigger. His single small brewery in St. Louis had grown into an industrial plant that employed 2,200 men and sprawled over forty acres like a city. It was fast on its way to becoming the largest brewery works in the world.

The temperance movement of the late nineteenth century was of little concern to most brewers, many of whom contributed to the coffers of politicians who enjoyed a drink, whether they said so or not. But a new adversary was organizing, and by late 1895 the Anti-Saloon League began to wage an ingenious strategic campaign to infiltrate and pressure major political parties. They first attacked the saloons, rather than going after the alcohol industry as a whole, and found some success passing laws that cut the number of direct-to-customer suppliers of beer. The prohibitionists were helped along by a series of national magazine exposés on commercialized vice and the corrupt alliances between brewers and politicians. Southern states were the first to dry up between 1907 and 1909—Georgia, Oklahoma, Alabama, Mississippi, and North Carolina.

In some ways, the complaints of the prohibitionists were legitimate. Competition among breweries had outfitted cities with a slew of saloons, and for every family-friendly drinking establishment there were four or five blood buckets. If a brewer opened a saloon at a vacant intersection, immediately three others would plant their saloons on the remaining corners, and employ attractions like sexy women or gambling to beat the competition. And because of competition, they almost never closed. By 1909, there was one saloon for every three hundred St. Louis residents.

Brewers tried to fight the Anti-Saloon League by encouraging regulation of the liquor traffic, the licensing of saloons, and penalties against the disorderly establishments, thereby quelling the League's most successful propaganda. In 1909 Anheuser-Busch began to set aside a chunk of money for an educational campaign, to show Americans the temperate side of consumption and booze's benefits to society, the virtues of beer. The company partnered with the Joseph Schlitz Brewing Co. to publish two-column probeer articles on the front page of many newspapers in the United States. But it wasn't much help against the wave of prohibition. Five states went dry in 1914, four in 1915. Sales fell. When war broke out, many Americans were hostile toward Germany and, by extension, anything that sounded German, including good German-American beer. This put the beer industry, and Anheuser-Busch, on its heels.

The prohibitionists capitalized on the sentiment after the German sinking of the British passenger ship *Lusitania*, and on the idea that banning alcohol and shutting down breweries would cough up laborers who could be diverted to help build boats, make artillery, or fight the war. The Anti-Saloon League went so far as to link drinking beer with rooting for Germany to win the war, declaring in a pamphlet: "Everything in the country that is pro-German is anti-American. Everything that is pro-German must go."

Cards fell left and right. Moral outrage boiled. Fear of immigration bubbled.

Brewing stopped at Anheuser-Busch in 1918 when President Wilson, dealing with crop failure and labor supply, forbade the wartime use of grain to make malt liquor. But by then Anheuser-Busch had become such an integral part of the fabric of St. Louis that businessmen and journalists across the city called on the president to allow the brewery to produce nonalcoholic beverages and other products. Busch had so diversified operations that he was all but prepared for the coming ban on the manufacture of beer. In late 1918, a *Post-Dispatch* reporter asked August Busch about his prospects should the states ratify the Eighteenth Amendment, which had already cleared the House and Senate. "If they do ratify it, I am ready," he said. "All I can say is that I am looking ahead and planning on the theory that the country will have prohibition."

By January 1920 it did. Signs went up in St. Louis saying:

BONE DRY FOREVER
BUY NOW FOR THE REST OF YOUR LIFE

The number of breweries in the US making full-strength beer fell from 1,300 in 1916 to none in 1926. Distilleries dropped by 85 percent. Wineries fell from 318 in 1914 to 27 in 1925. Tax revenues from distilled spirits dropped from $365 million to $13 million.

Only those that diversified could weather the change. The others faded away. One pioneer of St. Louis brewing, William J. Lemp II, shot himself to death in the brewery office in 1923. Friends blamed Prohibition and a closed production plant for his troubles.

The year Plennie arrived, Anheuser-Busch was holding strong. The valued local company covering seventy city blocks ran an advertisement in the *St. Louis Star*, spelling out its sustaining operation:

> *Originally in the brewing business, the company was compelled in 1919 to readjust its entire business structure and today it is actively engaged in the production of barley, Budweiser malt syrup, ginger ale, Budweiser Brew, yeast, refrigerator truck bodies, ice cream cabinets, corn products and Diesel engines.*

Almost immediately behind Prohibition came new and inventive and bloody enterprises organized to keep Americans as drunk as they wanted to be. The thirst for liberty could not be quenched.

* * *

As Plennie stood agape on the St. Louis sidewalk, the cop proceeded to handcuff his charitable, dull-eyed donor and place him in the squad car. The sound of the man's exasperated protests filled the city street. Plennie looked at the five-dollar bill in his hand.

That was the way it was, the way it had been for a decade. The ban made criminals of everyone, and their mothers weren't far behind. The law rushed the smallest infractions.

Plennie thought he was next when another police car pulled to the curb. He hadn't even made it all the way into the city and already he was in trouble, he thought. Alas, the police officer just wanted to escort him across the busy intersections. The year before, 156 people had been killed in car crashes in St. Louis, and 117 of them were pedestrians. "As far as the pedestrian is concerned, the situation grows steadily worse," read an editorial in the *St. Louis Star*, titled THE DANGERS OF WALKING. "Human life still is one of the cheapest things of our so-called modern civilization." Traffic enforcement had grown so lax the police chief was fuming. He accused his officers of lying down on the job and issued an order for stronger enforcement, or they'd be brought before the disciplinary board. The car ruled the road. There were no protected lanes or walk signals. The city lacked the infrastructure to protect regular-walking pedestrians, much less those going backward.

Plennie thanked the officers and told them he appreciated their interest. The driver grinned. "Oh, it's not you we're interested in," he said. "We just don't want to clean you off the streets after the traffic gets through with you."

The cops tooled along in front of him until he reached the Western Union. When he emerged walking forward, the same cop spoke up. "We just wanted to see if you could walk forward," he said. "I think you do better backward." Then they sped away—probably to bust a drunk.

The enforcement of the Prohibition laws had taken on a new seriousness. If the law was to work, it had to be enforced. In 1931, more liquor cases were brought—56,938—than any other year. Shockingly, the cat-and-mouse game had grown deadlier. In the previous fiscal year, five lawmen and seven civilians were killed during enforcement of the liquor law. But so far in 1931, deaths had shot up, with 70 agents and 162 civilians dead in the first six months.

In St. Louis, there seemed to be a new arrest every day. "My men," the police chief told reporters, "will make a practice of arresting patrons of cafés and restaurants when the patrons are found to be in possession of liquor."

The West End cafés were a favorite target. One in particular. Just past midnight on January 19, 1922, an undercover officer thought he smelled pre-Prohibition juice being served to customers and called in the raiders, who carted off twelve men, twelve women, and the proprietor, Silvio Mazza. Just two days later, twenty police officers and Prohibition enforcement agents kicked open the doors of Mazza's café again. Couples who had been dancing and drinking scrambled to flee. "We're pinched!" someone shouted. The jazz band quit playing as men and women smashed bottles of booze on the floor. Police arrested fifty-five people that night. They hauled off fourteen women, the African-American jazz band, and the three Mazza brothers, Silvio, Tony, and Pete.

* * *

Every Joe in St. Louis seemed to be selling something. The polished lobby of the eighteen-story Mayflower Hotel was filled with salesmen. Plennie met F. M. Stambaugh of Stambaugh & Sons selling tools and dies, and Fred G. Benson selling real estate and insurance and Joe Wolf from Wolf's Department Store, who wanted to outfit you and your entire family. In a strange twist of fate, Plennie even bumped into Dr. Geiber, the man who'd invented the rear-vision glasses he wore.

Most of them had read about him in the newspapers. He felt like a big deal, and they were enthusiastic about his venture but disappointed to hear he hadn't gotten a full sponsor for the trip. Several of them offered advice, as salesmen are wont to do.

"I think I know the reason you're having trouble," one told Plennie that night. "Right now, in the Depression, the whole world is going backward. Everybody's business is going backward. So why should they advertise it by employing someone like you, who is going backward, too?"

It made sense, but that was the whole gimmick. If he turned around and walked forward he was just a guy.

He desperately needed a sponsor, some way to liquidate this adventure so he wouldn't have to worry about expenses and so he could send some money back to his people in Abilene. Things had gotten so bad that his father and brothers were forced to resort to picking cotton again, which was a hell of a hard way to make a living. One of Plennie's earliest childhood memories was set in a cotton field, the sun white-hot and the air dry as jerky, with his brothers and dad hunched over, all. And while the memory wasn't happy, it was not sad, either. It was just a memory of togetherness and the hardest kind of work.

Also of concern were Della's letters, which were growing increasingly mysterious. Plennie tried to convince her to abide, to have patience. He promised his fortune would come, and every newspaper clipping he sent home was evidence of wide general interest in what he was doing. Had she not seen his photographs in the *St. Louis Post-Dispatch*, the daily newspaper in the seventh-largest city in the country, with a population of 822,000 people? In any event, having a benefactor might fix shut the wounds he'd left open in Texas. And St. Louis, Missouri, happened to be the shoe manufacturing center of the world.

Making shoes was a northeastern trade at first, based mostly in Lynn, Massachusetts. But a series of inventions—the sewing machine in 1848, the heeling and welting machines in the 1860s, the lasting machine in 1883—reduced the need for skilled craftsmen, and shoe production plants began to spring up in places where labor was cheap. On the backs of the Brown brothers, transplants from New York, the railroad, and the cheap labor of women and children, St. Louis had twenty-four shoe manufacturers in 1880. By the turn of the century, the city had emerged as a major shoe center, with factories staffed by German immigrants. By 1905, it was the third-largest shoe manufacturing city in the country. By 1913, St. Louis shoe houses produced and sold nearly twenty-eight million pairs of shoes in sixty-one factories for $70 million.

With the help of the salesmen, Plennie began to cobble together a list of companies he could approach, here and elsewhere, about sponsorship. Before long he had twenty-four names, including the Jarman Shoe Co., Johnston & Murphy Shoe Co., Commonwealth Shoe Company, and Stacy Adams Co. He decided to start at the top. But he left each meeting dejected, unable to sell anyone on the idea. The last shoe company on his list was the biggest and best, the leader of the shoe industry, which ran advertisements in newspapers and magazines across America: the Brown Shoe Company, makers of Buster Brown Blue Ribbon Shoes for boys and girls. Plennie remembered Buster Brown from his boyhood in

West Texas. A representative came to town once or twice a year on a horse-drawn wagon decorated with advertisements. And riding along with the shoe salesman was a little person dressed in a cute little red suit—Buster Brown himself, accompanied by his bulldog, Tige.

Plennie arrived at company headquarters full of vim and vigor, ready to pitch himself as a real-world backward-walking advertisement for Brown shoes. He prepared himself on the sidewalk, then pulled open the door and stepped inside the office. What he saw stole his breath. Sitting around the office were twenty Buster Browns, and twenty Tiges.

He told the lady behind the front desk that he thought the Buster Brown who came to West Texas was *the* Buster Brown, the only Buster Brown in the world. She just laughed and told Plennie that they actually employed forty-two little people for their advertising. And she shocked him again by casually mentioning that this was the only form of advertising the firm employed. He bowed his head, turned, and walked forward out of the office.

* * *

Plennie fished a business card out of his journal. Pete Mazza. He found a phone and dialed the number. Pete Mazza seemed happy to receive the call. He told Plennie he'd pick him up, and before long, Plennie was riding shotgun in Mazza's snazzy automobile toward his home in University City, a streetcar suburb west of downtown. Mazza lived in the most beautiful mansion Plennie had ever seen, with ten or twelve rooms, polished floors and cabinets, and ornate fixtures. He employed a staff of three to maintain his home and serve him meals. Mazza and Plennie made small talk as they ate lunch alone. Plennie wondered about Mazza's family when he saw no wife or children, but he swallowed his questions.

He also swallowed a stiff drink. Alcohol seemed to be plentiful at Mazza's house.

That afternoon, Mazza had a surprise. They loaded back into the car and drove a few miles to Sportsman's Park, on Grand Boulevard, on the north side of the city, to watch the Cardinals from St. Louis play the Giants from New York in front of 27,611 fans. The day was gorgeous, with highs in the low eighties. Plennie watched his first major-league baseball game with the eyes of a child. The Giants tied the game at seven in the top of the ninth; then the Cardinals drove in a run in the tenth to win and the place came alive with a sound Plennie had never heard before, a scream from twenty-six thousand throats.

The newspapers were selling quick around the stadium when the game turned out. The headline, big and bold and stretched all the way across the front of 1A, wasn't exactly shocking, but it was something. CAPONE INDICTED FOR EVADING TAX ON $1,038,654, it read.

The Feds had been investigating the man called "Scarface Al" for two years. They had questioned more than a thousand people, and the only evidence of crime they could use to bring a case was that Capone owed $215,089 in back taxes on underground earnings between 1924 and 1929. Capone had turned himself in at the federal courthouse in Chicago earlier that day, accompanied by his lawyer. Elsewhere on the front page, John B. Huesmann, a laborer, died from a skull fracture, becoming the seventy-seventh person in the city to be struck and killed by a car since January 1. And there were two apparent suicides in St. Louis, a demoted railroad clerk who jumped out a sixth-story window at Broadway and Pine, and a real estate agent who had become "inactive in business" a year before and was found forty-eight hours after death, lying beside a shotgun. In sports, Babe Ruth had homered in the ninth inning, his tenth home run of the season, pushing the Yankees past the St. Louis Browns in New York.

Back at the mansion, Pete Mazza broke out his booze again. They had a drink, then another; then Mazza said, "Come on, let's go to the club."

Speakeasies had been the target of intense prosecution, but it seemed like every time one place was shuttered, another opened somewhere else. Police were just wasting money. New York's new police commissioner, Grover Whalen, launched an effort to crack down, raiding fifty-five speakeasies. According to the wiseacre press, that left just 29,945 more in the city to raid.

Pete Mazza and Plennie pulled up to one in St. Louis after dark and walked to the door. Mazza introduced Plennie as his guest and they ducked inside. Plennie had never seen such a place. He gazed around through thick smoke. Women in short dresses puffed on cigarettes and clinked glasses. Men rolled dice and ringed poker tables two deep as dealers dealt twenty-one. Slot machines lined the walls. Mazza led Plennie to a pool table, where they played a few games. This was a day of firsts. The drinks flowed.

They left the club at 1 a.m., the Missouri cityscape blurring by outside the car. Plennie looked at Mazza.

"Believe me," he said, "if I had a home as nice as yours, I'd be staying home all the time."

Mazza surprised him. Maybe the liquor had loosened him up.

"You don't know how lonely it gets around here," he said. "I used to have a family and felt the way you do. But things have changed."

There was no stopping him now. He told Plennie how he'd come over from Italy, settled in St. Louis, got a job as a butcher. He worked long hours to get ahead, saving money, neglecting his family.

"I was a good provider, but I was too busy to spend time with them," he said. "One day, my wife told me she had decided to quit me and go back to her home in Italy with the children. Now I have the controlling interest in the plant, the largest in the city, with all the business I can handle. But I'm all alone. I try to be happy, but I can't."

Mazza had become a very wealthy man, but money doesn't mean much when your wife and kids are gone. Plennie could relate to part of that.

"That's why I keep inviting people like yourself to come and spend a little time with me," Mazza said.

The next morning, Plennie said goodbye to Pete Mazza and thanked him for everything, telling him what a pleasure it had been to visit with him. Mazza said the pleasure was his and he handed Plennie an envelope, sealed. "Keep this with you," he said. "Don't open it unless you are in need of help."

* * *

The next day's newspaper carried an update:

> ST. LOUIS, Mo.—It's kind of lucky for the engineer that Plennie L. Wingo is a man instead of a ship, because the way Plennie is walking around the world, he's going astern when he's going forward and he'd have to signal starboard when he wanted to turn port.
>
> Plennie is planning to walk around the world—backwards, and already has walked that way from his home in Abilene, Texas, to this city.
>
> As his eyes are normally placed, they're useless for seeing ahead—or should it be astern?—so he is equipped with "periscope" rear-vision goggles, the wide windows of which enable him to see what is coming toward him when he looks as though he was walking away from it.
>
> He's the only man able to see both front and rear at the

same time, anyway, because the special goggles have extraordinary glass in their center lenses so he can see what's behind him when it is in front of him, and the side-mirrors reflect what is in front of him when it's behind him.

His rate of progress is about three miles an hour when he's going full steam ahead in reverse.

13.

DON'T STOP

The fellow in the tollbooth on the Eads Bridge wouldn't take his money.

"Aren't you the man who walks backwards?" the man said.

"That's me," Plennie replied.

"Well, sir, you get to walk across the bridge without paying the dime."

Plennie thanked him and sold him a postcard, then started across, the first person he or anybody had ever heard of crossing the Mississippi River backward. He was halfway across the bridge, an engineering marvel envisioned and financed by a young Andrew Carnegie sixty years before, when he suddenly recalled the stories his grandpa used to tell about the Mississippi. He could practically hear the old man's voice settling into the story about how Grandma learned she could swim. She'd never before been in water deeper than a bathtub. But they'd been fishing the Mississippi in a johnboat when she hooked a massive catfish. In the process of wrestling the monster aboard, the boat turned over, and both parties went into the drink. "Swim or drown," Grandpa said. "Come on, Ma." When he reached the shore he finally checked to see if she was okay. There was Grandma, right behind him. They were both still alive and kicking back home.

Plennie wasn't more than a half mile into East St. Louis, Illinois, when he caught in his mirrors the stare of a big policeman. Something about the man's look told Plennie he was about to be stopped. He kept pacing backward until he saw the officer's big hand go up in his mirrors. He whipped around at the last moment, facing forward, before the cop could touch him. The harassment was getting tiring.

"You can't walk backward here," the cop said.

Of course. Plennie could see that the officer was somehow perturbed. Who knows why? Plennie explained yet again who he was and what he was doing, that he'd come backward 672 miles so far without issue or harm, but the cop was having none of it and demanded he turn around.

"You might get hurt," the officer said.

This was a city that had recently been through a period of great upheaval. The buildup to the war had sucked many laborers into active duty, and they'd been replaced by African-Americans migrating out of the Jim Crow South. By the spring of 1917, blacks were arriving in St. Louis at a rate of two thousand per week, many of them finding work with the Aluminum Ore Company and the American Steel Company, and in the East St. Louis rail yards, the nexus of dozens of regional lines. They were also called in to break strikes, adding to racial tensions that were already boiling by May 1917, when the National Guard was summoned to help disperse a violent march on the city by three thousand white men.

The bloodshed began in early July. A car full of whites drove through the black neighborhood, firing at houses. When a police unit accompanied by a local reporter drove to the same neighborhood to investigate, the residents opened fire on the car, killing one detective and mortally wounding another. The cops parked the bullet-riddled car in front of the police station the next morning, then stood by while the white residents got their vengeance. They set fire to homes of blacks, then shot the residents as they fled.

Others they lynched. Six thousand black residents were left home-less. The death toll climbed to nine whites and at least thirty-nine blacks. The police were never held to account. "All the impartial witnesses agree that the police were either indifferent or encour-aged the barbarities, and that the major part of the National Guard was indifferent or inactive," wrote the *St. Louis Post-Dispatch*. "No organized effort was made to protect the Negroes or disperse the murdering groups. The lack of frenzy and of a large infuriated mob made the task easy. Ten determined officers could have prevented most of the outrages. One hundred men acting with authority and vigor might have prevented any outrage." Ten thousand blacks marched in silent protest down Fifth Avenue in New York. Marcus Garvey said it was "time to lift one's voice against the savagery of a people who claim to be the dispensers of democracy." The city would be marked permanently by the event, and well into the next century whites would follow an unspoken rule of never stopping in East St. Louis.

Here, fourteen years after the violence, stood a man wearing the uniform of that apathetic organization, now concerned about the well-being of a fellow walking backward.

Plennie, in his nicest Texan voice, tried again to explain, said he appreciated immensely the good officer's concern, but he had nav-igated the entirety of the city of St. Louis proper without getting hurt, and, by and large, without police escort, and he felt certain he could get by all right here. He read nothing but obstinacy on the cop's face. So Plennie scanned the sidewalk for a stone and drew a line on the sidewalk where he'd stopped. He faced forward, brushed past the cop, and proceeded to City Hall. There, driven by no small amount of frustration, he asked to see the police chief, got a quick audience, and laid out his situation. The chief laughed.

"Sure, I've been reading about you, Mr. Wingo," he said. "I'm sure if you got through St. Louis alive, you'll be safe enough here."

The chief grabbed a pen from his desk, scratched a note on a piece of letterhead, and handed it to Plennie. "If anyone stops you, just show him this."

Back outside, back across town, back to his line on the sidewalk. He turned and began backpedaling. Sure enough, there was the exact same cop, waiting. Even more upset, the officer grabbed Plennie by the collar. "I thought I told you..." he said through gritted teeth.

Plennie reached into his jacket and held the note up to the officer. The cop's face grew red as he read the note. When he finished, he shoved it back into Plennie's chest.

"All right," he said. "Go ahead and break your fool neck for all I care."

An article appeared in the next edition of the *St. Louis Star*, on the front page, along with stories about Germany asking America to forgive reparations, and ten thousand striking miners in western Pennsylvania rioting against police:

Backward Hiker Has Run-In With Cop

Plennie L. Wingo, Abilene, Tex., who left Fort Worth April 15 in an attempt to walk around the world backward, ran into difficulty with East St. Louis police today. As he neared the east end of Eads Bridge, Patrolman Patrick Ryan stopped him and inquired: "What are you doing?"

After Wingo explained, Ryan said, "You can't walk backward here, you might get hurt."

Wingo turned around and walked forward until he found police headquarters and Chief of Police James A. Leahy. Explaining the situation to the chief, Wingo was told he might walk through the city any way he wanted to. The hiker returned to the point of his interrupted walk and resumed his backward march.

* * *

Plennie's aunt lived in Chicago, which was only about 260 miles away, as the crow flies. He was already planning to take a little break, to get good and fed by kin. And Chicago seemed like another decent place to try to land a sponsor.

He was on his way, about ten miles outside of East St. Louis on Route 66, when yet another cop pulled off the highway and stopped. The Illinois highway patrolman inquired about the nonsense, then informed Plennie that he was in violation of some state law prohibiting backward walking on Illinois roadways.

"You get off and don't let me catch you on again," the patrolman said.

The edict was disappointing, but it wasn't like Plennie could just bypass the entire state. He waited until the officer was well out of sight, then again faced the south and began backing up. He never saw the patrolman again.

He stopped long enough in Edwardsville to get a haircut and a bite to eat, to give his story to a reporter for the *Edwardsville Intelligencer*, to check in at the Western Union, and to get a new set of toe plates put on his shoes, his seventeenth set so far. He backed through Worden and Staunton and Honey Bend, Waggoner, Farmersville, Thomasville, Divernon, Glenarm, and Springfield, where Abraham Lincoln lived until 1861, when he left to take a job as the sixteenth president of the United States.

There had amassed in the state's capital that day an unusual band of pedestrians from all corners of Illinois, calling themselves the Hunger Marchers. More than three hundred unemployed men had been unceremoniously corralled by the state police despite having been officially invited to address the House of Representatives. Their complaint was common. They wanted the state to pass a worker unemployment bill, giving some social relief to the thousands of citizens who couldn't find work. Nationwide, more than six million men were unemployed. Even though the federal government planned to spend $780 million on public works projects that year (up from $260 million in 1928), and even though more than ten million veterans and government employees were supported in some way by the taxpayers, millions more went hungry. Many, including the Hunger Marchers, looked to the Soviet Union for inspiration. The hard times called for some sort of social security, but President Hoover was having none of it. The private sector, through charity and jobs, could handle the crisis.

"I am opposed to any direct or indirect Government dole," he said in his annual address of 1931. "The breakdown and increased unemployment in Europe is due in part to such practices. Our people are providing against distress from unemployment in true American fashion by a magnificent response to public appeal and by action of the local governments."

As Plennie backed out of town under a blistering sun, the president himself was headed toward Springfield by train, part of a Midwestern tour of Ohio, Indiana, and Illinois. The day before, Hoover had joined former President Calvin Coolidge to dedicate the tomb of Warren G. Harding in Marion, Ohio, the small town that saw Harding's rise from newspaper editor to president. They honored the scandal-tainted Harding by casting him as a good man betrayed by friends he trusted, and even suggested that the betrayal had led to his early death. Hoover's creativity was controversial.

Now Hoover was scheduled to tour Lincoln's old home and deliver an address at the Emancipator's tomb. Security was tight, with extra law officers and mounted police scrutinizing anyone who looked suspicious. An African-American choir sang "Swing Low, Sweet Chariot" while Boy Scouts scooped water out of buckets for the perspiring Civil War veterans seated near the stage. While a crowd turned out for Hoover's arrival, it wasn't nearly as big as the seventy-five thousand predicted, and, as reporters noted, those lining the streets "failed to applaud vigorously." Such was Hoover's predicament.

In the hilly college town of Bloomington, Plennie decided to call for his mail. He was expecting a package of postcards. It caught him off guard when the postal clerk recognized him.

"You are the man that is walking around the world backwards, aren't you?" the clerk said. His name was Bert Kelly, and without missing a beat he invited Plennie to sleep the night at his house. He said it would be his pleasure. He lived with his parents and had plenty of room.

"You'll be very welcome and comfortable," Kelly said. "And I'd like my dad and mother to meet you, too."

Plennie gave in and the two walked a few blocks to his home. Bert Kelly's mother and father were sitting in the shade of the front porch, trying to keep cool in a record-setting heat wave.

"Would you do me a great favor?" Bert asked.

"Yes," Plennie replied. "If I can."

"Walk backwards up to the house," Bert said.

"Why do you ask that?" Plennie said. The request seemed queer.

"Would you?" Bert said. "I'd appreciate it."

"Of course," Plennie said. "If that's what you want."

He turned his back to the couple and reversed up the walkway, watching in his mirrors as the old folks began to whisper. They shouted in unison, like children. "You're the backwards man!"

They invited the backwards man in for supper, and as they ate, Plennie learned that Bert had decided not to marry so he could stay home and take care of his parents. It struck him as a kind and noble act, in keeping with the Fifth Commandment. Plennie couldn't help but think of his own folks back home. A vicious

wind- and hailstorm had swept through West Texas over the weekend. It ruined acres of crops, dropping hailstones the size of turkey
eggs across the countryside. After the storm died down, neighbors
found Mrs. J. W. Yopp, seventy-seven, sprawled in the chicken
yard. The justice of the peace said she'd likely been beaten to death
by the hail, on account of the dead chickens surrounding her body.
Plennie hoped his folks were okay, but he wouldn't know until he
caught up to his mail down the line.

The next morning, as Plennie was starting north again, Al
Capone stood in a Chicago courtroom flanked by six policemen.
The curious filled every seat and packed the corridors and eleva-
tors. Young women stood on their tiptoes, trying to catch a glimpse
of the most wanted gangster in America. When proccedings began,
they all fell quiet. The assistant district attorney turned to face
Capone.

"Did you violate the United States income tax laws in 1924?"

"Yes," Capone said. "I'm guilty."

The lawyer ran through the same question for each of the following years, through 1929.

"Guilty," the gangster said.

"Did you and sundry others conspire to violate certain sections
of the national prohibition laws?"

Capone wet his lips.

"Yes, I'm guilty."

When it was over, still flanked by police, Capone turned and
left the federal building, free on $50,000 bond. His sentencing was
scheduled for two weeks later, around the same time a backward-
walking man would arrive in the Windy City carrying a binder
containing a newspaper clipping from Bloomington that expressed
in practical terms the physical toll of his odd effort to make a legal
living.

The Pantagraph, June 16, 1931

Walking in Reverse Around Globe, Wingo Finds It Health Aid

There's more than one way of reducing a "baywindow" waistline according to Plennie L. Wingo, Abilene, Tex., who arrived in Bloomington Monday evening walking backwards on his way around the world. Two months ago Mr. Wingo left a restaurant in Abilene where he worked, weighing 166 pounds. His weight now is 136 pounds, the "baywindow" is gone, and he says he is physically better.

Leaving St. Louis eight days ago Mr. Wingo made fast time coming to Bloomington, averaging 20 to 30 miles a day. Monday he traveled 24 miles in eight hours and 25 minutes. Mr. Wingo sends all his luggage ahead by bus from stop to stop and carries nothing except a fancy hand carved cane with a steer horn handle. He left the city at 8:30 a.m. Tuesday, north bound.

Mr. Wingo utilizes a pair of special glasses with mirrors to see "ahead of his back." He wears civilian clothes, is well groomed and has gained a heavy coat of sun tan during the first leg of his trip. He expects to complete his walk in three years. He is paying his own way.

* * *

The citizens of Joliet, Illinois, cast cold, hard eyes on the stranger from Abilene, Texas. Plennie had never experienced such a chilly reception. It hadn't been like this to the south, where he spent the night in a friendly couple's home and chatted up a man mowing the shoulder of the highway. Here, everyone in town seemed suspicious and difficult. When he stopped to have coffee at a roadside greasy spoon, two plainclothes detectives soon joined him and started asking all sorts of questions. When Plennie explained, they asked him to prove his identity. When he showed his credentials and the newspaper clippings, the detectives apologized for troubling him.

All of it was odd.

He learned why when Route 66 turned north toward Chicago and he saw the hulking gray hull of the Illinois State Penitentiary growing in his mirrors. The pen held eighteen hundred bank robbers and bankers, as well as maniac rapists and calculated killers like Nathan Leopold Jr. and Richard Loeb, the University of Chicago students who tried to commit the perfect crime by driving a chisel into the skull of poor Bobby Franks, fourteen. Just four months before Plennie's arrival, a five-man kitchen detail tried to make a break using a makeshift ladder and steel cable. They were caught in the searchlights and mowed down by machine-gun fire as soon as they hit the ground. Guards had been tipped off and were lying in wait. Some called it the Washington's Birthday Massacre. The prisoners still inside, who heard the fusillade and knew its meaning, screamed and hollered until the sun came up. A month later, following the March death of a prisoner in solitary confinement, eleven hundred inmates rioted, destroying the mess hall, setting fire to buildings and stealing kitchen knives and meat cleavers before one man was killed and three others wounded by guards with guns and tear gas. The treatment of inmates in the congested prison was now the subject of legislative investigation.

Plennie would've walked around the prison, but the highway ran right through the middle, between the high-walled canyons of convicts. He noticed the guards with guns manning the towers, watching him as he walked. A sign affixed to the stone wall read: KEEP GOING—DO NOT STOP BETWEEN PRISON WALLS. He followed instructions and was glad to be past the place and on out of town.

He followed his hunger to the first café he saw in the next town north. He backed in, spotted a seat at the far end of the counter, and backed his way to it. When he sat down, the other diners applauded him, the proprietor smiling and clapping along. "You don't need a menu," the man said. "Anyone that did what you just did is welcome to the best meal in the house." Plennie ate a T-bone steak that day.

He pushed on toward Chicago, introducing himself to strangers when the opportunity arose. He soon noticed an uptick in traffic, likely heralding the weekend. He watched a man with his family pass by, but the man continued to stare, watching Plennie over his right shoulder as he accidentally steered into oncoming traffic and collided head-on with a southbound car. The crash sounded worse than it looked, and so far as Plennie could see there were no injuries. He wanted no part of whatever might happen next, so he ducked behind a hedge bordering the yard of a suburban home and waited, hoping they didn't call the police. He'd been warned not to walk on Illinois highways, but he'd come a long way without incident, and he was so damn close to Chicago. He was glad when the motorists quit looking in his direction, returned to their vehicles, and drove away.

He popped into Joe Nejedly's barbecue stand at 111th Street and Archer Avenue in Lemont, Illinois, and the waitress brought his entire meal out at once. He felt folks watching him, so he gave them a little treat. He ate the dessert first, then the vegetable, then the barbecue sandwich, then the salad, then the soup, then drank his entire iced tea. As he wiped his mouth, curiosity got the best of one of the men in the joint.

"We were watching you eat," the man said sheepishly. "Is that the way you always eat?"

Plennie couldn't muster a witty retort on the spot.

"No." He smiled. "I just happened to be craving something sweet."

He arrived at his aunt Marie Oldham's house at 4753 Lake Park

Avenue in Chicago that Sunday, June 21, having walked backward almost exactly 950 miles from Fort Worth in sixty-seven days. He was due for a rest, but his aunt Marie phoned a reporter for the *Chicago Daily News*, who hustled over, chatted awhile, then convinced Plennie to put his shoes back on. Yes, Wiley Post and Harold Gatty were taking to the skies to fly around the world faster than anyone in history, and Al Capone was scheduled to be sentenced to prison a few days later, and it had just been announced that the US government was ending the fiscal year with the first deficit since 1919. But the world wanted to see Plennie Wingo do his thing.

They were going to make a moving picture.

14.

AN OUNCE OF ATTENTION

On June 25 Plennie and his aunt Marie settled into their cushioned seats in the little movie house and waited for the film to start.

He still needed a booster, and maybe this was his ticket to fame, or even a little dough he could send back home just to let Della know he was actually working. Her letters had begun to concern him. If he could answer the next one with a chunk of money, enough to help her get by for a few months and convince her he was doing his best in a bad situation, perhaps his dear wife would cut him some slack. So far he'd sent nothing but words on paper. He reckoned there was some cash in the envelope Pete Mazza handed him in St. Louis, but he felt like he'd made a promise not to open it unless things got really bad. Besides, he still had to get to Europe and through Asia and across the Pacific and home—another twenty-four thousand miles or so. He needed money.

Their anticipation grew as the theater fell dark and the hubbub died down, and then the screen flickered to life. The first Universal Newsreel clip featured Otto Hillig and Holger Hoiriis, in jittery black-and-white, embarking on a daring flight to Denmark from the quaint Catskills town of Liberty, New York, in a 300-horsepower Bellanca monoplane. Then they watched footage of the opening of a new traffic artery into New York to help alleviate bridge jams, and a wild wine-barrel-rolling race in Vincennes, France, and a Tacoma, Washington, man named Jack Rousseau building an eight-foot-tall house of cards using 135 decks. Impressive.

Then the next clip started, three minutes into the newsreel.

Texan on round-the-world walking tour! the opening slide read. *Plennie Wingo of Abilene is different ~ he does it in reverse.*

The streets were packed with pedestrians, dozens of them, women wearing long-sleeved dresses and cloche hats and men in suits and ties and skimmers. They carried newspapers and purses and shopping bags, and they each looked to be headed somewhere important. The camera captured shots from various angles to show little Plennie Wingo in all his unlikely glory. Wearing the same suit and tie he wore when he left Texas, Plennie crossed streetcar tracks like a professional, dodged two halting automobiles, weaved through a cluster of urban pedestrians streaming off a curb at Madison Street, and navigated up a wide set of stairs. Near the end, the camera focused on his face, his mirrored glasses, fedora, and broad smile.

No one seemed to notice or care that walking among them, dodging cars at busy Chicago intersections and weaving his way through oncoming throngs, was a man turned the wrong way. No one besides a Chicago police officer, that is, and he appeared to offer some firm instruction to the backward walker. The striking thing was that nothing was all that striking. If there were gawkers, the cameraman missed them. One man walking behind Plennie turned to the buddies flanking him in a get-a-load-of-this-guy sort of way, but that was the extent of the wonderment captured. Perhaps the ballyhoo bubble had popped, or the ulterior motives had become a little too obvious and commonplace. Maybe F. Scott Fitzgerald was right, that the new generation had grown up to find all Gods dead and all faith in man shaken. Maybe Charles Lindbergh had spoiled it for more mundane madcaps. But the *Chicago Daily Tribune* was giving large play to Post and Gatty, who were trying to circle the globe in record time, stopping for fuel in England, Germany, Russia, Siberia, Alaska, Canada, and Cleveland. Banner headlines captured their every move. The only competition for space on the front pages seemed to be from Al Capone. Maybe he was what people wanted to see.

Capone was Chicago and Chicago was very much Capone. The Neapolitan transplant from New York's Five Points gang had risen from "second-hand furniture dealer" to American potentate with seven hundred men at his disposal in a matter of years. The first time Capone's photograph ran in the *Chicago Daily Tribune* was May 1924, when he emptied a six-shooter into the skull of a thug named Joe Howard in a barroom. Three people saw him. Two got amnesia, one went missing, and Capone never saw a courtroom. His rise as the symbol of subversion was meteoric. By 1931, he controlled the mayor's office, a handful of judges, and the lion's share of liquor sales to Chicago's ten thousand speakeasies, and he ran the East Coast supply network between Florida and Canada. He tipped waiters $100 and hatcheck girls $25 and opened a soup kitchen for the down-and-out. He was pursued by the media *en masse*. In the first six months of that year, just nineteen editions of the *Chicago Daily Tribune* failed to include a story about Capone, which means that regular readers of the largest daily newspaper in the second-largest city in the United States read something about Public Enemy No. 1 on 162 of 181 days before his scheduled sentencing on June 30, 1931. And the average daily net paid circulation of the newspaper climbed from 795,000 to 820,000 in the same six-month period.

Plennie had read the headlines himself. Editors with business interests in the city's reputation wrung their hands every time "typewriters" rattled in the streets or a bomb went off in town, and no fewer than 157 were found or exploded between October 1927 and January 1929. In that wild decade, there were more than five hundred gang murders, and few, if any, convictions. Capone held the city in his hands. He had the best seats at the theater and at baseball and football games, and he rode the streets in an armored car. He gave orders to politicians from the Lexington Hotel on Michigan Avenue and held press conferences where he played the part of an innocent businessman servicing a needy world, and so what if he had found ways to circumvent an unjust law? Hadn't we been doing that here since the Molasses Act of 1733?

People pored over the stories about the entrepreneurs of the underground industry, the rose floats following gangsters to their graves, and the king of crooks and killers in the hot seat now, trying to avoid hard time at Leavenworth for not giving the federal government its cut of the millions he'd made in illegal trade.

Could a man walking backward capture an ounce of attention?

Plennie felt good about his odds. In fact, he was downright pleased at the good fortune of making it into the newspapers and onto the movie screen. As he left the theater, he felt sure he'd get a sponsor. Three and a half million people lived in Chicago, the second-largest city in America, the biggest he'd ever seen. It was 13 times larger than Dallas, 21 times bigger than Fort Worth, 150 times the size of Abilene. There had to be some man of business in a city this size who would want the kind of good publicity that Plennie could offer. The newsreel would be shown in theaters across America. Imagine how many eyeballs would land on a sign on Plennie's chest advertising Johnston & Murphy Shoe Co. or Stacy Adams Shoes or even Goodyear Rubber.

He gave it the college try. Plenty of companies were willing to grant him an audience, but he couldn't convince any to give him money. He visited the Bird-Sykes Company on Automobile Row and Van Camp Products Company on East Illinois, and even R. K. Mulholand, who was selling Rupture Cure on West Sixty-Third.

After eight days in Chicago with no luck, after Hillig and Hoiriis landed in Copenhagen before a crowd of thousands, after Post and Gatty made it around the world and back to New York, after Al Capone had delayed his ordeal by withdrawing his guilty plea, Plennie packed his suitcase in his aunt Marie's home on Lake Park and rode in her car to the Western Union. He checked his luggage for Fort Wayne, Indiana, said goodbye to his kinfolk, then started down Michigan Avenue.

Before him were the Wrigley Building and Tribune Tower and 333 Michigan Avenue in all their glory. On his right as he backed south, down at the end of Randolph Street near the remnants of the SS *Commodore*, there had sprouted a village of more modest measure which locals were calling "Hooverville." The shantytown had sprouted quickly the past winter, with a dozen or so shacks built from discarded *Commodore* scraps, and faintly defined streets named Prosperity Road, Easy Street, and Hard Times Avenue, all in the shadows of Michigan Avenue's famed skyscrapers. The shantytown even had a mayor at one time, a blue-eyed Irishman named Mike Donovan. "Building operations may be at a standstill elsewhere," Donovan told a reporter, "but down here everything is booming." The police had recently sacked the place and chased the men back under the monumental Michigan Avenue Bridge. Plennie kept going, past the Art Institute of Chicago, and Al Capone's room in the Lexington Hotel, and on out of town.

15.

ARE YOU CRAZY?

Sometimes bad things happen to men chasing fortune, and if you manipulate the chronology a little, slow the time line down here or speed it up there, the picture comes clear and stands as a lesson of sorts. So start here, in Fort Wayne, Indiana, with Plennie Wingo framed in the window of his room on the fifth floor of the Randall Hotel, "the best $2 hotel in Indiana." He was overlooking the railroad yard, where a circus train was resting on the tracks, waiting to open a show the following day. He had backed 150 miles from Chicago, east along Route 30, without incident. He had slept in Valparaiso, Hanna, and Hamlet, and had gotten a paragraph on page five in the *Indianapolis News* while at Warsaw, the standard fare, beneath a story about an electrician who fell into a well and expired before aid could reach him, and another about a young mother suffering from "mental aberration," who wrapped her newborn in a blanket, placed it in a shed, and went for a walk on the railroad tracks until a Big Four passenger train removed her.

Plennie saw below him a man expertly riding a white horse and he knew without hesitation the man's identity, for they had met some four months before in Texas. The man was Tom Mix—many called him "king of the cowboys"—and truth be told, they had not technically met. Plennie had been near Mix once while he was advertising for the Fort Worth Fat Stock Show. He recognized Mix just the same. The man's legend was swollen. He had ridden with Teddy Roosevelt and the Rough Riders in the Spanish-American War. He'd served as sheriff, US Marshal, and Texas Ranger. He was a hero of the Wild West.

Alas, most of what people knew about Mix had been invented by publicists. True, Mix had enlisted in the army, but he went AWOL when he married the first in a string of wives. He'd worked on a ranch before migrating into Wild West shows and then, starting in 1909, moving pictures. He'd appeared in 291 of them, at one point reportedly making more than $17,000 a week. He and his wives knew how to spend it, too. He'd defined the Western genre and was its biggest cowboy star, wearing a ten-gallon hat before they became comical. He introduced John Wayne to acting and be-friended Wyatt Earp. When Hollywood gave out on him, he signed with a circus. Then he was charged with tax evasion. Then his marriage fell apart. Then the market crashed and he lost his Arizona ranch and the great majority of his fortune. This is the state in which Plennie saw him down on Harrison Street in Fort Wayne— a broken man on horseback. But it's not the end of the story.

Mix would marry a fifth wife, appear in a few talkies, buy his own circus, and claw his way back. That circus would fail and he'd blame his own daughter and cut her out of his will. He would visit a friend on a fine October evening, then head north on Highway 80 under a persimmon sky in his Cord 812 Phaeton, toward a washed-out bridge south of Florence, Arizona. He would swerve, slide, and not be able to stop, and an aluminum briefcase containing $6,000 cash, $1,500 in traveler's checks, and several valuable jewels would dislodge from a package shelf behind him, fly forward, and strike him in the back of the head, breaking his neck and killing Tom Mix, king of the cowboys.

Plennie went to sleep that night in Fort Wayne knowing nothing of what would become of Tom Mix, just that he was a man people recognized from fifth-floor hotel windows, a man who had found fame and fortune, and Plennie wanted that, too, all of it.

* * *

By the time he reached Van Wert, Ohio, it dawned on him that he had to move faster if he was going to make New York by September and England by October. He hustled down the Lincoln Highway through Delphos, Lima, Beaver Dam, and Williamstown, and carried a sack lunch out of Kirby on advice that it was a good walk to the next café.

Plennie backed through Bucyrus, Mansfield, Wooster, and little towns in between, stopping only to eat or sleep or when motorists pulled onto the shoulder to inquire about his behavior. He took down their names dutifully, in careful penmanship.

Sometimes he made notes for himself in the margins. Miss Donna Seiz of Lima, Ohio, for instance, "MAY WANT MY BOOK." Mr. John Bosch of St. Louis: "Will help if I need it." Tom Clark of Jeromesville, Ohio: "WISE CRACKER. We had a cuss Fight."

W. W. Alexander of Waxahachie, Texas, met Plennie way back in April, on the second day of his journey, then spotted him again outside Chicago and stopped to congratulate him. C. G. Warrick rode a high-wheel bicycle for Plennie's amusement. "The bike was purchased in 1890 by him," Plennie wrote. T. M. Forrester of Wanatah, Indiana, was a "Farmer" with whom Plennie had a "Tree discussion." Thomas McGorvey of Hanoverton, Ohio, had evidently been "Convicted for manslaughter." He met Carl O. James from Frankfort, Indiana, and was surprised to learn he personally knew the Abilene doctor who had brought Plennie into this small, small world.

He reached Canton and planned to stay a night or two with an aunt and uncle he had not seen since he was six years old. They welcomed him as though the past thirty years had been a day, and he was glad, but times were difficult for them. They were living paycheck to paycheck and Plennie didn't want to be a burden, so he hoped to land some work in Canton. He took advantage of the downtime to send a letter back to Abilene.

Canton, Ohio

July 24

Dear mother and all,

I will write you tonite. I am at Aunt Nola and Uncle Warner's. They both are natural to me. I recognized Aunt Nola and spoke to her calling her Aunt Nola and she sure was supprised to see me. She is real heavy and Uncle Warner is still slim as ever. I am going to stay over until Monday. I am going to advertise for a picture show here Monday. I feel a lotts better about every thing some how.

Seems like I am getting better publicity up here.

How is every one? Fine I hope. I got a good letter from Aunt Marie today. They sure are interested in my stunt now and want to see me do good. I bought me a new pencil today. It is a good one. Maybe I won't mind writing now. I didn't hear from Della in the last week. I guess they are getting along allright. I hope so. The people are all so much better up here than in Missouri. I sure am glad too. I am only about 487 miles from N.Y. City now. Just think. I will be sailing in less than two months for Europe if everything turns out right.

Mama, I have decided I will write a book on my trip when I get back. It will be called Around the World Backwards and I will continue my stunt walking backwards in cities selling my books so if my plan works I will have a long job, won't I? I think I will have a good book when I get through also.

I don't think it will be long until I can send the kids some money along. I sure hope I can.

How is dad getting along with his trucking? Well I have just got up so will finish my letter. I am going over to another town today and see about some advertising so I have to wait until Monday to advertise in Canton. Aunt Nola said she would write you after I am gone and am in a hurry to mail this one. I don't know anymore news. Will write again later. I hope I hear from you before I leave Canton.

Lots of love to all from Plennie.

He planned to stay only a few days, but found a little work advertising toasted sandwiches, waffles, and plate dinners for D&E Sandwich Shop on Tuscarawas Street West, where proprietor Bill Steiner was so savvy he fit four mottos on the same business card: BEST COFFEE IN CANTON, WE MAKE OUR OWN PASTRY, A MEAL A MINUTE, and YOUR TIME TO EAT IS OUR TIME TO SERVE. Plennie thought he'd stick around for a bit and see if there was more work.

A vicious bilious attack came on, and the headache and constipation immobilized him for two days longer than he'd planned. He had not received a letter from his mother nor Della since leaving Bucyrus, Ohio, ten days before, and the anxiety was eating at him. He sent one more letter to Texas letting them know that he'd kindly like to hear how things were going back home, and that he'd likely be in New York by the end of August, barring unforeseen challenges. He wrote that he was enjoying Canton and the company of Aunt Nola and Uncle Warner, and he listed the cities through which he expected to pass next: Pittsburgh, Greensburg, Bedford, Chambersburgh, Gettysburg, Lancaster, Philadelphia.

He set out again on Monday, August 3, and it felt good to stretch out his legs after the rest. He was booking backward over rolling hills covered by curly dock and horse nettle, and by noon he had reached Robertsville, ten and a half miles from Canton, full of energy and confidence. He ate lunch in a roadside café, then picked up at the spot where he'd left Highway 30. His eyes were up, watching for traffic, as he took a step backward and plunged his foot into a sizable hole. It sounded like a limb breaking off a Texas ironwood in a strong wind.

Plennie saw stars. Not like in the cartoons; his eyes went dark but for little pinprick flashes of light. So much ran through his mind all at once. He knew his ankle was broken, but how would he get to a hospital? And what would this mean for his trip? He had a few bucks and Pete Mazza's mysterious envelope, but he couldn't afford a doctor bill right now. Maybe he could advertise for the hospital?

He felt confident, lying on his back under the Ohio sky, that his adventure was over.

He heard voices above his head, the folks from the café. They'd rushed over when they saw him fall. A man asked Plennie what hurt, and if he'd like to call an ambulance. Plennie told them he had no money, so maybe they should leave him on the roadside to fend for himself. The man said he was going to call the sheriff, and a government car pulled up a few minutes later and carried Plennie the ten miles back to Canton in severe pain and feeling every bump in the road.

When the nurses informed the doctor what had happened, the doctor shook his head.

"Well," he said, "he ought to have broken his ankle then, if he was doing that."

The only redeeming elements of the experience were that his treatment and stay were free of charge, courtesy of Mercy Hospital, which was run by Sisters of Charity of St. Augustine; that he enjoyed conversing with Carl McCauley, his roommate at Mercy for much of his stay; and that the downtime gave him a chance to catch up on correspondence with people he'd met so far.

He spent the next three weeks at Mercy, and got a kick out of the fact that the hospital was built where former president William McKinley's home once stood. McKinley was the first president Plennie could remember, taking office when Plennie was two years old. He led America to war in 1898 against Spain, which had been trying to repress revolution in Cuba, and after three months claimed the spoils of victory: Puerto Rico, Guam, and the Philippine Islands, the westernmost land under the American flag. Critics called him an imperialist, but he cruised to a second term and was cheered by thousands on a tour after inauguration in 1901. At the end of the tour, in Buffalo, New York, he was standing in a receiving line when an unemployed Detroit mill worker and anarchist named Leon Czolgosz fired two bullets into his chest from a .32-caliber revolver hidden under a handkerchief. McKinley died eight days later, joining Andrew Jackson, Abraham Lincoln, and James Garfield on the list of presidents shot or shot at. The nation mourned, named roads and public buildings in his honor, arrested anarchists in cities across the country, and put Leon Czolgosz to death. His revolver, made by Iver Johnson, a company that also built bicycles, went to a museum.

A week into his hospital stay, Plennie received a letter postmarked Plano, Texas. His little friend Tom Robbins had read in the paper that Plennie's trip was delayed. "I heard that a car had ran over you and we all was worried to death for they said you was killed and we had no way of finding out whether it was true or not," he wrote. "And I sure was glad to get your letter because that showed that you were still alive." Tom was over the mumps, as was his brother Bill. He was also excited to be promoted to the fourth grade. He wished Plennie good health and good luck and asked him to write more, promising to save his letters so his friends could see them.

To know that an eight-year-old in Texas cared and was paying attention made Plennie feel good.

When his leg was properly mended, he tied his brogans tight and told the sisters goodbye, being sure to write their names and addresses in his journal so he could thank them properly when his trip was finished. Most he entered with the simple description: "Mercy Hospital, Canton, Ohio, Nurse." Miss L. G. Christie, however, was "blond nurse," and Miss Virginia Parker was "Red Headed Nurse," so he would remember.

He caught a ride to Robertsville, and the small-town residents remembered him. Betty Devaux gave Plennie a sack lunch to take along. L. E. Glasser repainted his sign for no charge. He walked to the café and the hole in front that had nearly done him in. He put his foot into the hole, turned his back toward the Atlantic Ocean, and started again.

* * *

Just three miles of the Lincoln Highway ran through rural West Virginia, but it was the most treacherous three miles of Plennie's trip so far. He crossed the Ohio River into his seventh state and stopped for traffic at an intersection in a town called Chester. Two cars came to a stop beside him, one behind the other. Plennie watched the man in the back car climb out, run forward, and drag the other driver from his vehicle by the hair. Then the two went at it, fists and feet flying, right there on the highway. They tore each other's shirts off and continued fighting bare-chested. Bystanders filed out of buildings nearby as the fight wore on, and soon there was a small crowd watching the two pummel each other. A patrolman pulled up and tried with difficulty to pull the men apart. The two were panting by the time the officer wedged himself between them and got them separated. "That'll teach you to run people off the road," shouted the man from the rear car. Plennie thought that was funny, because the man doing the shouting seemed to be the bloodier. They finally calmed down and both took a ticket from the cop for disturbing the peace. Welcome to West Virginia.

Plennie walked the next three miles along a narrow two-lane highway with gravel shoulders that squirmed through foothills on the Allegheny Plateau. The walk was quite pretty, but replete with insults and vulgarity from drivers, many of whom drove so close to Plennie that he was forced off the paved portion of roadway. "What the hell are you doing?" one man shouted. "Get off the road!" hollered another. "Are you crazy?"

He couldn't stop thinking about Della. He still had not heard from her. As he walked, he imagined scenarios as a way to prepare for what might come.

He checked into a roadside hotel, his only stop in West Virginia, and woke the next morning covered in bites from bedbugs. He was glad to be on his way.

16.

MOPERY IN THE SECOND DEGREE

He thought he'd seen people on hard times, but nothing so far compared to the human misery clustered roadside in the western mountains of Pennsylvania. Ten thousand miners were on unofficial strike and the number was growing by the day. It was unofficial because the unions hadn't yet called it a strike, but the elements were there. A big darkness had crept across the soft-coal and coke region, up and down the Monongahela River, and the shafts had stopped smoking, the steam shovels were idle, the trains and coal wagons stood at rest, and the blood of miners was spilling in the streets. By the time Plennie walked through, the strikers numbered ten thousand, arguing for shorter hours, better conditions, and more pay. Their numbers would grow to seven times that. Many were so ill paid that they had to go on government relief, and shopkeepers in coal towns told reporters about miners handing over sixty-nine-cent pay envelopes—all they got for a week's work. Any kind of economy in Pennsylvania's coal patches was grinding to a halt.

The Pittsburgh Coal Company bosses gave strikers a deadline to vacate company-owned housing at the Montour No. 10 line near Library. The sheriff used tear gas to break up a union meeting at Cedar Grove, and women were arrested for having the audacity to stand beside their husbands on the picket line. Strikers outside the Warden mine threw stones at a truck full of strikebreakers that sped perilously close. In Arnold City, sheriff's deputies and mine police opened fire after a little boy threw an egg at strikebreakers. Their bullets injured four miners and killed a shopkeeper who was trying to break up the fight.

Little clusters of men stood outside the entrances to mines across Fayette, Washington, Westmoreland, Greene, and Allegheny Counties, and lines of the rank and file unspooled along roadside shoulders all over the blue and brown and green hills, the pinkish mist of the mountains on the horizon. They aimed to live like human beings.

Plennie noticed that the names on the mailboxes were mostly Dutch and German, and he was happy to see a farmer and his wife sitting on the front porch of a large farmhouse west of Pittsburgh. The two watched as their dog snarled at Plennie, then made a wild charge across the yard. The dog got bigger in Plennie's mirrors until he finally raised his cane as if to strike, and the dog tucked tail and ran, disappearing under the house. The farmer walked out to greet Plennie. "You know, that's the first time I ever saw my dog scare for anybody," he said.

The farmer was W. H. Werkheiser, and Plennie was soon sharing supper, his first real German meal, at the Werkheiser table with seven Werkheiser children. He walked out of the house backward for their amusement and the old dog saw him coming again and ran, again, and everyone laughed.

In Pittsburgh, he got a room in the moderately priced American House on Liberty Street, paid thirty-five cents for a haircut, and wrote his mother again, letting her know he had decided to change his route to visit Washington, DC, before heading to New York. He wanted to get President Hoover's autograph while he had the chance. The way people in coal country talked about Hoover made hard the fact that he wouldn't be in the White House much longer. Plennie advised his mother to send future correspondence to Greensburg, Pennsylvania, as he'd decided to stay on Route 30 eastbound.

Pittsburgh, Penna

Aug. 27, 1931

Dear Mother and all.

I got your letter today. Was glad to hear from you all. I am well and my foot is doing fine. I didn't hear from Della. Was disappointed too. But I guess she is like me, don't have good news to write and hates to write. But I may have good news some of these days.

I am working hard to get hold of some way to make good. This is a large city and pretty, too. It sure is hilly and has a large river near it also. Will write again later.

Lots of love as ever,
Plennie

He was running low on money after three nights at the American House with no favors. He called on the friends he had met at a roadside park in Missouri, beside whose names he'd jotted "colored." He was expecting nothing more than to tell them hello, but when he called the Trumond home, Mrs. Trumond told him to stay put and her husband would be by on his lunch break to pick him up. When George Trumond arrived, he invited Plennie to be his guest while in Pittsburgh rather than wasting money on a hotel. So that's what he did. The Trumonds and Walkers lived side by side in beautiful two-story homes on Monticello Street, in a majority-black neighborhood called Homestead.

The city's racial dynamics were fascinating to Plennie. A renaissance had shot forth from the massive migration of African-Americans, who had come from the South for jobs in the mines or steel industry during and after the war. They smelted with other immigrant groups already established, and while there were sometimes raw spots, the tribes fed off one another in a great give-and-take. Before the end of the year, there would be mob lynchings in places like Salisbury, Maryland, and Lewisburg, West Virginia, but never had there been nor would there ever be unhinged racial violence of that kind in Pittsburgh, Pennsylvania.

Smoketown, the black folks called their section, and it was home to a bumping art and theater scene. The city's jazz had even more tickle and pang than the sound coming out of New Orleans. Everybody read the *Pittsburgh Courier*, the black newspaper, and believed it and followed its advice, and the ladies taking turns bringing Plennie his chicken and biscuits were two of the darlings of the *Courier's* women's pages. He spent a few happy days being doted upon. "I can't remember having a better visit and being made to feel more at home," Plennie told them. He meant it, and he would correspond with both couples for the rest of his trip.

On August 28, as he backed his way out of the city, a Pittsburgh police officer shouted at Plennie to stop where he was. The cop was tall and broad-shouldered, with close-cropped hair, thick eyebrows, and large ears. Seemed to be in his midfifties. He looked Plennie over, then pulled his citation book out of his pocket.

"I hate to do this," he said, "but it's the law."

Yet again. Plennie tried to summon the nerve to protest.

"What's the ticket for?" he asked.

"Mopery in the second degree," the cop said without looking up.

The way in which the words came out of the lawman's mouth, so clear and direct, frightened Plennie.

"Mopery?" he said. "I never heard of that. What is it? Is it serious? What did I do?"

"You'll find out how serious it is at the trial," the officer replied.

"Trial?"

"Yeah," the officer said. "You got a good lawyer?"

Plennie was starting to come undone. Thoughts of courtrooms and fines he could not pay rushed into his head.

"I don't have any lawyer," he said.

"Well, buddy," the cop said, "better get one, because you're going to need one."

Sometimes men in such situations consider running, the old fight-or-flight dichotomy.

"But Officer," Plennie said, "I don't understand. Is it because I'm walking backwards?"

"That's only the beginning of it," the cop said.

Plennie was flummoxed. This was it. The end of the line, a month short of Manhattan. All for mopery.

"Maybe you can get off with a couple years up the river," the cop said, tearing off the ticket and forcing it into Plennie's hands.

Plennie looked at his citation.

"GOOD LUCK ON YOUR TRIP AROUND THE WORLD."

Now the cop was laughing. Now he was doubled over. Now Plennie smiled and shook his head and started laughing too.

"I just couldn't resist the opportunity," the officer said, trying to catch his breath. "I had been reading about you and when I saw you I thought I'd have a little fun."

Harry Hart was a good cop. He'd worked as a firefighter for eleven years before joining the police department in 1913. He was one of the city's first traffic cornermen before advancing to lieutenant in the East End district, and he would go on to lead a colorful career as a homicide detective, solving murders and working hard right up until the day they rushed him from the station to the hospital where he died.

"I'll never forget you," Plennie said. "That's for sure."

* * *

A columnist for the *Pittsburgh Post-Gazette* wrote a story about Plennie the day he backed out of town, calling him a "pleasant chap" who "decided to cut loose for a little vacation." Even if that wasn't totally true, it might have been a fair interpretation. The column explained that he wore mirrored glasses to prevent "running into telegraph poles and autos." It mentioned how odd it was for Plennie to walk normal after checking in at Western Union, how "the act of turning around to walk the natural way was something like stepping out of a pair of overshoes—or recovering from a sleeping foot." It mentioned the book he planned to write, and that he supported himself by selling postcards and advertising for businesses.

The column made its way into the hands of R. C. Williams, a special representative of the Sulphur Products Co. of Greensburg, Pennsylvania, makers of McKeon's Liquid Sulphur, the natural conqueror of things like Rheumatism, Catarrh, Piles, Sore Throat, Hives, Prickly Heat, Eczema, Poison, Skin Diseases, Bites, Whites, Inflammation of the Womb, Ulceration, Chronic Enlargement, and all ovarian disorders. Liquid Sulphur did not have the "vacillating buoyance so often noticed in those addicted to the use of patent concoctions and alleged stimulants, but rather the slow but sure and persistent climbing upwards, always upwards, toward the pinnacle of absolute physical and organic perfection."

Mostly it might make your sore feet feel healthier, and who

better to advertise that than Plennie L. Wingo? Williams tracked Plennie down at his hotel and proposed the idea. Plennie agreed wholeheartedly and made himself immediately available. He'd run his savings short in Pittsburgh and couldn't sell any postcards in coal country. Money was so tight he had begrudgingly opened the envelope from Pete Mazza and found twenty dollars, a significant sum, which meant sleeping indoors instead of on the highway.

"How would you consider walking around town tomorrow," Williams said, "for let's say four hours, with a placard advertising Liquid Sulphur for tired feet?"

"I'd be glad to," Plennie said.

"Shall we say twenty-five dollars for the job?" Williams asked.

Plennie was so flabbergasted by the rate, the largest offer he'd ever received, that he didn't answer immediately. Williams took this to mean he was hesitant.

"Naturally," Williams interjected, "I'll pay expenses at the hotel, and meals."

"Okay," Plennie replied, trying not to sound too eager. "I guess I can stay over an extra day for that."

There would rarely come a day when the money in his pocket qualified as anything more than sustaining, but this recent good fortune had left him financially secure. With Pete Mazza's gift and Williams's payment for labor, he had enough to sleep in a two-dollar hotel room every night for more than three weeks. He could have, that very day, in that very vicinity, paid one month's rent on a six-room brick house, bought thirty plain linen dresses in rose, blue, green, or pink, or walked off the used-car lot with a 1927 Ford Tudor Sedan, free and clear, and driven it back to Texas. Had he kept what he earned from Williams and sent Pete Mazza's gift home to Della and Vivian in Abilene, where that very day the Texas governor was calling an emergency legislative session to save cotton farmers from complete disaster, his wife and daughter could have bought five pairs of leather high-heeled shoes, a new Simmons Slumberking Mattress, eight hundred loaves of bread, or eighty-six pounds of sliced bacon.

The next thing Plennie knew, he was "stuck"—his word—at a beautiful resort on a mountaintop outside a tourist town called Breezewood, Pennsylvania.

17.

CHOICES AND CONSEQUENCES

She had not complained, so far, in the strictest sense, in that she had not explicitly written to say that what he was doing was selfish, self-serving, egomaniacal, and unbelievably, unquestionably irresponsible. Della had not yet expressed the outrage a reasonable woman might have felt if her husband of sixteen years and the father of her teenage daughter had packed a suitcase and left home in the thick of one of the worst and most difficult years in the history of man.

So when Plennie stopped at the post office in Breezewood, Pennsylvania, and found that there was a letter from the wife from whom he had not heard in fifty days, he tore it open with no small amount of anxiety.

There in the letter she articulated her feelings. She wrote that she was sick of his silly project. She wrote that she was tired of clawing to survive, and that if there had been any chance his original scheme was going to work he would have sent money home by now. She wrote that she wanted him to knock it off and return home, immediately.

Vivian wrote her own letter, which was included, and it, too, was hurtful. She wrote that her mother had lost a significant amount of weight since he'd been gone and was in poor health.

Plennie would later recall that it "looked as though the entire trip would be a hand-to-mouth affair and she was tired of getting along without me and with no amount of money coming in," and he would fail to acknowledge the reality of his recent financial windfall. "I was not prepared for what the letter said!" he would write.

That Sunday in Breezewood, September 6, he wrote to his own mother, opening with platitudes and then cutting to the chase.

Mother, I am going through with something now. I finally got a letter from Della and Vivian. Oh, mother. I did not intend to tell you yet, but I might as well. It was the saddest and heart-breakingest letter I have ever read in my life. Della and Vivian have both turned against me and ask for freedom.

Mother, what in the world will I do? I can't eat or sleep. I never was so shocked in my life to think they had been writing encouraging letters all the time and all of a sudden I got this letter that I am telling you about. Mother, I am doing my best to hold up under this and am doing so by the help of God. God has answered my prayers. He has forgiven me of my sins and I am getting a relief by praying to God.

Mother, the poor girls don't know what they are doing. I am praying for them and the letters they both wrote have broken my heart. Mother, by the help of God I am going to make good on this trip and I guess that is the way I will gain them back by finally doing good.

Oh, mother. I can't give them up this way but they are determined to quit me so it looks like I am doomed to be left without them. I am worried about Della's health. Vivian said she only weighed 90 lbs. I know she is in bad health some way. If I possibly can I am going to help them if they let me.

He took a break from writing and slept some. It is unknown whether he prayed, too, or dwelt on the significance of the fact that his wife was underweight by thirty pounds or more. He continued when he woke, appealing for sympathy and exaggerating his walking routine.

Mother, this is Monday morning. I was so tired I laid down and slept a little but not much. I have been doing my best to get in some money with this stunt so I could help them, but I guess the money part will come too late to do any good. I have walked every day, even when I didn't feel like it, but would be compelled to keep going in order to sell enough cards for the next night's lodging. But this is what I have got for that.

I know I have not made them a good living the past two years, but I have done my best. But mother, they are two sweet girls and are both real ladies and I love them, too. I can not say a thing against them and mother, I know that you love them too. If there is anything I can ever do to redeem myself and get their forgiveness and respect I will do it. Mother, pray for them that they may be happy in their undertaking and that I may be able to bear such burden even though it is heartbreaking. Well mother, I will close for today. Will write again later. You can answer this at Washington, D.C.

I will be there in a week or so.

May God bless and keep Della and Vivian for I love them and you, mother. I know my mother's love.

From one who is sad and broken hearted,
Plennie

He tucked the letter inside an envelope addressed to Mrs. T. H. Wingo and affixed to its face a five-cent stamp. On the back he wrote a calculating postscript:

Mother don't let Della know I ask you to write her a letter and put this letter in with it. That will let her know that I was not talking against her, won't it. Will you please do that?

Love to all—Plennie.

He picked up his trail outside the resort on the top of Sideling Hill Mountain and started backward toward McConnellsburg, where he left the Lincoln Highway. He was eating that evening in the Harris Hotel when the proprietor, James J. Harris, joined him. They talked awhile and Plennie shared some stories. Harris sensed Plennie's dour mood and interrupted.

"What's bothering you?" Harris asked.

Plennie tried to convince the hotelier nothing was wrong, but Harris kept asking until Plennie let it all out, unable to control himself. He thought he'd overcome the pangs of depression. He had not.

"You decided right," Harris said. "Don't you ever go home when things are going as good as they are."

18.

PERSEVERING PEDALIST

He stood at the base of the Washington Monument and looked out over the Mall, the delayed civic reflection of what America had been and aimed to become. Indigenous tribes had once hunted and gathered food along the Tiber Creek estuary on the east, but they were displaced by European settlers who used the flood-prone lowlands for grazing. When Washington was chosen for the capital, the land before Plennie was set aside for a grand avenue flanked by gardens and embassies. The brilliant Frenchman Pierre L'Enfant, who planned the Mall, lost support and was either forced to resign or fired, depending on the teller. He tried to get Congress to pay him and died penniless.

The first two public buildings housed the president and Congress and would have to be rebuilt after the British burned the city in 1814. Politics, lack of funding, and an anti-immigrant group nearly doomed the Washington Monument behind Plennie, which was not more than a stump for two decades before rising tall. The War Between the States gave lift to a smattering of new buildings and monuments here and there, and some cohesion, but it was still very much a strip of earth in flux, a place that would someday host museums to peoples not yet respected, and monuments to men not yet called great—to the man who would become the very next president, for instance, and to a black man who was then a two-year-old boy in Atlanta, Georgia. Hoover had just recently dedicated the District of Columbia memorial to the world war nearby. He used the opportunity to warn Americans that the world was more heavily armed than at any time before the world war, with international conflicts probably no fewer than they were before actual bloodshed in that war began.

Plennie had visited the US Capitol on the east end, where a statue of Jefferson Davis had been unveiled just three months before, and Davis's name and likeness would carry controversy into the next century. To the west, Plennie gazed upon the Lincoln Memorial, dedicated nine years before, the work described by James Truslow Adams as "perhaps the finest example of sculpture in the last half century."

Wasn't it interesting the men we chose to remember, and what we remembered? The first president, both a slaveholder and a war hero. The sixteenth, who jailed editors and suspended habeas corpus, and then ended slavery. It seemed to be more about timing than anything, or maybe it had to do with corners on which the light of history had shined.

The long, linear, open expanse that stretched before Plennie was for the people, a void upon which to rest and relax, to protest, to be seen and heard. They'd come already, unemployed workers called Fry's Army, then Coxey's Army, when things got bad in the 1890s. Thousands of women came in 1913 to demand suffrage and enfranchisement, and they got it, though things in Washington move slowly. Thousands of members of the Ku Klux Klan poured onto the Mall in 1925, their dusty autos bearing stickers professing the legend 100 PER CENT AMERICAN. They burned a big cross in Virginia, then went home. Also American was the editor of the *Buffalo American*, who wrote about the Klan that "50,000 men are a mere drop in the bucket of 115,000,000 and the rest of the nations have chuckled with glee at this attempt to purify the sins of 300 years with such attempts as these."

Gathering energy on their move toward Washington even now were the Hunger Marchers, some of whom Plennie had passed in Springfield, Illinois. Their numbers were growing. They'd been arrested in Oklahoma City, teargassed in St. Louis, clubbed in Indianapolis, provided with hay for beds in Columbus, Ohio, fed warm meat and potatoes in Owosso, Michigan, and labeled communists everywhere they went. The sentiment—that the marchers were all communists—has lost the edge that it might've had in the early 1920s, during the Big Red Bolshevist Scare, when books and movies were scrutinized, radical college professors were fired, and high school teachers were made to sign oaths against communism. "You cannot have from five to eight million people wanting work and unable to get it without knowing that this constitutes a challenge to our social order," Maryland governor Albert Ritchie told the annual conference of governors, "and that it is the strongest argument for communism unless it is solved."

Whatever they were, they were coming. Washington civic and trade organizations resolved to extend no free hospitality in the way of shelter or food to the marchers, and the police were forming a "welcoming committee" to deal with them. They would fail to break the White House or Capitol, despite demands to be heard. And right behind the Hunger Marchers were the marching farmers, and right behind them came Father James Renshaw Cox, a Roman Catholic priest from Pittsburgh, and twenty-five thousand unemployed Pennsylvanians called Cox's Army, and right behind them came the Bonus Army, twenty thousand veterans of the Great War demanding their bonus pay immediately. These were to be long months in the capital.

The man standing beside Plennie asked why he hadn't gotten President Hoover's autograph.

"He wouldn't care to give it to me," Plennie said. "He's the head man in this depression and the cause of my starting out on this jaunt."

The maligning was mild, and only partly true. But it was Hoover, it must be said, who had warned President Coolidge that his bull market was madly out of control.

If ever there was a man made for the challenge of a moment like this, he might've had Hoover's pedigree. An orphan by the age of ten, Hoover had hustled his way through Stanford University and roamed the world as a geological engineer. By twenty-four, he was running a gold mine in Australia, and by twenty-seven, he managed a coal mining operation in China and was hailed as the highest-salaried man of his age in the world, earning $30,000 a year. As the unpaid head of the Commission for Relief in Belgium from 1915, the great Quaker humanitarian fed seven million starving Belgians and French, then directed food to Russians in the same shape. He was touted as a brilliant progressive technocrat at the Commerce Department and was one of the key Americans in rebuilding Europe after the war. Just before the market crashed, he'd received a standing ovation at the last game of the World Series in Philadelphia.

Now, though, his name was synonymous with hard times, even if they weren't entirely of his creation. As H. L. Mencken wrote: "there was a volcano boiling under (Coolidge), but he did not know and was not singed. When it burst forth at last, it was Hoover who got its blast and was fried, boiled, roasted and fricasseed." Hoover would attend another World Series baseball game the month after Plennie passed through DC, and he'd be booed unmercifully, an unprecedented public embarrassment for a sitting president. Already, men were lining up to take his job, including the wiry governor of Oklahoma, Alfalfa Bill Murray, the same man who'd sent his National Guard to fight Texas at the Red River. He had not occupied the governor's office in the Sooner State for a solid year yet but was already considering a run to replace Hoover. He would throw his hat in shortly, and his campaign platform for the highest office in the land would promise people the "Four B's: Bread, Butter, Bacon, and Beans."

Hoovervilles had popped up in cities across the country. Out-turned empty pockets became Hoover flags. Newspapers covering homeless men on park benches were Hoover blankets.

Hoover was saddled with a sad situation, and he had too few fingers for the crumbling dike. He had tried to pit the government against the economic cycle, the first president to do so, by starting more public works projects than anyone had in the past two decades. He grew the government by creating civil service jobs; just recently more than ten thousand men and women had applied to be new Prohibition enforcers. He rammed constructive legislation through Congress while trying to limit the swell of bureaucracy and government debt. And often when he tried to distribute larger sums, Congress would slash the aid. Many Americans were still repulsed by the idea of living off the public dole and chastised those in need. In his boldest move, Hoover had proposed a yearlong debt payment holiday for European allies—Great Britain, France, and thirteen other countries—that owed money to the US, if they in turn would forgive German reparations for the same period. Germany was complaining that the burden of paying reparations to the victors of the world war was "unbearable," and the country was on the brink of total economic failure. Hoover thought that by pausing debt payments for a solid year he could give the world economy a chance to recover.

Ultimately, in spite of his efforts, Hoover was restrained by his own ideals. He believed that if the government was the source of relief, it would create dependency. Welfare would beget sloth. "This is not an issue as to whether people shall go hungry or cold in the United States," he explained. "It is solely a question of the best method by which hunger and cold should be prevented."

Plennie thought about a little boy he'd seen on the outskirts of Hagerstown, Maryland, a few days earlier. The kid was wearing a harness on his chest, and a long rope was tied from the harness to a tree in the center of the yard, staking the boy in place. Upon seeing Plennie coming backward, the boy jumped to his feet and scrambled toward the house. He must've forgotten that he was tied down, and when the slack ran out of his rope it jerked him flat on his back. The boy's mother ran outside screaming. She blamed Plennie. Plennie blamed the rope. The boy just cried. And that seemed like a fine analogy for this moment.

There at the foot of the Washington Monument, he joked with the man beside him. Both he and the president were champions at going backward, he said, and the man admitted Plennie had a point. They chuckled. That was about all anyone knew to do.

Back in June, when Plennie was less than a month into his trip, the Washington *Evening Star* ran a cartoon on its front page by the famed illustrator Clifford K. Berryman. It depicted a sign titled NEWS BULLETIN, and beneath that, MAN FROM TEXAS STARTS TO WALK AROUND THE WORLD BACKWARDS. In front of the sign stood a well-dressed elephant in a top hat labeled GOP and a tweed-suited jackass in a fedora labeled democrat. One was saying to the other: "THAT'S NOTHING NEW! WE'VE BOTH GOT LOTS OF CHAPS BEEN DOING THAT FOR YEARS."

On the day Plennie left the District, the *Star* ran another Berryman cartoon, this one depicting Miss Democracy leaning on her umbrella as Plennie Wingo backed toward the White House. "NOW MEBBE I COULD CATCH THE REPUBLICANS UNAWARES AND BACK A DEMOCRAT INTO THE WHITE HOUSE."

Clifford Berryman cartoon from the Washington Evening Star, author's collection.
(Courtesy of the Washington Evening Star)

The same paper ran a story about Plennie under the headline TEXAN, WALKING BACKWARD, USES 5 MONTHS AND DAY TO GET HERE.

At first glance, it looked like Plennie L. Wingo, the 36-year-old Texan, who is walking around the world, was on his way home to Fort Worth to meet himself coming back.

"Hey," shouted an interviewer, who caught Wingo on the wing today, en route between Washington and Bethesda, or rather Bethesda and Washington, "if you are walking back to Texas by way of that Atlantic you'd better turn around."

But Wingo, although his smoked glasses were turned full on the questioner, was looking in the other direction. And that, it developed, was the way he was walking.

For Wingo, the globe-trotting pedestrian, was travelling in reverse. He was looking in reverse also, through periscopes in his glasses.

What with so many motor cars on the highways these days, Wingo said, when his interviewer caught up and got behind him, it is better to look behind you if you're going in that direction.

Wingo made Bethesda last night, five months and one day after leaving Fort Worth. He came into Washington last night, face first, to look over the street layouts.

After that Wingo returned for his official entry today. He expects to see the sights that lay behind him and then walk on for New York, as he will allow himself only three years to get back to Fort Worth backwards via the Atlantic and Pacific.

"Maybe I am walking backwards," said Wingo, "but I'm not behind my schedule."

The *Washington Post*, too, ran a feature story about the "persevering pedalist" on his "odd enterprise" to "girdle the globe." If nothing else, Plennie gave reporters a chance to test their alliterative acumen.

He faced the Washington Monument and started out of town, catching Highway 1 to Baltimore, then Highway 40 north. He did some fishing with a kind man in Perryville, Maryland, on the beautiful Susquehanna River, but caught only a crab. "Figures," the man said. On September 28, he crossed into Delaware, his eleventh state, and was again hassled by a police officer. "What in the hell do you mean by walking backwards?" the officer said. "I don't think anyone would try a thing like that unless he is crazy or a damn fool."

Maybe he was right.

"I won't stop you," the cop said, "but if you get hit by a car the State of Delaware will not be responsible."

In Wilmington, the clerk at the Western Union refused to look at him or sign his book so he signed it himself: "3:17 p.m., September 29, 1931." He checked into a boardinghouse and took a stroll around town, stopping to inspect the whipping post called "Red Hanna" in the town square. He asked a local about it. The man said Delaware still had a law on the books that allowed public flogging as punishment for crimes like robbery, adultery, and embezzlement, and they sometimes whipped folks passing through just for fun.

On his way out of town the next morning, another police officer shouted at him.

"Get out of town," he said. "We don't allow folks like you here."

"My pleasure," Plennie said, starting backward, which must've seemed odd to the cop.

"Why don't you walk right?" he said.

"As far as I'm concerned, I am walking right," Plennie said. He didn't stop until he crossed the state line.

He rubbed his fingers along the crack in the Liberty Bell in Philadelphia, sold postcards to the friendly policemen on the superhighway leaving town, got bit by bedbugs at a fifty-cent motel in Trenton, New Jersey, and mostly just spent his money, day after day. The largest and most expensive city lay ahead. He needed to catch a break. He needed something big.

19.

BAMBOOZLED

The police roped off the streets as the crowd began to gather, men and women heaving and shoving and squinting against the October sky, trying to get a glimpse of the strange fellow in the homespun suit up on the ledge, twelve stories above the hard concrete sidewalks of Elizabeth, New Jersey.

The man on the ledge was glad they had come. Plennie had arrived with exactly eleven dollars in his pocket, and if he had any hopes of making it on to Europe, he needed to relieve the people below of their money.

* * *

He had left the dust storms in Texas and Oklahoma, backed past barren fields and stalled tractors in Missouri, Illinois, and Indiana, past shuttered factories and mines in Ohio, West Virginia, and Pennsylvania, and hungry men and women along the way. The healthy wheat crop in Kansas was practically worthless, drawing the lowest prices in history, so bad that counties quit collecting taxes. A plague of grasshoppers was scourging Iowa, Nebraska, and South Dakota. In the last week U.S. Steel had cut wages for 220,000 workers by 10 percent, then Bethlehem Steel and General Motors and U.S. Rubber Co. followed suit. But nowhere was the collapse as obvious as it was in New York. Everywhere he looked, the people seemed despondent, depressed. Bread lines stretched for blocks and apple vendors plugged sidewalks and men with nothing better to do smoked cigarettes on corners. Even the clothes people wore seemed to betray a collective poverty, ill-fitting and weak-seamed, women's hemlines dropping like the stock market. The papers were filled with stories about more strikes and government debt and marchers banging at the doors of city halls.

Much was made of the out-of-work silk weaver who drank poison in the Fifth Avenue Presbyterian Church during the Sunday morning sermon, and of the stockbroker who ate mercury tablets, and of the dahlia grower who leaped on purpose from the wing of an airplane and landed in Lake View Cemetery in Jamestown, New York, a convenient suicide, no mess. Capone was going to prison for eleven years. Alfalfa Bill Murray was going to run for president in '32. Okies and Arkies and Texans were going west to find work and escape the increasingly frequent dust storms, which were growing tall as mountains. Here in New York, the Depression was stagnant, and no one seemed to have anything to do but stay put, stuck like day-old molasses on a kitchen table. It all felt like something was missing, the chirp of birds or the clang of hammers, but nobody could say exactly what.

Plennie would've been in a terrible situation himself were it not for the charity of J. Walton Green, his chummy boyhood friend from school back in West Texas. Growing up, Walton had been a standoffish and unpopular boy, always in his books, studying while the others played. He had taken a correspondence course in hotel management while they were in high school and had landed a job as assistant manager at the luxurious St. Regis Hotel on Fifty-Fifth Street in New York and he was really making it, the rare eastbound migrant. Everyone at the hotel liked and respected him and, when

Plennie called him up, Walton greeted his old friend with open arms. Plennie had no intention of sponging. In fact, he was too embarrassed to tell Walton how short on cash he was.

"I know lots of people around town, and maybe I can help you," Walton said graciously. "Anyway, come what may, I know you're going to succeed in what you started out to do, no matter how discouraging it looks right now."

"Thanks, Walton," Plennie said. "If you think you can help me with your connections, fine. But if you put out any money on me, I want you to keep books, and even if I have to wash dishes, I'll pay it back."

Walton was having none of it. He insisted Plennie move in with him at the hotel, and the two soon commenced calling on shoe manufacturers across the city, looking for a sponsor. But as in St. Louis and Chicago, everyone was pinching pennies. They must've called every shoe shop in New York, with no luck. Walton suggested trying to contact shipping companies to see about getting Plennie a working passage to Europe on a big boat, but the Depression had hit the water, too. Massive ships were bobbing idle at the Hoboken port. The *George Washington* was the most recent victim, bringing the total tonnage of big liners resting at Hoboken to 144,000 tons. The biggest—the *Leviathan*, weighing nearly 60,000 tons—had laid off its crew of 856. Nearby bobbed the *America*, a 21,000-ton liner, and two others, *Resolute* and *Reliance*, 19,000 tons each. They weren't scheduled to leave on cruises until late in the fall, if then. Thousands of out-of-work seamen waited on the docks, desperate for any job available. A man with no maritime experience or union card didn't stand a chance.

Plennie was finally able to get some publicity, thanks to an accountant he met who shared a telephone triangle with the *Brooklyn Eagle*. The paper ran a photograph of the "ODD STEPPER" who was "back-tracking after the fickle dame" of fame. "A young man with a

Texas drawl walked backward into Brooklyn today and announced that he had been walking that way for months and would continue to do it for years," the story read. "After all, he asked, isn't the whole world going backward these days?" The story went on to say he was angling to get passage on a ship bound for London, and Plennie hoped the right person would see the story and throw him a hand.

As the days slipped by without his landing a sponsor, Plennie thought more and more about giving up. He was tired of being a burden on his friend Walton, so he took a job and moved into a boardinghouse. He told his mother she "may call it an appartment."

I am going to work at a caffeteria until I get some kind of a proposition on my stunt. I am going to work nites and that will give me a chance to work on my stunt at day time. I got the job last Friday. I am doing bussboy work. I am getting two dollars a day and my meals. I can soon get on my feet at that for I can buy clothes awful cheap and my room cost three dollars a week.

The financials were not ideal, but Plennie felt sure he could soon get a job behind the counter that paid three dollars a day. The manager liked him and said he expected an opening soon. Plennie was glad to have any job because they were hard to find.

"I am going to work at getting my transportations to Europe and my passports every day until I get it then I will continue my trip," he wrote. "Getting this job will give me a chance to do something toward my trip."

He'd made it to the East Coast backward, no small feat. But his prospects of continuing were dimmer by the day. And he had not heard a word from Della since that fateful letter in Pennsylvania. "I guess she is going to quit even writing to me," he confided to his mother. "Well, all I can do is to make my trip some way and make a lot of money and that is what I am going to do if I possibly can. If I don't make good I will never go around them again, but I am determined to make good and where there is a will I know there is a way."

If he did quit, it wasn't like he had a job waiting for him back home. His dad and brothers were out of work, looking again for cotton jobs, the bottom of the employment barrel, work so hard it made men run, or pick up rifles and kill one another.

What he was doing was crazy. He knew that. But he hadn't predicted the practical difficulties of financing his stunt and keeping things together back home.

That's when he met Schwartz.

* * *

He was looking out over Times Square when a man sat down, struck up a conversation, and introduced himself as Alexander J. Schwartz. His business card said he was an auctioneer and appraiser who conducted sales throughout the United States, and it listed an office address in Elizabeth, New Jersey, a half block from the Union County courthouse. He wore a fine suit and silk necktie and he struck Plennie as a man of means, a smooth talker, and an interesting fellow to boot. And maybe a little shady, but Plennie wasn't the suspicious type. Plennie told Schwartz his story over a cup of coffee and betrayed to his new acquaintance his recent financial troubles.

"I've tried about everything I can think of except maybe walking around the ledge of the Empire State Building," Plennie said.

Schwartz's eyes lit up. He snapped his fingers.

"That's it!" he said. "We'll get a permit. We'll sell advertising at our own price!"

Plennie was only kidding, but Schwartz was earnest in his excitement.

"And if I slip," Plennie said, "that will be the end of my trip right there."

"Oh, don't worry about that," Schwartz said. "I'll take care of that, too."

He told Plennie he knew an engineer at the new Empire State Building who could get them to the top floor, and they'd figure out a way to fasten a safety wire around Plennie's waist so the people on the street 102 stories below couldn't see it. Plennie politely said he wasn't interested in a scam to make money, but Schwartz wasn't taking no for an answer.

He dragged Plennie to meet his engineer friend. The building was simply incredible, shooting 1,250 feet into the sky above New York, and everything about it pointed to how grand the previous decade had been for mankind. The building stood because of a bet between two men with lots of money, such were the times. Walter Chrysler of the Chrysler Corp. and John Raskob, a financier and advisor to General Motors, wagered to see who could erect the world's tallest building. Chrysler finished his first, in 1930, a shining example of art deco architecture and the tallest building in the world...for a few months. It was then exceeded in height by Raskob's 10-million-brick, 365,000-ton Empire State Building, which took just more than a year to complete. Herbert Hoover himself was on hand to dedicate it that May. It was as impressive in its compact, narrow rise toward the heavens as the clearing of the Plains was in its expansive breadth. Plennie had never seen anything like it.

Schwartz's friend, the engineer, laughed in their faces but played along and showed them to the express elevator, and they ascended quickly to the top, more than a thousand feet in the air. When they pushed open the door to the roof, Plennie could see what the man was laughing about. The wind gusts were so strong that none of them dared to step outside the cavity. There were 58,322 insane people in New York in 1931, and Plennie Wingo wasn't about to add to the number.

"Well, we tried," Schwartz said.

"What do you mean *we* tried?" Plennie said. "I'm the guy who was supposed to risk his neck on that stunt."

"You know what I mean," Schwartz said. "It's like a fighter's manager telling the fighter, 'We ain't afraid of that guy.'"

They rebooted their plan over another cup of coffee, both men brainstorming stunts that would grab attention. The Hersch Tower in Elizabeth, also completed that year, was only twelve stories high, Schwartz said, his excitement growing. "I know Mr. Rosen, the manager there, and I know we can get a permit to walk that one. Not only that, I know all the merchants in Elizabeth. Selling advertising will be a breeze."

"Don't talk to me about a breeze," Plennie said.

He gave Schwartz his telephone number at the St. Regis, and the next morning Schwartz sent a car for him. Plennie brought along his cane, his rearview glasses, and his scrapbook, heavy now with newspaper clippings. When he arrived in Elizabeth, he inspected the roof of the Hersch Tower. The ledge was eighteen inches wide, and each side of the art deco gem had architectural rises that would prove difficult to back over. The stunt would be tricky, but Plennie thought he could do it.

Schwartz surprised Plennie with a stack of new business cards.

FROM FORT WORTH, TEXAS
AROUND THE WORLD BACK WARDS
PLENNIE L. WINGO

They spent the next few hours looking for sponsors. The merchants of Elizabeth all seemed to know Schwartz, but Plennie got

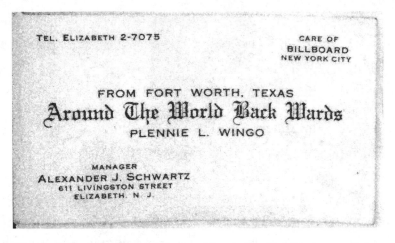

With the help of Alexander J. Schwartz, Plennie distributed business cards in
New York and New Jersey, trying to raise money and add credibility to his stunt.
(Courtesy of Pat Lefors Dawson)

the sense that they weren't fond of him. Many promised to pay
only upon the completion of the stunt. A good businessman made
smart decisions and knew full well what the newspapers were saying about the rise of corruption in the past year. You couldn't even
trust the law, anymore. Hoover's Wickersham Commission had just
denounced lawlessness in law enforcement, singling out New York
City.

On Saturday morning, the day of the advertised walk, Plennie
visited Elizabeth mayor John Kenah, who honored the Texan with
his autograph. Then he filled the next two hours parading heels-
first through the streets of town wearing advertisements for the
various shops that had signed on. He was something to behold, and
the people of Elizabeth stopped and stared.

A few minutes before noon, he arrived at the Hersch Tower and
walked backward up the stairs as the crowd swelled. He figured
the police ropes were keeping people back in case he fell.

He should've been nervous but found his legs steady as he

stepped up on the ledge and waved at the throngs below, the hotel men standing nearby on the roof. He began backing around the building, slowly at first, and heard the people on the ground gasp each time he stepped up and over an architectural feature, carefully navigating with his cane and mirrored glasses. The people cheered when he had cleared each obstacle. He traipsed the entire rectangle without so much as a wobble, and when he arrived where he'd started, he dramatically jumped to the roof and waved again. The crowd went crazy.

He was miffed to see that Schwartz wasn't standing on the roof with the hotel manager, but Plennie was so satisfied to have completed the stunt safely that he didn't give it much thought. He looked over the ledge again and realized he had just risked life and limb for a few dollars. He'd later have nightmares about the walk and swear never to do it again, but then and there he was pretty proud.

Schwartz didn't show up for dinner. Nor was he back at the hotel. Plennie visited one of the merchants who'd sponsored him, and the man said that Schwartz had come around after the stunt and collected his fee. The other businessmen told the same story.

Plennie was growing suspicious. He went to Schwartz's house and found his mother and father, who seemed like good and honest people. Schwartz's mother said he'd been home earlier but rushed out when he got an urgent call to go to New York City. Schwartz had told her he had to hustle across the bay to meet a man named Plennie Wingo.

Plennie's heart fell like a popped balloon. He'd been bamboozled. Hoodwinked. He felt stupid for being naive and enraged over the wasted time. The merchants had collectively pledged $86, enough to get him through a month without terrible want, and Plennie and Schwartz had agreed to split it down the middle. Now Plennie was back where he started.

He never thought he'd see Schwartz again, and he didn't have the time or money to stick around town and search for the bastard. Bitter lesson learned, he thought.

He did want to get a letter of endorsement from Mr. Rosen, manager at the Hersch Tower, in the event he had to make other ledge-walking deals on his own. So he stayed in town Sunday and paid Rosen a visit on Monday morning. Rosen's receptionist asked him to have a seat because Rosen was in a meeting. As Plennie waited, the door swung open and there stood Schwartz. He ran past a stunned Plennie, pushed into Rosen's office without knocking, and slammed the door behind him.

"What on the face of the earth is wrong with that guy?" the receptionist said.

Plennie waited and thought through the confrontation. He was ready to give Schwartz a piece of his mind and demand his money. Five minutes slid by. Then ten. Then twenty. It was becoming clear that Schwartz wasn't coming out so long as he was there. After waiting forty-five minutes, Plennie got up to go.

"I'm leaving now," he said loudly and slowly to the receptionist. "I'll come back this afternoon."

In the lobby, he summoned the elevator, then pushed the button for it to descend without him. He hoped Schwartz could hear the chime in Rosen's office. He then ducked beside the stairway and waited. Twenty minutes later, Schwartz poked his head out of Rosen's office and looked up and down the hallway before hustling for the stairs. He was looking over his shoulder when Plennie lurched out from his hiding place.

Even as a kid, Plennie had never been in a fistfight with anyone but family, and he wasn't sure he knew how. But his arms seemed to act without his volition. A fire raged inside him as he pounded Schwartz about the face and skull. He landed blow after blow as the man begged him to stop. In the struggle he somehow managed to hook his thumb in Schwartz's mouth and pulled out his dentures. Schwartz fell to the ground and Plennie kept slugging him, demanding his part of the money.

"I don't have it!" Schwartz screamed as the blows fell.

The beating did not stop until Schwartz said he'd give Plennie everything he had. Plennie let him up off the ground and Schwartz started fumbling around in his pockets. He eventually produced six crumpled dollar bills.

Plennie snatched the money, and the rage came back up in his throat. Schwartz tried to scramble away, down the stairs, but Plennie was on top of him like a cat, scratching and kicking him now. At the bottom of two flights of stairs, Schwartz broke away and ran outside and down the street as fast as he could.

Plennie checked himself for injuries. His knuckles were busted and his heart was pounding, but otherwise he was fine. He tossed Schwartz's bridgework on the sidewalk and looked again at the money. Six measly bucks.

The scuffle had caused a scene. He was trying to decide what to do next when a police officer spotted him. Schwartz had flagged down the cop and made a complaint. The cop cuffed Plennie, drove him to headquarters, and put him in a cell by himself on a charge of aggravated assault. There he remained for an hour before a group of the merchants who heard about the beating paid his $100 bail.

Schwartz and his lawyer showed up at Plennie's hearing the next morning. Plennie pleaded his own case, calling on the merchants to testify that Schwartz had collected the money. He argued that he didn't owe Schwartz any money for his broken bridgework and most certainly had not robbed him, as Schwartz's lawyer contended. He told the judge he was still angry about being swindled and he'd get even with Schwartz, no matter how long it took.

"I believe you will," the judge said. "I am not going to fine you or Schwartz. I can't make him pay what he has not got. But Mr. Schwartz did you an injustice, so I'm going to let him pay for his own bridgework."

Plennie was free, and as broke as he was when he arrived.

* * *

Back in New York, he told his friend Walton the whole story.

"The thing I liked the best was the way you beat the hell out of that crook," Walton said. "If I'd known what was going on I'd have come over and helped you out."

"You've done more than enough for me already," Plennie replied.

He was still in dire need. He had the $11 he'd had when he arrived, plus $12 from postcard sales in Elizabeth, plus the $6 he'd taken off Schwartz. All together it wasn't nearly enough to pay for passage on a ship to London.

He received a letter from his mother that made him crave home like nothing else. She was worried about him. She wrote that she'd had a dream the night before so real it stole her breath. In it, Plennie walked into her bedroom and sat down, and they had a nice conversation, just chatting like old times. When she woke, there was an empty space where he sat.

As he was on the edge of giving up, a thought struck him. He'd met a man, Paul Jones, on the highway outside Philadelphia. Jones was interested in his stunt and told Plennie he worked for the Hood Rubber Company, and maybe there was a chance the heel and sole department of the company was in need of some advertising. He gave Plennie the name of a colleague in New York, C. H. Carpenter. He was Plennie's last hope.

Carpenter was glad to see him, even had a postcard sitting on his desk when Plennie arrived, courtesy of Paul Jones, Philadelphia. Carpenter didn't have work but suggested Plennie keep walking north, to Boston, to visit P. R. Drew, head of the heel and sole department at the main factory. The recommendation was a glimmer of hope, two hundred miles away.

"It's a good lead," Walton told Plennie, adding that he'd enjoy the walk through New England. "It's beautiful country and the people are friendly."

Plennie and Walton tooled around New York for the next few days while Plennie weighed his options. They saw the World Championship Rodeo at Madison Square Garden and met up with a couple of cowboys from Abilene. They ate in Chinatown and visited an opium den, where green-eyed men smoked long pipes and looked to be in the throes of fever dreams. They walked across the brand-new George Washington Bridge, which had just recently opened to traffic and was used on its first day by 56,000 vehicles and 100,000 pedestrians. And they visited the flamboyant mayor, Jimmy Walker, a proud moment that Plennie would talk about for the rest of his life.

"Well, if he walked backward all the way just to get my autograph," Walker said, "he certainly deserves it."

Plennie bragged to his mother in a letter. "So you can see that I can get something done when I try, can't I?" he wrote. "I feel like I am going to make good and don't intend to ever give up until I back into Fort Worth, Tex."

Walker was easily the most famous person he'd ever met and he equated the encounter with success, writing to many friends and family about it.

"I don't blame you for being proud of having his signature," replied Hilda Beck of Fostoria, Ohio, whom Plennie had met in the Midwest. "I would be proud of it too."

The following Tuesday, Plennie put on his hat and glasses and grabbed his cane and new stack of postcards and walked into the Western Union to continue his journey. When the stationmaster stamped his booklet, he started up the street toward Yonkers, family on his mind.

He'd been dreaming about Della and Vivian. Since her last letter in Pennsylvania, demanding he come home, he often engaged in mental subterfuge. He told himself his own affairs had soured. If he'd had surplus, he would've sent it home. "I was having trouble enough to keep going without having extra money to send to her," he would later write, "but to tell her so would only add to her ire, so I decided to remain silent." In a letter to his sister, he'd tried to explain himself:

Yes, Lula Mae, it almost kills me to think of Della and Vivian in the way that I have to think of them. I thought I was doing this to suit them but I have decided that they never did like the idea and would not tell me until I left home. But I guess if I had made good it would have been all okay with them. Well, I am going to make good all right, but it may be a long time before I do. I think after I have finished my trip I will have plenty of money but I will have my hard time while I am doing the trip.

The fact that Della was living with her own family, and he couldn't imagine her people letting her go without, helped stifle his guilt.

He would press on, backward.

He had made his decision, come what might.

Two hundred miles to Boston.

20.

REVERSE IN WEDDED STATE

In June 1630, the tall ship *Arbella* was coming to anchor in Salem Harbor after a harrowing three-thousand-mile journey from England. *Arbella* was the flagship in an eleven-vessel fleet carrying a thousand Puritans on the front end of the earliest great migration in the new land's written history. A few other colonies had been planted and were deemed successful, thanks mostly to replenishment by immigrants. Jamestown, Virginia, despite "the starving time," had survived. The Pilgrims up in Maine complained of "muskeeto" bites and lost half their population when a hundred people died that first winter, but they were making it. A fishing village had begun to thrive at Cape Ann. By the time the *Arbella* made anchor, about seven thousand English settlers were living along the Atlantic coast, and their survival had become a beacon for those across the sea. Settlement in the New World remained dangerous and difficult, but for those on the margins in England, America was a land of pristine hope.

By and large, none of the early settlers had organized governments, but to avert the anarchy or dictatorships from which they'd fled, they had all agreed to abide by an expressed *common* will. It was a simple solution, perhaps uniquely British, and it was a fix that would be repeated again and again by the settlers of America, grafting democracy into the new world.

Aboard the *Arbella* stood John Winthrop, forty-one, leader of the Massachusetts Bay Company, which aimed to plant a new colony with an organized government. Winthrop observed disorder among his shipmates long before they saw the shoreline of the New World. One seasick maid "drank so much strong water, that she was senseless," Winthrop wrote in his diary, "and had near killed herself. We observed it a common fault in our young people, that they gave themselves to drink hot waters very immoderately." Later, someone found out that a servant was conducting a dubious economy. He was buying biscuits off a boy, marking them up, and reselling them to other servants. "We caused his hands to be tied up to a bar," Winthrop wrote, "and hanged a basket with stones about his neck, and so he stood two hours." So it was that alcoholism, youthful abandon, financial chicanery, and punitive justice were imported to the colonies. Before landfall, perhaps to set things straight, Winthrop wrote a memorable sermon in which he spelled out his ideas for the new settlement. Chief among them was this: take care of one another, and don't be selfish and greedy. Those who seek riches for themselves alone, he wrote, will receive the wrath of God.

"Now the only way to avoid this shipwreck, and to provide for our posterity, is to follow the counsel of Micah, to do justly, to love mercy, to walk humbly with our God. For this end, we must be knit together, in this work, as one man," he wrote. "We must entertain each other in brotherly affection. We must be willing to abridge ourselves of our superfluities, for the supply of others' necessities. We must uphold a familiar commerce together in all meekness, gentleness, patience and liberality. We must delight in each other; make others' conditions our own; rejoice together, mourn together, labor and suffer together, always having before our eyes our commission and community in the work, as members of the same body. So shall we keep the unity of the spirit in the bond of peace."

The next part would lay the groundwork for a doctrine of American exceptionalism that would define the country for centuries to come. It would for generations be on the tongues of men who would at times forget or ignore the first precipitants about community and liberality.

"For we must consider that we shall be as a city upon a hill," Winthrop wrote. "The eyes of all people are upon us."

The members of the Massachusetts Bay Company disembarked, and Winthrop, the colony's first governor, settled at Boston and set about taking slaves and banning gambling, adultery, and Christmas.

And so it came to pass that almost exactly three hundred years later, on December 23, a man from Texas walked backward up the steps to Boston City Hall at 5:30 p.m. and pulled on locked doors.

They're at a Christmas party, said a man nearby. *Why don't you try the back doors?*

He did, and he found them unlocked, and as he backed down a hallway he came upon Wilford J. Doyle, Boston city clerk, and J. P. Meahoney, secretary to the mayor, who saw to it immediately that he was part of the city employee Christmas party. The basement was packed with people, mostly elderly women, who began doting upon and fussing over young Plennie L. Wingo of Abilene. He was full of stories, and they were happy to hear.

He had backed up US Highway 1 through Yonkers and New Rochelle, and stopped at Stamford, Connecticut, to advertise a vaudeville act opening at the Strand Theater, twenty dollars for two days' work. He'd gotten a letter from the Strand manager to present to his cousin, who worked for Paramount Pictures in Berlin, should Plennie make it as far as Germany. He'd gained the autograph of Stamford mayor Joseph P. Boyle, and gotten his picture in the newspaper shaking the hand of Bridgeport mayor Edward T. Buckingham behind his back. He'd advertised again in New

Haven, for a movie called *Local Boy Makes Good* at the Roger Sherman Theater, and the coincidence wasn't lost on Plennie. He'd eaten fried smelts at a café outside New Haven, and they were delicious. In several towns, his reputation had preceded him, and curious onlookers had lined roadsides, cheering as he blew by. Reporters hustled to keep up with him. He'd paused for a night in Providence, Rhode Island, for two reasons: he wanted to hike the entire way to Boston in a single day, so he needed good rest, and he had to meet with a lawyer.

* * *

Perhaps there was a certain irony to the fact that Della's letter caught up with him in a place called Providence. She had to think about her own future. She was done with marriage. She had dutifully presented him with a chance to turn around, to go home and retake his seat at the head of their table and give up the ridiculous exhibition that had brought his loved ones zero benefit and noticeable harm. The test of love, commitment, loyalty, and obligation had come and gone, and Plennie had failed.

Men do strange and terrible things sometimes.

He backed into the office of James H. Kiernan, counselor-at-law, on Weybosset Street. With Mr. Kiernan's guidance, Plennie waived his right to appear before a jury and agreed to pay court costs. There was no use in fighting anything, for his wife was always right.

Plennie wrote "Dec. 21—1931," on James Kiernan's business card. "Signed divorce papers." He stepped back into the sunshine, completely unaware that his fame had brought him into vaulted and unenviable regard among the American press corps. The papers, of course, carried the scandalous news.

Reverse Walker Has Reverse In Wedded State

If Plennie Wingo of Abilene, who has walked backward farther than any other known man, carries out his intentions of going around the world in reverse, he will have to about face when he gets home to regain his wife's affections. Mrs. Wingo has filed suit for divorce in the 42nd district court. Mrs. Wingo and her sixteen-year-old daughter live in Abilene. She was married to Plennie in 1914, according to the petition filed in the name of Mrs. Idella Wingo.

* * *

The ladies at City Hall couldn't get enough of Plennie. Someone brought him a plate of food from the potluck buffet. He was famished after twelve hours of backpedaling. He'd worn shorts for the thirty-mile hustle from Providence to the city upon the hill, and they made him seem younger, boyish. A reporter for the *Boston Globe* wrote that he wore "sawed-off knee-pants" and looked like "an escaped yodeler from the Tyrolean Alps." The ladies and the reporter asked him what everyone else asked him: *Why are you doing this?*

"Just because," he said.

They pried, trying to get him to articulate why, of all the various avenues of human achievement, he chose this one. He told them he liked the outdoors, and liked walking. He told them it was a great chance to see the country, albeit backward. He explained that he wanted to do something that would make people notice, make them stop and think.

"It's an ambition I've had for many years," he said. "There's no competition in it, either, and that's something in this day and age."

He'd walked more than two thousand miles through sixteen states and the District of Columbia, and below the hems of his knee pants you could see that his calves had moved around to the fronts of his legs.

All that remained between him and the next leg of his journey was passage to London, and the next morning, after a quick rest at Hotel Haymarket, courtesy of the City of Boston, he called on P. R. Drew, head of the heel and sole department of the Hood Rubber Company in Watertown, a few miles west. When he walked into the office he was happy to see one of his postcards on Drew's desk. Drew was kind and good-natured, and he seemed genuinely interested in doing what he could to help. But he told Plennie it would have to wait until after the New Year. Meanwhile, Plennie got a passport and spent Christmas alone.

When he next saw Drew, it didn't look good. The company viewed the stunt as a liability and therefore would not be using Plennie L. Wingo for advertising. But there was an ounce of hope. "I am going to make you acquainted with our traffic director," Drew said. "He might be able to assist you in getting a boat job."

The two men walked down the hall to the office of Mr. Webster, and Plennie explained himself, doing his best to sound desperate and grateful.

"Tell you what," Webster said. "You go back to your hotel and I'll call you."

Plennie *was* grateful. Neither man needed to be so kind. He returned to Hotel Haymarket to wait. He shoved his hands in his trouser pockets and paced in the lobby, weighing his situation. If this didn't work, he'd soon be out of money. That would leave him homeless, divorced and broke, and two thousand miles from home. His spirits were lower than they'd been in a long time.

The desk clerk called out for Plennie. He had a phone call. Webster was on the other end.

"Would it make any difference to you," he asked, "if you went to Germany instead of England?"

21.

VENGEANCE

If you take a man who has never seen the open water, who has spent all thirty-six of his years surrounded by the assurance of firm earth, and put him on a ship upon the vast and rolling sea, surrounded by ocean for days, you should not be surprised by the man's discomfort. It might take a few days, perhaps more, for him to get oriented and present himself upright. This is why the crew of the *Seattle Spirit*, which set sail from Boston for Hamburg, Germany, on January 12, 1932, got to know Plennie Wingo's back better than his face, much like the rest of the world, on account of the fact that he spent the first few days of his ocean voyage facedown on his bunk, holding the loose sheets balled up in his hands, as if that might help.

He had boarded with such pizazz, walking backward down the gangplank even, as his crusty shipmates watched from the deck, some curious, some sneering. "Hello, everybody," he said when aboard. "Here I am!"

His entrance had earned him no great benevolence among the seafaring men beside whom he'd soon be sleeping. He was granted passage as a favor, and was told he would not have much work to do, and the seamen seemed to know as much. Plennie's chaperone introduced him to the crew, working his way down the line until at last they came to the steward, who was in charge of the housekeeping department. The man appeared to be equal parts German and Italian and had the hulking build of a professional wrestler.

"I'm glad to meet you," Plennie said, extending his hand.

"I'll bet you are," the steward replied. Then he glanced at his crew. "He may be walking backwards now," he said, "but I'll have him turned around by the time we reach Hamburg."

Their meeting began a relationship people would come to describe as emotionally abusive.

"We serve dinner at five," the steward said. "You can start work in the morning."

The next morning Plennie was put to the task of squeegeeing fourteen cabins. He was nearly finished with the first when he felt a powerful phlegm rise in his throat, a sickness he tried to hold down by swallowing. This worked for a few moments, but eventually he acquiesced to the impulse to vomit, and the putrid discharge erased considerably his squeegee productivity. He crawled on hands and knees to his bunk, whereupon the mattress began to shift from under his weight as though it were attempting to overpower him. A great battle thus ensued. Plennie managed to reverse onto his stomach and latch on to his resilient adversary. He maintained the posture, void of concern for life, until the steward's assistant breached the crew cabin.

"I've been poisoned," Plennie managed to moan.

The steward's assistant was indifferent. "You're seasick," he said. "Give it a few days."

Plennie lay there alone for hours in the looming disquiet, unwilling to unleash his disobedient bedroll, until a crewman came in. Plennie couldn't remember his name from the introductions, but the mate seemed friendly enough. They talked for a while and Plennie mentioned that he was surprised to have been given a chore, having been told on shore that there was little work to be done. The man hadn't been gone long when the steward burst in, put his meaty hands on little Plennie, and flipped him upright, like a child, jerking him to his feet.

"So you don't figure to have much to do, eh?" he bellowed, spitting profanity. "You're going to work now, and work every day until you get off this ship."

* * *

"I want to give you some advice," the man in the next bunk whispered a few days later. Plennie couldn't see him in the darkness, but his name was John Hall, and if Plennie had a friend on the *Seattle Spirit* it was him. "You talk too much," John Hall said. "And to the wrong people. That fellow you told about not expecting much to do is the steward's right-hand stool pigeon." The entire ship was a giant grapevine, and the steward was the root. Whatever anybody said made its way back to him.

Plennie was sick for four days. Anything he ate came back with involuntary force. He was growing weaker and weaker, but the steward watched him closely, demanding he work eight hours each day, not including time spent on his knees in the head.

John Hall was working his third trip across the ocean, and he kept his nose clean because he didn't talk to anybody. He told Plennie that his son, on the opposite bunk, was the same way; he was no trouble because John Hall had trained him to keep his mouth shut. Plennie thanked Hall for the lesson and resolved to stay quiet.

* * *

He tried to eat again on January 16 but couldn't keep food down. He found success, finally, on January 17, and his stomach retained his first solid meal in five days. By then he had squeegeed seven of fourteen cabins. His friend John Hall whispered that he'd never seen a sick crewman run as ragged. Plennie was keeping his mouth shut and showing the steward, who was nearly twice his size, all the courtesy he could feign, but he couldn't work fast enough. The big man grew more disagreeable by the day. He seemed to enjoy insulting Plennie, threatening to lock him in the hold on bread and water, even suggesting he wouldn't give Plennie a release once they arrived in Germany. Plennie was dubious about the prospect and slipped out of the cabin one night to track down the captain.

"I have to tell you, son," the captain said, "we have rules at sea and we can't interfere in another man's territory. Unless he tried to murder you, I couldn't lift a finger."

"Could he prevent me from landing in Germany?" Plennie asked.

"He sure could if he wanted to," the captain said. "For any reason."

A propeller broke on the sixth day at sea, delaying arrival by three days. Plennie had finished his squeegee work on the cabins by the time it was repaired.

"I guess they will pass," the steward said begrudgingly.

Plennie was hoping to relax a little the next few days, but the steward put him back to work cleaning grease from the ceiling and walls of the dining room. When that was finished, he was made to clean the galley.

Plennie celebrated his thirty-seventh birthday in silence on January 24, a Sunday, and within a few hours he saw the white cliffs of Dover—as close as he'd ever come to England—and the big ship entered the English Channel. Just six months earlier, an Austrian named Karl Naumestnik had become the first human to walk across the dangerous twenty-mile stretch from Cape Gris Nez to Dover, wearing on his feet eight-foot-long bamboo water skis buoyed by inflatable bladders. What would they think up next?

The five-thousand-ton ship pushed up the River Elbe toward Hamburg as Plennie hustled to finish cleaning the galley, fantasizing the entire time about ways to get even with the steward. Plennie was a Texan, by God, and there was no justice in his current arrangement. When the city came into view, Plennie wondered if he'd be allowed off the boat given the steward's disposition. Then he was summoned.

"I have to go to Italy while the ship is in port," the steward told him. "I'll be back before sailing time on January twenty-ninth. The second mate has your passport and will release you after my orders are carried out, and not before." If Plennie wasn't finished by sailing time he could finish on his way back to America.

Plennie was boiling mad, but what option did he have? He went back to work, daydreaming about evening the score. He changed the linens in all fourteen cabins and put the dirties in the laundry. He defrosted the two walk-in freezers and cleaned them. He had begun to straighten and clean the large storage room near the mess when his plan revealed itself as he was moving several cases of lye. Some of the powder had spilled out of a broken can. With a mean notion in his head, Plennie wrapped the lye in a cellophane bag and tucked it into his pocket. The big bastard would never know what hit him.

He collected his clothes and notebook and swapped out his suitcase for a spare knapsack. He double-checked his cleaning, then, as twilight approached, reported to the second mate, who handed him his passport. Just before he disembarked, he slipped into the steward's room when no one was looking, took care of his business, then, full of anxiety and flushed from the effort, headed for the gangplank. The second mate was there to see him off.

"Are you feeling all right?" the mate asked.

"I feel fine," Plennie said. "I guess the idea of entering a foreign country makes me nervous."

He bade the man farewell, put his glasses on, faced the *Seattle Spirit*, and started backward down the gangplank. Europe was behind him, finally, and he hoped hard that the big ogre didn't appear in his mirrors. What he had done felt something like setting fire to the long fuse on a stick of dynamite, then walking away, hoping to be out of the blast zone by the time the thing blows.

* * *

He hustled, forward this time, down the backstreets of Hamburg, occasionally looking over his shoulder, until he found a rooming house where to his surprise the proprietor spoke perfect English. Some of the crew of the *Seattle Spirit* got rooms at the hotel overlooking the port, but he wanted to remain anonymous until he was certain the ship, and the steward, were at sea. Still, he found sleep difficult and interrupted by attacks of anxiety. He tossed and turned until morning, picturing the fruits of what was most certainly a criminal act, even by the lax standards of maritime law. When the sun rose, he walked to the harbor like a spy, peeking around buildings, until he was sure the ship had departed. He paced to the dock, then continued his backward walk away from the Elbe into the brick canyons of the portside city. Soon the curious were rushing to the curb, then rushing away and bringing back friends and family. Before long the streets were packed with Germans puzzling over the man wearing the sign with English wording. Soon a reporter was at Plennie's side, asking questions in English, telling him he had read about a backward-walking Texan but had not believed it. After a short while they arrived at the American Embassy, where Plennie shook hands with the American consul from Pittsburgh, Pennsylvania, and showed him the clippings from his hometown newspaper. He left with two cartons of American cigarettes and the consul's good-luck wishes.

Plennie made one final stop before carrying on with his second leg in an unknown land.

"What do you wish?" asked the doorman at the police station, which covered an entire city block. Plennie explained slowly that he would like to talk to someone who might make it okay for him to stay in Germany for a spell. He was shown inside, to a giant room, and from what he could tell there was not a single interior wall or partition on the entire first floor. He walked forward past a jumble of crooked desks to a long table in the center of the room where the bearded men seemed most official. Several studied his sign.

"Are you American?" one of them asked. "The one who is going around the world backward?"

"I am," Plennie said.

"You must be crazy," the man said.

"Perhaps," Plennie conceded. He handed over his passport and the men perused it, speaking to one another in German.

"Are you planning to walk backwards in Germany?" the man asked.

Plennie confirmed. That was the plan.

The men talked some more.

"We do not believe it is safe," the one finally said.

Plennie whipped out his glasses, his ace in the hole. He pressed them into the German's hands. The men all looked them over. Two tried them on and attempted to walk backward. They weren't convinced.

Plennie put his glasses on.

"See that door in the front?" he asked, referring to the door far behind him, through which he'd come. He paced backward toward it, zigzagging around the desks and down crooked aisles without bumping anything. He reached behind him finally and grabbed the knob. The cops seated around the room began to applaud, then more joined in, and the bearded men in the middle of the room nodded. But what about finances?

Here he had less confidence.

"Sufficient," he said. "I won't be a bother to anyone."

*   *   *

He gave instructions at the post office to forward any mail for Plennie L. Wingo to Berlin. A kind man down the street agreed to paint a new sign on the back of the scrap he'd worn across America. He tied his shoes tight and slung onto his back the knapsack containing his extra clothes, two hundred postcards, two cartons of American cigarettes, and his journal, which contained a new clipping from the Hamburg newspaper *Altonaer Nachrichten*, headlined WELTREISE RÜCKWÄRTS! He left Hamburg on February 1, 1932, wearing a newly painted sign, saying:

RÜCKWÄRTS
Rund um die
WELT

22.

POWDER KEG

He'd been warned. The reporter for the Hamburg newspaper had told Plennie to be careful in Berlin. Something was different there. Something had changed.

All of Germany was facing a national crisis: millions were unemployed, and banks were failing left and right after Austria's big Creditanstalt bank declared bankruptcy in May 1931. But Germany's largest city, with a population of more than four million, felt like a powder keg waiting for a match. Broken, out-of-work men filled the squares. Their factories were closed, smokestacks eerily still. Their government dole swelled. Their leaders were impotent. Even with President Hoover's moratorium on repayment of debts, the country's economy was failing. "Gray desperation" was what a publicity man named Joseph Goebbels called it. "The people are divided, torn in two," he wrote just before Christmas in Berlin's *Der Angriff*. "People have every reason to despair of the future. Were there no National Socialist movement as the last hope of those of good will, millions of people in Germany would long since have plunged into the abyss of chaos and anarchy. We have raised the banner of a new faith."

By the time the backward ambassador from Abilene arrived in Berlin, men in brown uniforms were hanging posters on city walls, advertising a speech for the following week at the Sportpalast by the leader of the National Socialist Party, or the Fascists, the group Joseph Goebbels was referring to in his Christmas column.

The charismatic party chief was growing more popular by the day, riding a tide of unhappy people who seemed to enjoy being told that they were unhappy. In 1929, his political party had fewer than half a dozen members on the national legislative body, the Reichstag. By 1930, it had won an astonishing 107 seats. By September 1931, the party had garnered six million votes in national polling to emerge as the second-largest political party in Germany.

They viewed their leader as a martyr. Years before, he had tried to take over the government by force in Munich. The coup attempt started in a beer hall, and it failed. He went to prison for nine months, but this served to bring attention to his cause and give him time to write a book called *My Fight*.

He was chauvinist. He was fascist. He was nationalist. People loved him. Those who didn't were scared of those who did. Those who did came by the thousands to see him, packing halls and waiting, waiting, for he was perpetually late. They did not mind waiting. The stadiums and arenas where he was to deliver speeches felt festive, like carnivals. The observers stood because there were always more bodies than seats. It was next to impossible to leave because the crowds were so thick they blocked the exits. And when he emerged to shouts of *"Heil! Heil!"* it was as though the people were in bondage to him, would do anything he asked.

The establishment treated him like a joke at first, an outlier and extremist, until their laughter was stifled by the sheer number of people who believed the things he said. He tailored his speeches to his audiences. Before businessmen, he talked about economic policy. But when he spoke before the masses of disenfranchised citizens, his speeches were all blood and thunder and racist rhetoric. He frightened them and comforted them.

He promised an assortment of government reforms, but chief

among them, at the top of his list, was the jingoistic and immea-surable vow that he would make Germany great again.

And swift was his rise. He claimed now that he represented 15 million voters, and his party viewed 1932 as the "year of decisions," moving its headquarters from Munich to Berlin. German president Paul von Hindenburg issued an emergency decree in December 1931, imposing a stoppage on political activities during the holi-days. That expired on January 3, 1932. The American press was calling the upcoming season "one of the most dramatic periods in the history of the German republic." Democracy hung in the bal-ance.

In the early months of 1932, everyone was talking about whether Hindenburg would run for president again. He was eighty-five years old, and another election cycle might negatively impact the old field marshal's health. German chancellor Heinrich Brün-ing was toying with the idea of asking the parliament, the Reich-stag, to extend Hindenburg's term in office. That meant changing the constitution, and changing the constitution meant convinc-ing the National Socialist Party to get on board with the idea. So Brüning sent his defense and interior minister to meet with the National Socialist party leader, to see if he'd support the idea. "A likeable impression, modest, orderly man who wants the best," was Minister Wilhelm Groener's take on Adolf Hitler. "External appear-ance of an ambitious autodidact. Hitler's intentions and goals are good but he's an enthusiast, glowing and multifaceted."

A week later, Hitler rejected the offer, hypocritically citing con-stitutional concerns when everyone knew that the first thing he'd do if he took power was gut the constitution. A week after that, Hitler's publicity man first proposed the idea of *him* running for president against Hindenburg. "Hitler has to become Reich pres-ident," Joseph Goebbels wrote in his diary. "That's the only way. That's our slogan. He hasn't decided yet. I'll continue to drill away."

The problem was that Hindenburg was very popular among right-wingers, and if Hitler ran, he stood a good chance of losing, and losing might shatter the image he was trying to create, of an invincible savior who could not be defeated.

"Hitler is waiting too long," Goebbels wrote on January 28.

"When will Hitler decide?" he wrote on January 30. "Does he not have the nerve?"

The elections were six weeks away. Hitler talked to the press at Weimar, then traveled to Munich, then returned to Berlin to deliver a speech at the Sportpalast, the days ticking by with no word about whether he would run. He was trying to wait out Hindenburg. If the prodemocracy camp threw its support behind Hindenburg, whom they'd vigorously opposed in 1925, Hitler was better situated to get all the support of the nationalist right wing.

"Machiavelli," Joseph Goebbels wrote. "But correct."

On February 15, 1932, before the Night of Broken Glass and the Night of the Long Knives, before the burning of the Reichstag and disposal of the Treaty of Versailles, and before an ethnic genocide the world would never forget, Paul von Hindenburg announced he was again running for president, to save the Weimar Republic, and his announcement paved the way for the nationalist newcomer Adolf Hitler to begin preparing an unprecedented presidential campaign, gushing, "Now the battle has been declared."

And a man from Texas, wearing a pressed and mended suit because he wanted to look his best, walked backward into Berlin.

*　*　*

"Misery and poverty are guests in the farmhouses," Joseph Goebbels had written in his Christmas column. Plennie Wingo was a guest in the farmhouses too, and he found poverty but no misery to speak of. The folks he met in the German countryside between Hamburg and Berlin were nothing but kind and gracious, giving freely of their food and inviting him to spend the night in their homes. He was a curiosity, a walking carnival. His story in the Hamburg newspaper helped explain what he was doing to those who spoke no English. The American cigarettes helped break any ice. Many were curious about his scrapbook, and he was surprised at the number of Germans who understood who Jimmy Walker was and wanted to see his autograph.

He realized early on that he would have to rely on friendship to get him through, since public inns or motels were difficult to find. This meant fewer daily miles. What had been short roadside conversations in America took more time here and involved a more universal form of discourse, like pantomime or charades. He was glad for the sacrifice because he was just as interested in the daily lives of the citizenry as they were in him.

He spent one night with a doctor on a feather bed in the guest room, and one at a mission, shivering in a barn in a pile of hay. He stopped at a lunch counter and tried to order a bowl of stew. The waitress couldn't understand him, so he said, "Moo?" She shook her head and said, "Baa." Late one evening, he walked up to a swanky resort-type establishment, sat at the bar, and ordered a glass of beer. The bartender mistook him for a vagrant and called security, and security called the city police, and the police took his passport and put him in a one-room jail cell, where he slept on a wooden bench. They turned him loose in the morning and he was on his way.

Postcard sales had fallen off, until he met an English-speaking German who told him he was charging too high a price. A German mark—what he'd been asking—was roughly equal to a US dollar. From then forward he charged only what those interested could afford. Sales spiked immediately and depleted his supply, but by the time he arrived in Berlin he had thirty marks in his pocket and two weeks of mostly rewarding experiences.

On the outskirts of Berlin he reached a traffic circle connecting a half dozen roads. One signal, perched atop a concrete base, appeared to be servicing all lanes, and several police officers were directing traffic. When Plennie was utterly confused, one of the officers came to his aid, but he only spoke German. The two tried in vain to communicate until finally the officer grabbed Plennie's elbow to move him across the lanes of traffic. He seemed terribly confused when Plennie began to walk backward. Once they had made it to the safety of the raised island, the flabbergasted officer released Plennie and looked him over. Plennie raised one finger, then fished the Hamburg newspaper clipping out of his journal. The officer read the clip and finally understood, and he helped Plennie the rest of the way, pointing down a cobblestone road toward downtown.

* * *

He checked the building number twice against the piece of paper. This was it. Paramount Pictures Corporation. He walked inside, introduced himself, and reported that he was looking to speak with Guss Schaefer, cousin of Louis Schaefer, manager of the Strand Theater in Stamford, Connecticut, USA. When Guss emerged, Plennie handed him a handwritten note.

My dear Guss:

This will introduce to you, Mr. Plennie L. Wingo, who is walking around the world backwards.

I used Mr. Wingo for a stunt here in connection with the opening of our new vaudeville policy, and he turned out a very effective job. If he gets into your neck of the woods, you may be able to give him the right kind of a steer.

With all good wishes from all the family, to you and Clara.
Your cousin,
Louis J. Schaefer

The next morning, a Paramount Pictures sound truck pulled up outside the YMCA where Plennie had spent the night. The men drove him around Berlin for two days, filming as he backed past the famous historic structures. People lined the streets to watch the American and struggled to get into the newsreel. They filmed Plennie scooting in reverse near the Brandenburg Gate, not far from Hotel Kaiserhof, where Hitler was staying. He scooted past the Reichstag building, across Alexanderplatz, and in front of the thirteenth-century Marienkirche, which contained on its walls 362 ancient verses, the oldest evidence of poetic creativity in Berlin. The poem explained the dance of death, that we all die and it's best to be humble.

* * *

Tempo
  Backwards around the world
  Berlin, 16 February 1932
  I am no longer able to move forward, thought Mr. Plennie L. Wingo, when he took off last season from Texas, in order to walk around the world backwards. Yes, people today really have the craziest ideas. Here we have this good fellow, owning a well-going bar, and he really doesn't have to worry about anything or anybody in the world.
  He lives satisfied and his needs are met, until one day, he sud-

denly has the odd idea to wander these great roads of the world backwards, and then write a book about it. He practiced for six months with a special trainer in his hometown of Abilene. Then he had himself built a special pair of glasses which allowed him to see from backwards, forwards. James Walker, the mayor of New York, gave him a letter of recommendation and of congratulation, and all American newspapers dedicated column upon column to him, walking backwards, showing his back to new parts of the globe.

Currently he is in Berlin and he still wants to make it through all parts of Europe, and wants to be back at the beginning of 1933 at the world's fair in Chicago. Good luck on your return trip.

Hitler had plenty of critics before everyone on the planet knew his name.

"If there is one thing we admire about National Socialism," said Social Democratic Party deputy Kurt Schumacher as Hitler was preparing to run for president, "it's the fact that it has succeeded, for the first time in German politics, in the complete mobilization of human stupidity."

"Hitler in place of Hindenburg means chaos and panic in Germany and the whole of Europe, an extreme worsening of the economic crisis and of unemployment, and the most acute danger of bloodshed within our own people and abroad," the Social Democratic Party leadership wrote in the party newspaper.

But Hitler and the National Socialists were launching a massive campaign as Plennie wrapped up his stay in Berlin. The party plastered posters on walls around the city, strong and shrill propaganda with slogans like "Down with the system! Power to the National Socialists!" Joseph Goebbels distributed fifty thousand gramophone records of a campaign speech, and the party produced a ten-minute sound film, meant for broadcast in city squares, that depicted Hitler as the coming savior of the German people. Hitler's campaign stops grew into massive spectacles as he bounced from city to city, telling his swarming fans to prepare for the "gigantic battle ahead."

"The people were beside themselves," Joseph Goebbels noted. "An hour of euphoria. Hitler is a true man. I love him."

Plennie packed his bag and stopped by the American consulate, where he got two more cartons of cigarettes and a letter from his mother addressed to "the man who walks backwards." He said goodbye to Guss Schaefer at Paramount Pictures.

"We don't usually make a practice of paying for newsreels," Schaefer told him, "but I feel your case is different."

He handed Plennie a hundred-mark bill.

"You've made my visit here the happiest of my trip," Plennie said.

With that, he backed south out of Berlin and away from the gray, dull, suffering army that would soon go to the polls and vote for the man they believed would change their lives.

23.

HINTERLANDS

The snow began to fall before he reached Dresden, 120 miles south of Berlin, an astonishing and sometimes painful thing for a man from the desert, so Plennie ducked into a roadside tavern, kicked the ice off his shoes, and sat at a table near the fireplace. It didn't take long for the proprietor, Weiber Hirsch, who spoke a little English, to grow interested in Plennie. Between waiting on others in the tavern, he paused at Plennie's table to ask questions, before finally inviting him to stay the night in a cabin out back. The snow fell heavy outside the window. Plennie accepted the man's kind offer, and Hirsch showed him to his room and quickly built a fire to warm Plennie up.

When dinner rolled around, Plennie's suit still had not dried and he was embarrassed by his appearance. He apologized to Hirsch for how he looked.

"You know, me and some of the fellows have been discussing that very problem," Hirsch said. "We wondered if it would embarrass you if we were to pitch in and fit you out with some of our clothes that we could spare."

"I think that's wonderful," Plennie said, and soon Hirsch and three other men came to him bearing clothes that looked brand-new: suits, shoes, fresh shirts, socks, heavy underwear. They even brought a short all-weather coat and a gray felt hat that fit perfectly over his considerable ears.

Germans were proving to be the kindest people he'd met.

* * *

The hotel in Dresden looked beautiful from the outside. Plennie had a little money to spare and the slog from Berlin had worn him out, so he walked into the lobby and gave his name and passport to the clerk, who spoke no English. He was waiting to pay, wondering how much he owed, when the clerk took his arm and directed him into another room lined with rows of individual lockers. The fellow who seemed to be in charge handed Plennie a key and pointed to one of the lockers. He made some odd noises and pantomimed taking his clothes off, then pointed to Plennie, who did not much like what was happening. The man, however, was insistent. Plennie began to disrobe, the man hovering nearby, now indicating for Plennie to remove his undergarments and put those in the locker too.

Plennie was a funny-looking man with clothes on. Nude, his appearance was downright comical, with his thin chest and narrow shoulders and his oddly muscled legs from backpedaling what now was more than 2,300 miles. He stood there naked as the German looked him over, walked around to his backside, and gave him a hard shove forward toward a heavy door. Plennie nearly fell into the next room, where the ceiling was lined with rows of long perforated pipes spraying warm water. It felt like walking into a warm summer rainstorm, but for the fact that other naked men were standing around the room.

The German grabbed a mop, plunged the head into a five-gallon bucket of liquid soap, then walked behind the men, bringing the mop down on the top of each man's head. He barked instructions for them to wash. When he was satisfied, he shoved them into another room, tossed them towels and nightgowns, then showed them to a fourth room, filled with rows of long tables and benches where stoop-shouldered men and boys were eating hard bread and bowls of soup.

When everyone was finished eating, a chaplain of some sort led them in group singing and said what Plennie took to be a heart-felt prayer. This was not the First Baptist Church of Abilene, but it wasn't all bad. The men and boys filed into yet another room filled with rows of cots, each with a pillow and single bedsheet.

Some hotel.

The room was warm, thank goodness, but Plennie had trouble sleeping. Some kind of chemical odor, maybe a fumigant, hung heavy in the air. He lay there well past midnight, wondering what he'd gotten himself into. Whatever the case, it was better than a hayloft or a jail cell, and the way he looked at it, he was a shower ahead in the deal.

The grits and weak coffee the next morning weren't satisfying, so after Plennie dressed and picked up his passport, he went in search of a proper meal along the River Elbe, which divided the newer part of town from a cluster of breathtaking old buildings and stone streets. He was digging into breakfast at a restaurant when the man behind the cash register asked in good English about his sign.

"Does that mean what it says?"

"It sure does," Plennie said.

The man smiled and shook Plennie's hand warmly. He had read the story in *Tempo*.

Plennie had been longing to meet an English-speaking local so he could ask about the hotel in which he'd spent the night. As he described the place, the man got tickled, then started belly-laughing.

214

"Do you know what they call that place?" he asked. "The delousing joint."

He explained that it was a mission for unfortunates, and that Plennie should rest assured that he was free of bugs and lice. He recommended Hotel Pension Hofer instead. His friend owned it and would probably even offer a free room. The friend turned out to be so welcoming that Plennie stayed two nights.

* * *

When he set out again, he followed the River Elbe southeast, against its flow, through the glorious snowfall, wearing his warm secondhand clothing and all-weather jacket. He narrowly avoided being robbed once more by "gypsies," as he called them, outside Niedersedlitz. Like in Oklahoma, the handsy groping was interrupted when an automobile came to a stop nearby, and the men and women slunk back into their inert caravan. Simple men made easy marks.

Walking through the snow grew exceedingly difficult, and his pace slowed as he entered the rural Bohemian Highlands. He came to a fork in the road and chose at random the path he soon learned did not run into the nearest town. The snowflakes, thick as nickels, caught the sun and looked like moths lit by a street-lamp. Deep in a borderland German forest, he came to another unmarked split in the road and wasn't sure which path to take. The snow had stopped and the sun fell in patches through the trees, dancing and glistening magically upon the drifts. He had never beheld a more beautiful sight, and he was saddened to think he might never again. He stood for a long time, watching, listening, his breath visible, the full moon rising over the woods. He had walked at least twelve miles in the wrong direction. He was happy to be lost.

He pulled a coin from his pocket and flipped it into the cold air with his thumbnail.

"Heads," he said into the stillness.

He faithfully started down the empty white road to his right, going backward as though the traffic were heavy and people were watching. The snow crunched under his brogans.

When he crested a hilltop he noticed distant lights glimmering in his mirrors. He walked another four miles, praying for a sign of life. He soon realized he'd stumbled across a lumber camp. At the largest lit house, a bearded man answered the door and shook his head when Plennie began to talk. Plennie whipped out his clipping from *Tempo* and pushed it into the lumberjack's hands. The man left him standing in the cold and returned with another man, who introduced himself in broken English as I. H. Honeger and invited Plennie inside.

Plennie shook off the cold as he told the men of his wrong turn and tried to explain how he had accidentally arrived at their camp. They seemed dubious, so two other men, much younger, walked into the night and returned ten minutes later, having followed Plennie's tracks some distance, to confirm his story. They had not believed it possible to walk all that way.

The foreman's name was Lutzengauser and his wife was a fine cook. Lutzengauser pulled out a gallon jug of red wine and poured a round, then another, toasting the backward American until the bottle was empty. They talked well past midnight, and when Honeger stood to leave, Plennie passed out on the floor, his belly full of wine, the fireplace crackling, and a handful of lumberjacks hovering overhead, laughing.

In the morning they walked Plennie to the Czech border. Honeger slipped a folded bill into Plennie's pocket. "To use as you journey along," he whispered. He then produced a pencil and asked to see Plennie's journal, where he wrote:

216

There came a man out of nowhere
    His boots were wet, his bag was heavy
    He looks at the world with a different view
    That's how we should look
    That may be the clue

24.

A YEAR ON FOOT

He had barely made it through the gate of the fortified village at the foot of the ancient Bohemian castle when he noticed that the peasants seemed to want to kill him.

The signs were all there. They were angry and shouting. They were spitting in the dirt. And they were scuffling, holding one another back violently, the whole time staring through hard eyes at the backward stranger. Something was amiss. Plennie didn't know what, but he readied his fists just in case. The entrance to the village, 340 miles southeast of Hamburg, was flanked by stone walls, and inside the walls were rooms, and the deeper he progressed into the village the more peasants poured out of the rooms and advanced toward him.

Just before they reached Plennie, a uniformed constable appeared and ordered them to stop the commotion. He escorted Plennie into the little square, then into another stone room that housed a tavern of some sort. The bartender recognized that Plennie was speaking English, motioned for him to wait, then ducked out the back door. He returned accompanied by a man named Schultz, who spoke English and began translating for the constable. The constable informed Plennie that the peasants hated Germans, and they'd seen Plennie's sign and assumed he was German. They were all set to rough him up when the constable heard the commotion.

The village was part of Aussig but across the river from the industrial city. It sprouted up at the foot of Castle Střekov, a fourteenth-century stone fortress perched atop a blackstone cliff, rising high above the River Elbe. Richard Wagner was a guest once, wandering around at night wrapped in a bedsheet. Johann Wolfgang von Goethe stayed here as well and savored the views of the Bohemian hills. Now came a Texan in soiled clothes wearing a German sign.

Schultz, the English-speaker, was a Czech, and he invited Plennie to be his guest for the night. He'd been deported from London with his British wife and three sons after the war and wound up back home, struggling like everyone else in Czechoslovakia. His wife had lost all her teeth, and they didn't have money for a false set. She prepared a meal in the kitchen while the two men talked. When she finally brought food to the table, Plennie looked it over: cornmeal dumplings cooked with a ham bone. The woman picked the meat off the bone and put it on Plennie's plate.

"Are the stores still open?" Plennie asked.

They were. Schultz asked what he wanted to buy.

"I want to do some shopping," Plennie said. The bill that Mr. Honeger had slipped in his pocket at the border was a hundred marks, more than twenty US dollars. He'd never had more fun buying groceries. When he returned, he splayed the bounty on the table: bacon, ham, beef, bread, butter, eggs—the woman's eyes grew wide—coffee, potatoes, onions, and a jar of pickles.

"I want to show my appreciation for your wonderful hospitality," he said.

Mrs. Schultz began to sob. She wrapped her arms around Plennie's neck. Mr. Schultz began to cry as well, and then their sons, and then Plennie cried a little too, of course.

* * *

Eastern Europe was a glorious and terrifying romp. As the Great Depression grew worse and nationalist attitudes strained relationships between the neighbors that shared this small slice of the globe, the sun continued to rise over the Balkans. On March 13, Paul von Hindenburg beat Adolf Hitler in the German general election, but by a slim enough margin that a runoff was scheduled for the following month. Police began raiding Nazi headquarters across the country, searching for evidence of a Nazi plot to plunge the country into civil war. Hitler launched a flying tour of Germany by airplane, which would take him to dozens of campaign stops where he addressed more than 150,000 people in a matter of days. Back in the States, as Plennie plodded south through Czechoslovakia, someone kidnapped the Lindberghs' baby from his bed at their home in Hopewell, New Jersey, and left a ransom note on the windowsill. Four people were killed and dozens wounded when unemployed protesters clashed with police outside a Ford plant in Dearborn, Michigan. President Hoover signed a law giving workers the right to organize and pick representatives to negotiate contracts.

Plennie made friends with a wealthy man in Prague and inherited a swell new suit. In Vienna, the city that inspired Mozart and Beethoven, he walked the stone streets of Old Town, admiring the churches, then walked seven miles through an enormous cemetery outside the city, thinking about how fleeting life is. The Vienna newspaper carried a story that day about the "special world traveler."

In order to gain interest, which his kind barely gets anymore, he walks around the world backwards. Although people have no eyes in the back, Wingo had himself fashioned glasses, which function like the mirror of a motorcar and allow him to look backward.

His trip is being financed by a rubber sole company. He has

traveled through the various cities of the Union, such as St.
Louis, Chicago, Washington, and New York, where he got an
autograph from Mayor Jimmy Walker. From there he went to
Boston and by ship to Hamburg. From Hamburg to Berlin,
Dresden and Vienna. He carries with him a book of clippings
from American newspapers which report his travels.

 From Vienna, he wants to go to Budapest, Bucharest, and Con-
stantinople, straight eastward to Japan. Had he gone in reverse
order to America, it would have been a simpler trip for him.

He reached Budapest in five days and was surprised and delighted to learn that the American consul, Fletcher Warren, was
from Wolfe City, Texas. A reporter for the leading daily newspaper
interviewed him for a story in which he used the Hungarian word
for "peculiar." Near Sebeş, Romania, he accidentally knocked his
cane from a bridge railing into the water below. He had carried the
cane 2,952 miles so far and nearly lost his mind at the thought
of continuing without it, so he scrambled down to the base of the
bridge, stripped, and jumped into the murky water. He plunged to
the bottom three, four, five times, gasping for air at the surface,
until, on the sixth dive, he found it, and he celebrated in his own
mind the personal triumph.

In Sebeş, he checked into a hotel and noticed the date for the
first time in a long while. April 15, 1932. He'd been on the road a
solid year. The fact gave him only minor pause, and little satisfaction.

Two hundred miles later, in Bucharest, he walked ten blocks
and solicited four different hotels in hopes of finding someone who
spoke English. This effort he performed in his usual reverse manner, so by the time he accomplished his goal, a healthy crowd of
Romanians had begun to follow him, which delighted the English-
speaking desk clerk at the next hotel. He checked in with the

American consulate and retrieved a stack of mail that had been for-warded from Hamburg to Berlin, Prague, Vienna, Budapest, and finally Bucharest. He tore into a few letters from siblings in West Texas and several from his loyal mother, who expressed concern and, as always, love. He was also interested to see one from John Hall, his only friend on the *Seattle Spirit*, dated March 15.

Dear Mr. Wingo,

It has been a good while since I last saw you. I don't know if you will get this letter or not. But if you do I certainly would like to hear from you.

I know that you will like to hear what I am going to tell you about what happened aboard the Seattle Spirit *after you went ashore the night we sailed out of Hamburg. If you remember, and I am sure you do, the steward was due to get back from Italy at nine o'clock that night. Well, he came in right on sched-ule. All the ship's crewmen had everything ready for sailing and we were all in the bunkhouse just chewing the fat, waiting for twelve o'clock to cut loose to sail out to sea. Arthur Cook, the second mate, I know you remember him? He was just wait-ing and talking in the bunkhouse, too. When the steward came aboard he wanted to see Arthur to ask about you.*

He had an armful of magazines when he came into the bunkhouse and was all tuckered out and dirty from the long car ride from Italy. The first thing he asked of Arthur was, "How did Wingo do with the cleaning?" Arthur said, "I think he did a very good job." The steward said, "Is he gone?" Arthur told him yes, that you left ship at five that afternoon. Steward said, well, good riddance, and he was tired and he was going to take a bath and hit the hay. He went into the cabins. We just kept chewing the fat and some of the boys were playing pinochle. In about twenty minutes we heard the awfulest noise, screaming, hollering, and cursing, and we all run to see what happened.

When we got to the cabin hallway he was running up and down the hall without a stitch of clothes on and acting like a maniac. We were all afraid of him and he could see that we were, so he said, "Please don't be afraid of me. I need help." Arthur said, "What in the world is wrong, steward?" He said, "Hell, I don't know, but I am stinging and burning up. Do something!" Arthur said, "What happened, what have you done?" Steward said, "Nothing. I took a bath and went to bed. I think there is something in my bed." So Arthur checked and found the lye. Arthur said, "I think it must be lye or something," and it turned out to be lye. In the meantime, the steward went back to the bathroom and tried to wash off and that just made things worse. After we decided it was lye the second cook ran to the storeroom and fetched two gallons of vinegar and poured it in the bathtub and it took almost all of us to put the steward in it, but we gave him a good vinegar bath and he got some relief.

Then he asked if anyone knew where you were staying in Hamburg? And the two fellows that had talked to you at the restaurant had already told everybody about seeing you and that you were stopping in the hotel that most of us boys stop at when we are in Hamburg.

He dressed as soon as he could and left the ship for shore without saying anything at all. I was uneasy about you because I was sure he would find you and beat you to death. So before the ferry took off to shore with the steward, I told Arthur that he would kill you if he found you. So me and Arthur decided to go along to keep him from killing you. But I don't believe we could've prevented it if he had found you. You know how much of a man he is.

He went straight to the hotel and asked where your room was.

The hotel man said you had gone back to the ship that you came over on and was going to America. That you had been gone for over an hour. The steward said he knew better than that. He made the man show him every room in that hotel but couldn't find you.

Boy, I don't know where you went, but it was a good thing you wasn't there. He went to every hotel on the shore street asking about you, up until almost sailing time, and me and Arthur right with him. I thought he was going to jump ship and stay in Hamburg to find you, but the Captain talked him out of it.

He wouldn't talk to any of us on board about it, just mumbled to himself.

We sailed at twelve and he was aboard, so I was somewhat relieved. But if I were you, Mr. Wingo, I would steer clear of him because I believe if it is twenty or even thirty years from now he would kill you if he ran into you. I remember how you and me talked about not being able to give things up with him for the way he treated you. But I would never have thought of doing it the way you did. But believe me, you sure did a good job evening things up with him.

All the boys talked and laughed their heads off about how the steward acted. But not before him, because he was so burned up about it. But they all said they thought the steward had it coming to him. You should have seen the place, his room where he had stacks of books and magazines on a chair by his bed. When he left the bed in such a hurry, he knocked them over. His books and clothes and shoes were scattered everywhere. I guess that is about all I can tell you about the steward, but I just thought you would like to know how well you did even things up.

From your friend,
John Hall

* * *

Why do you walk backwards? asked one of the cluster of Romanians gathered around Plennie in Giurgiu, on the bleak Bulgarian border, examining him as one would a sideshow oddity.

"How many of you would be here now, watching me, if I were walking forward?" asked Plennie Wingo, who was ready to back down the gangplank onto a ferry to cross the Danube. "How many of you would remember that I had ever walked in your town if I walked through it in the usual way?"

And what do you do for money? one of the men asked.

Plennie told them about the postcards, how he had sold out, and how he was now relying on the goodwill of his friends in Europe. The man took off his hat, plunked a few coins inside, then began passing it around. The offering filled Plennie's pocket.

He got a haircut in Ruse, Bulgaria, passed the iron gates and the wild plum thickets, then spent a few complimentary nights in a hospital on a hill, on the advice of a kindhearted Methodist minister who felt Plennie could stand to relax a bit and put on some weight, lest he fall ill and die.

Not far from the hospital was an undiscovered archaeological site where four settlements were stacked one on top of the last. The oldest, at the bottom, dated back eleven thousand years. Excavated in reverse—descending, backward through time—the settlements would reveal a gradual primitivization. The higher strata contained currency, bookkeeping tablets, jewelry, and religious artifacts. The lower strata contained practical tools like eating utensils, pottery, knives, scrapers, and awls. Farther down still, the remains of the bottommost settlement held crude tools meant to kill: stones, boomerangs, spears, and arrows. The consistent element across thousands of years was the treatment of the dead. They were laid to rest outside town, sprinkled with red ocher, which was believed to symbolize blood and life and passage into the afterlife. And they were crouched, knees tucked, lying on their left sides with their heads toward the northeast, symbolizing a return to the womb of Mother Earth.

Plennie left Ruse as April turned to May, with a letter of endorsement from the minister and from one of his doctors, who wrote that "this will remain as a memory to our hospital, because this fearless human was here in person." A man had come, and would be remembered, and what more could he ask?

He slept the night in a mansion in the Balkans with four dogs and the widow of Captain William H. Northington, a seaman from Cardiff who'd been dead fifteen years. He nearly vomited when, in a restaurant in Kozar Belene, he was offered "horse flesh." He thought for a long while about that combination of words, and how "horse roast," or "horse chops," or "horse steak" sounded so much better.

He backed through Yablanitsa, where the thick carpet of stars lit the inky purple sky like they did over West Texas. Then came Botevgrad, then Sofia, the capital city, where dubious police officers escorted Plennie backward to jail and the American consulate sprung him five hours later.

His soiled map showed ten towns scattered along the 350-mile ribbon of road that stretched through a sliver of Greece to Constantinople, Turkey. He hurried backward, encountering very little traffic but considerable dust, choking and penetrating dust. He slept one night on the ground, the rest in roadside motels. He narrowly avoided a snake, which he estimated to be twenty feet long and as thick as a telephone pole.

As he moved through the land of the Parthenon, the land of Homer, he briefly encountered another American. Robert Edison Fulton Jr. was riding his two-cylinder Douglas motorcycle around the world. He had bought into the notion that although men have dreams of being poets, artists, discoverers, philosophers, scientists, few are permitted to realize any one of them in their daily lives. But in travel he could have them all. He could be anyone while moving through the world. Travel was eternal change, limitless contrast, unending variety. Fulton was full of joy. "Was not this the best of all possible worlds?" he would write. "Was not life worth striving for, fighting for and suffering for, so long as one achieved a destination? This was the land which had cradled ancient beauty which fills the hearts of many men with its inspiration to this very day."

As Fulton sped along, he caught a glare through the dust. Visibility was terrible, so he throttled back his machine. The glare grew brighter. The sun seemed to be bouncing off some kind of mirror. The figure of a man emerged on the shoulder of the Greek highway.

"There was a sign on the man's back," he would write in his book, *One Man Caravan*. "As I approached, the letters grew enormous: 'Look out! Look out! Walking around the world backward.'"

25.

MURDER JAIL

Things began to look bleak for Plennie around day seven in the Turkish jail. He counted the days by the sunlight, and by the muezzin's punctuating calls to prayer, for the authorities had seized all his possessions, his clothes, passport, money, journal, and his sign, which now worthlessly displayed the Bulgarian phrase for *Around the World Backwards*—*Okolo sveta nazad*. He had no proof of who he was and no way to communicate that he was a red-blooded Texan, by God, trying to set an unusual record and to help his family through the worst hard times. He wasn't even certain whether the city he'd entered a week before was Constantinople or Istanbul. He'd heard it called both. And he had no way of knowing that the inscription on the main gate of the jailhouse—DERSAADET CINAYET TEVKIFHANESI—said "Capital City Murder Jail."

What he knew was that he had been harassed by authorities at the Turkish border and locked up there several days, until an English-speaking man showed up and asked him what his plans were, what his financial situation was like, and whether anyone in America could send him enough money to get him through Turkey. He had informed the man that his family in America was too poor to send money, that he could do all right on his own, and that he just wanted to pass through the country on his way to Pakistan,

228

then India, then China, then Japan, where he'd catch a boat to California.

Simple.

"You don't want much, do you?" the man had said.

Plennie knew that when they'd released him at the border they had phoned the authorities in Istanbul, because when he arrived and approached the train station, a handful of police officers appeared in his mirrors, surrounded him, stuffed him into a car, and hurried him to the Sultanahmet Jail. And he knew that he slept at night surrounded by men accused of committing crimes, that every day a half dozen or so new prisoners were packed into the cell. Every morning since he'd arrived, he'd been carted from the jail to a courtroom, where he pleaded and mostly pantomimed to a judge. But how does one conjure up the physical expression for *Please let me speak with the American consulate because I don't like being stuck in jail in Turkey?*

His emotions oscillated among anger and shock and frustration. Days ticked by. He gave up trying to talk to the other prisoners. No one spoke English. He felt helpless, victimized, naive. He was about to break. That was when he heard the voice.

* * *

It came from somewhere outside the cell, he couldn't tell where. And he had no way of knowing to whom the voice belonged. But he recognized the rhythm and the glorious beat of syllables because he had heard the same singsong sounds in Mansfield, Ohio, and Frederick, Maryland, and McKeesport, Pennsylvania. He drew in a breath.

"Are you American?" Plennie shouted.

There was a pause.

"I am," the voice outside said. "Why?"

Plennie wasn't sure what to say.

"I am an American too!" he yelled. "And I would like to talk with you, if I may."

"Just a minute," the voice said. He heard it continue talking, possibly to a Turk, possibly to a Turkish lawyer. A few moments later, Plennie beheld a sight he was quite certain he'd never again see. There stood a man in a business suit, very clearly American. The man introduced himself as E. M. Hedden, assistant to the American ambassador at the US Embassy in Istanbul.

Plennie's good fortune manifested itself on his face. He told his story and Hedden listened carefully, then told Plennie he would check into the matter. *It may take a bit,* he said, but he left the impression that he was sincere.

Meanwhile, the Associated Press learned about Plennie's arrest, and a dispatch from the international desk made newspapers around the world, especially in the United States. TEXAS CRAB IN JAIL, proclaimed the *Bedford Gazette* in Pennsylvania. BACKWARD WALKER FINDS POLICE ARE NOT, said the *Albuquerque Journal*. TURKISH POLICE ARREST BACKWARD WALKING TEXAN, announced the *Baltimore Sun.*

The *Chicago Tribune* ran a two-column photo of Plennie in Oklahoma on page 12, reminding readers of his backstory and informing them that Turkish police arrested him at the border because "they couldn't decide whether he was coming or going." The *Pittsburgh Post-Gazette* ran the story on the front page, headlined WINGO OUGHT TO KNOW THEIR LINGO.

Plennie Wingo, of Abilene, Tex., is in a bad way. If he only knew the "lingo" spoken in Istanbul, Turkey, he might be able to help himself. As it is, he is resting in one of their jails, without a visa, without money, and, apparently without a friend.

Even the *New York Times* reported the trouble on page 10, on May 6, 1932: TURKS HOLD CRABLIKE TEXAN, WALKING BACKWARD FOR RECORD. The papers said he was "unable to get out either backward or forward." A few said he had blisters on his feet. One guessed at the harsh treatment in a Turkish jail, though no evidence exists to suggest he was the victim of abuse.

The *Des Moines Register* took the opportunity to point out an odd but interesting coincidence, under the headline NEVER THE TWAIN SHALL MEET, UNLESS YOU'VE GOT A VISA:

An Afghan and a Texan left their home countries and traveled to the ends of the earth.

The Afghan, at latest reports an inmate of the state hospital for the insane at Clarinda, Ia., was Abdul Ruouf, 32, son of a Mohammedan religious leader.

The Texan was Plennie Wingo of Abilene, in the Lone Star state, at latest reports Thursday night in a jail at Istanbul, Turkey.

Afghanistan, as a matter of geography, is located some 900 miles east across Persia from Turkey. And Iowa is some 450 miles north of Texas. But Plennie in the east and Abdul in the west have much in common.

When Abdul was traveling across Iowa in a bus last November his western fellow passengers couldn't understand why he knelt on the floor and recited his foreign prayers five times a day.

Jailed for causing a disturbance, he was examined, declared insane and committed to the hospital at Clarinda.

Plennie Wingo of Texas was walking backwards around the world when he came to Turkey. The Turkish people couldn't understand that.

Easterners, whether Turks or Afghans, probably wouldn't understand such American and western customs as flagpole sitting or dance marathons, not to mention the lesser diversions such as peanut pushing or pie eating competitions.

Little wonder then that Plennie, who didn't understand the eastern and foreign necessity of visas, was jailed by the Turks who didn't understand the western and foreign idea of walking backward around the world.

When Plennie finally heard back from Assistant Ambassador Hedden, it was bad news. The American consul, an older man named Charles E. Allen, was not interested in helping and wanted no involvement, Hedden said. The old man thought the stunt was meaningless and dangerous, and that anyone who set out to do something so stupid should expect to take care of himself. Plennie tried to point out that he was quite capable of taking care of himself if he was released, and he had 3,509 backward miles to prove it.

Hedden was determined to learn the charges on which Plennie was being held. He reported back to Plennie that his charge was twofold: he didn't have enough money to get through Turkey, and his reverse walking was a nuisance and a public hazard. If he wanted out of jail, he needed a responsible, credible person to sign papers swearing to take care of him and make certain he was not violating the law.

"You get me out of here," Plennie said, "and you may be sure I will back on out of Turkey just as fast as I can travel."

But Hedden was unsure. The diplomat didn't know if he could afford controversy if Plennie got into trouble again, especially now that the press was watching. Another dispatch from the AP circulated widely in American newspapers, giving a fuller account of the legal struggle, saying the authorities were dragging Plennie each day to the passport office in an attempt to sort out the matter.

"If they'd only let me go backwards, it wouldn't be so bad," Plennie told the reporter. "But I get all tuckered out now when I have to walk forward. It uses such different muscles."

Plennie eventually told Hedden that he had some money tucked away, enough to get him well out of Turkey, but he hadn't known whom he could trust. That was partly true, and it worked. Hedden agreed to sign the papers and he made arrangements for Plennie's release. But he could not convince the Turks to cough up Plennie's passport. It was outside his purview.

"The consulate might do *that* much," he said.

When Plennie walked out of Capital City Murder Jail, he finally got a chance to look around the vibrant old city, where the alleys were packed with chattering street merchants and rug salesmen and the minarets atop massive mosques rose into the sky. The stately buildings followed the contours of a hillside, and busy streets wrapped back and forth down toward the cerulean Sea of Marmara, and the Bosphorus Strait, which bisected Europe and Asia.

Up on top of the hill sat the Hagia Sophia, and nearby the Hippodrome, dating back to 330 AD, when Constantine the Great, victorious in battle over his rival and the undisputed emperor of Rome, moved the imperial capital to the ancient Greek city of Byzantium, which became Constantinople in his honor. His son built the cathedral and you could still see the Roman skeleton poking through its Islamic skin after a millennium. The Hippodrome had been Constantinople's political and sporting arena, and Constantine had covered its infield with treasures taken from other conquered lands in the empire.

The city fell to the Ottomans in 1453, and during the fighting there was in the sky a full lunar eclipse, and the bodies of Christians and Turks floated like melons on the sea under the orange moon. The siege was all that remained of the fifteen-hundred-year Roman rule, the last gasp of the Middle Ages. The end came for the Ottoman Empire after the First World War. It had aligned with Germany. Its territory was divided up by the Allies. The West had just recently started calling the city Istanbul.

Cities fall. Empires fade. History favors the persistent.

Hedden pointed out the United States Embassy, the American consulate, and a nearby YMCA with a vacancy; then he insisted that Plennie take ten dollars so he felt like he had at least one friend in Istanbul.

Plennie marched up to the consulate to take a shot at getting his passport back so he could get out of Dodge. But Charles Allen had gone for the weekend, and Plennie soon found himself laying his case out to the vice-consul, a friendly younger man named Loften Moore, from Chicago. Plennie was curious about Allen's negative attitude. Moore told him the boss was older, a former schoolteacher and principal before he joined the foreign service, and he was not the frivolous type. He said his boss thought Plennie's stunt was foolish. Moore, on the other hand, thought the journey was pretty gutsy.

Plennie told Moore he'd come back when Allen was in the office, and the two shook hands.

On his way out he noticed a well-dressed man sitting in the foyer. Plennie took him to be Italian on account of his complexion, but he spoke perfect English. The man said he had overheard Plennie's conversation and he was interested to know more. Just as Plennie was about to whip out his journal, the man cut him off and told Plennie to meet him in his hotel the following day, at two o'clock sharp.

* * *

The next afternoon, A. R. Ceretle showed Plennie to his four-room suite in the Vila de Pera Hotel. He was a smooth talker, cordial and gracious, and evidently very wealthy. He told Plennie his name was Albert, but friends could call him Al. He fixed them both a drink from a well-stocked bar, then offered a short tour of the posh suite as he talked. He said he was a native of Naples but had a sister in Barcelona, and his business was wholesale department store merchandise. He showed Plennie two sample rooms that were full of shiny new furniture, beautiful rugs, lamps, and modern interior decor. As they moseyed around the suite, Ceretle told Plennie he liked to do business in the morning, then shut down and enjoy himself in the afternoon and evening. He often entertained merchants and prospective buyers over cocktails in his suite. He knew nearly every language spoken in Europe.

He pointed out his bedroom, which had two full-size beds, and then a living room, and a kitchenette. Natural light filled the room. Plennie was dazzled by the reception room, and primarily the bar. It was good to be out of jail.

When the tour was over, Ceretle wanted to hear about Plennie's trip. He listened patiently, pouring drinks, asking questions, and examining Plennie's clippings.

"It is just amazing what a person can do if he sets his heart on it," he said. He mentioned Plennie's troubles, what he had over-heard the day before at the consulate.

"Mr. Wingo," Ceretle said, "why don't you check out of the YMCA and share this apartment with me? I will be so pleased if I can do anything to help you."

He sensed Plennie's awkward hesitation.

"Maybe you would prefer to join me a bit later," Ceretle said. "You do whatever seems right for you."

That was Saturday.

* * *

"If you were allowed to go on through...would you attempt it?"

Charles Allen looked across his desk at Plennie. This was on Monday. To go on through meant to walk backward to the land that the Western maps still called Persia, home to one of the world's oldest continuous civilizations, with settlements dating back to 7000 BC. It was an area beset by war and conflict and pestilence, but also life. There was Mesopotamia, the cradle of civilization, the Garden of Eden, the birthplace of us. There were hundreds of terrible ways to die and hundreds of glorious things to see.

"I sure would," Plennie said. There was but one way in his mind to go.

"Well," Charles Allen said, "I am not going to okay it."

Plennie felt like he was falling downstairs. The man who could stop him was doing it.

"I would not be any part of it," Allen said, "because there are places in these countries where there are no roads at all, just desert, jungle, mean people, heathens, wild animals, snakes."

Allen was no neophyte. He had worked nearly twenty years in foreign service, in Adrianople, Algiers, Nantes, and Damascus. And he'd done three separate stints in Istanbul. There were unrest and civil war in and around Persia, and a country in the throes of chaos, Allen said, and he would deny Plennie a visa without a legitimate reason for passing through. He also knew that Persia was one of the most isolated countries simply because of its geographical features. It was the size of the entire southeastern United States, and the high central plateau that made up the bulk of the country was almost entirely rimmed by lofty mountain ranges, and their crests were often snow-covered. The rest of the region was home to large, choking deserts.

"You have proven your point," Allen said, his eyes fixed on Plennie. "You have walked through the walkable countries. I tell you,

Turkey is doing you a favor by compelling you to abandon your walk at this point."

There was nothing more to say. Plennie stood to go, forward, not feeling like walking backward now.

"A man entering would be doomed," Allen told Plennie. "It would be impossible for him to survive."

26.

GOING BACK, FORWARD, UPRIGHT

When the Ottomans sacked Constantinople, the warfare sparked a massive migration of Greek scholars to Italy. The immigrants were orators, teachers, humanists, poets, writers, printers, musicians, astronomers, artists, philosophers, scientists, politicians, architects, and theologians. They had soaked up knowledge and experiences in the Middle East, on the lively edge of the Orient. They brought with them to Italy books and texts, and they served as revivalists for intense Greek and Roman studies, for perfecting the things they knew were good and pleasurable, and their work, in turn, led to the Renaissance, when men were more than themselves, when they strived to achieve greatness and to touch the hymn of heaven. That's the bright side of the fall of an empire. Sometimes a hand is forced and the correct card is played, and men return home with ideas about how to live life more fully.

"I think it's a wise decision," Charles Allen had said, and Plennie had bowed his head, understanding that he was out of options. He resigned himself to his new fate. He would return home, and he would be a changed man, better than when he had left.

The reality depressed him for a short while, until he hatched a new goal. He would make his way to New York, then to California, where he would begin his final leg of backward walking to Texas. He would finish in Fort Worth, claim his purse from the chamber

of commerce, write his book, then live comfortably for the foresee-
able future.

* * *

A. R. Ceretle was glad to see Plennie standing in the hotel lobby.
He made his way through the crowd.

"Coming over to stay with me?" Ceretle asked.

Plennie did not cry, but he did tell his new friend what Charles
Allen had said, and how he must now try to get onto a States-
bound ship, even if he had little money. Ceretle comforted him.
He bought their lunch, and their drinks, and paid for a taxi across
town. Then he bought dinner, and more drinks, and a ticket to a
picture show. Plennie tried to protest the charity.

"I can afford it," Ceretle said. "You are my guest and you can
spend your money when we are apart."

"It is very kind of you to befriend me this way," Plennie said,
"when you have only known me a few days."

"I have traveled a great deal," Ceretle replied. "Most of the time
I've been alone. I have seen just about everything. Now it is a pleasure to have companionship, fun to show somebody the sights who
has not seen them before."

Plennie had been suspicious. Ceretle's generosity was unusual.
In fact, Plennie had gone out of his way to ask several people at
the US Embassy about Ceretle, including Mr. Allen. He asked
whether they thought it was okay to befriend such a man. But now
Plennie was warming up to his new friend.

"If that's the way you feel," Plennie told him, "I certainly am in
a position to appreciate your hospitality."

The two playboys palled around Istanbul on Ceretle's dime as
days turned into weeks. They went to a carnival, where they played
games and watched a single man with instruments attached to every

moving part of his body perform songs as though he were a ten-piece band. They slipped into shoe coverings and padded into the Fatih Mosque, built in the fifteenth century, and gawked over the patterns on the original rugs. They ate and drank all over the city.

Plennie had never seen a camel, so he felt lucky to sit near a wooden bridge in Istanbul and watch as caravans of camels loaded with herbs and rawhide and other commodities were inspected before passing over the strait. Their feet were most interesting to him. They looked as big as washtubs. He visited the docks, too, and watched as fishermen brought their catches to the market. Men carried fish upon padded wooden trays on their heads, shouting in strange tongues, passing fish to the highest bidders. He and Ceretle visited a professor—an acquaintance of Al's—at Robert College of Istanbul. The man was surprised to meet Plennie, and laughed, and let them know he had read about the backward-walking Texan in his hometown paper, the *Philadelphia Inquirer*. Still laughing, he phoned his wife. He wanted her to meet Plennie as well. The three of them drove to the professor's home, where his wife was entertaining Queen Maria of Yugoslavia, who was the wife of King Alexander of Yugoslavia and daughter of King Ferdinand of Romania. Plennie joined them for tea.

Plennie left Ceretle alone one evening to go on a date with two Turkish girls he met at the consulate. Both spoke English and were in their twenties, single, and attractive, so when they invited him to an overnight picnic on the coast of the Black Sea with a group of young people, he obliged. He hated to leave Al alone but had a wonderful time with the friendly young women. They barbecued a whole pig on the beach and drank beer and wine as the sun fell, and Plennie wasn't feeling so bad about Turkey or his predicament anymore.

One of the women was Priscilla Ring, a correspondent for the Associated Press, who had recently scored a rare interview with the Russian revolutionary and Soviet architect Leon Trotsky, who had been exiled by Joseph Stalin and was "camping out" on the Princes Islands in the Black Sea, surrounded by books and newspapers, writing a history of Russia and needling Stalin from afar. Plennie told Priscilla Ring that he didn't read much but he was going to write his own book someday, about walking backward, and he might mention her in it.

One afternoon, while Plennie and Al were sauntering around the slums, they saw an old fellow picking through a trash barrel. When the man heard Plennie and Ceretle talking, he stood up straight.

"You are American?" the bum asked.

"He is," Al said.

The man looked like he'd seen a ghost.

"I'm an American seaman," he said. "I've been stranded here for years."

His story was that he'd gone ashore one day, had a few drinks, and woken up without a ship, a passport, or money. Plennie could see himself in the man. His appearance, his smell, the desperation in his eyes. It scared him immensely. Al gave the seaman twenty liras and they kept walking.

* * *

The Turkish newspaper dropped the *o* from *Wingo* and called Plennie "Mr. Wing." He was fine with that. He was also okay with the fact that the story made him sound like something of a jailbird. But he was saddened to read the very first reportage on what had been his climax, his turning point. "Now he says jail is not for him," the story said, "and he had been advised to end his backward trip here by some American officials, because the Asia Minor country is so hazardous and Mr. Wing said he was tired of jails."

He hoped primarily that the new bit of publicity would help him get home. He'd been stranded nearly a month, failing twice to get a job on board a Standard Oil tanker bound for New York. He visited Charles Allen, the consul, to see if he had any mail waiting. Allen caught Plennie by surprise.

"It is not natural for anybody to be so kind as Mr. Ceretle is being," Allen pointed out. He suggested Plennie keep his eyes open. He let on his suspicion about Ceretle asking for some kind of favor down the line.

A few days later, Ceretle finished his business in Istanbul and began packing his things. His next stop was France. He told Plennie he was sad to be going. Plennie was sad, too. He imagined the seaman with the crusty beard bent over the trash can.

"If it wouldn't hurt your feelings," Ceretle said, "I would like to pay an extra fare when I sail for France, and you can go along. I feel sure you can get a boat from there."

"Oh, no, you don't," Plennie said. "You have done so much already that I could never live long enough to repay you. As much as I would like that, I could not accept."

Ceretle stopped him. "Just consider it settled and say no more," Ceretle said. "I would do nothing but worry about you if I were to leave you behind."

Ceretle's love seemed too convenient.

While the vast majority of Plennie Wingo's later account of his backward adventure squares with independent sources, this portion deviates in important ways from the various accounts by Mr. Allen and other State Department officials whose correspondence can be found in the National Archives at College Park, Maryland, inside a box labeled SUSPECTED NARCOTICS TRAFFICKERS, 1927–1942, inside a file folder titled WINGO, PLENNIE L.

The accounts seem to agree that a man paid Plennie's fare from

Istanbul to Marseilles aboard the steamship *Sphinx*, and that Plennie raised a concern just before launch about suspicious cargo entrusted to him, and that American consul Charles E. Allen contacted French authorities with the information, and that Plennie spent a few days in Paris before setting off for New York on the steamship *Exeter*.

Here's where they diverge.

In the book he'd write years later, Plennie spelled the man's name Ceretle, though his journal contained the following name written in pencil in handwriting that does not appear to be Plennie's: "A. R. Ceretti, Lista de Correo, Barcelona, Espain." Nearby, in Plennie's hand, is this: "Paid Boat fare from Constantinople to France."

According to Plennie's book, he reported his good fortune with "Ceretle" to Charles Allen three days before setting sail, and Allen "got really suspicious." Plennie would write, "and in like degree, I got annoyed. For a man who had not cared enough about my troubles to get me out of the stinking Turkish jail, he was taking an awful interest now."

On sailing day, Plennie said goodbye to his new friends, retrieved his passport, boarded the *Sphinx* several hours early, then retired to one of the side-by-side cabins Al had purchased. When Al boarded a little while later, a porter was following with two large trunks on a dolly. "Mr. Wingo," Al said, "we have the right to carry two trunks on your ticket. Since you have none and I have such a great amount of luggage, I am going to take advantage of this and save money I would have to pay on excess freight." Plennie would later write in his book that though he said okay, he was increasingly uncomfortable with the arrangement, especially when Al said: "If any of the ship's crew ask, just tell them the trunks are your personal property, and it will save me paying extra duty."

Plennie would write in his book that he wondered why the man who splurged on food and drinks was suddenly trying to save on extra baggage fees. He recalled that Al always conducted business in Turkish, and that his colleagues would often look at Plennie and chuckle. Plennie would write that "almost with no volition," he rushed to the deck, down the gangplank, and found Mr. Allen conveniently standing on the dock, visiting with the captain. He would write that he pulled Allen to the side and told him about the trunks, and about the possibility that they contained contraband, to which Allen replied:

> *"You have just done it, my boy!" He pointed out if the trunks were filled with narcotics, and I had said nothing to him about them being put into my possession, I would have been in for no end of trouble. If the man was only trying to save on duty, time would tell. I was to behave normally. He would get in touch with the proper agents in France and clear me of any responsibility for the cargo.*

According to Plennie's account, he was then overwhelmed by guilt for possibly betraying his friend. It haunted him, kept him awake at night, as they ate and drank and visited ports in Greece, then Italy, then Barcelona, before arriving at France. In Plennie's version, the two visited a museum in Athens, ate in Al's favorite Naples restaurant, where he was known by everyone, met beautiful women at nightclubs in Italy and Greece, and met his family in Barcelona. "I struggled mightily to be natural and appeared to be enjoying the voyage," Plennie would write. "The thought that I might be wrong, and my benefactor would discover that I had reported him hung heavy over my guilty head."

Per Plennie's book, the ship neared Marseilles after fourteen days, and Al mentioned that he never had trouble with customs because he knew the right ones to tip. When they docked, Plennie would write, Al instructed him to hold back, then follow later with the trunks.

Suddenly he frowned at me. "What makes you so nervous?"

I tried to look surprised that he should suppose me upset in any way. "Nothing that I know of," I responded.

"Don't worry about a thing," he said solicitously. "Wait here in your cabin and I will send the porter with a dolly to pick up your trunks."

I did not miss that reference to "your trunks."

When they cleared customs without issue, they both climbed into a carriage while men loaded their trunks. Just then, two police officers approached the dray and asked, "Which one of you is Mr. Wingo?" Plennie signaled.

"Then you are Ceretle?"

He would write that Al jumped to the ground and tried to make a break for it before being grabbed. They were both marched into the customs house and placed in separate cells. About an hour later, Plennie was released to the American consulate. He asked the French officer about his friend. Was he being held?

"Yep, I'm afraid so."

"Would you mind telling me why?"

"No, not a bit," the official said. "He had enough stuff in those two trunks to set this whole town crazy. You did the best thing you ever did in your life when you notified Mr. Allen before you sailed."

It seems likely, however, that Plennie's version is less than truthful, because the State Department documents do not mention an Al Ceretle, or Ceretti, or anyone besides Plennie Wingo.

Charles E. Allen, American consul at Istanbul, wrote of his suspicions to the secretary of state in Washington, saying Wingo approached him just before departing Istanbul with intense concern that he'd been suckered into being a drug mule. Allen wrote that Wingo realized the improbability of meeting a high-class businessman in the cheap hostel in which he'd been staying, and was suspicious when the businessman asked him to carry trunks of samples aboard the ship. "Mr. Wingo was therefore convinced that the trunks could not reasonably be expected to contain legitimate commercial samples and he was obviously very much worried lest they be opened and found to contain contraband."

What puzzled Charles Allen was that Plennie was completely calm and collected when he arrived at Marseilles, as if nothing had happened. His demeanor at arrival, Allen wrote, "would seem to indicate that something had transpired in the meantime to calm his fears, for example, the unloading at Piraeus or Naples of the original contents of the trunks and the substitution of other contents." Allen suggested that an investigator should interview Plennie with that in mind.

"It would be particularly interesting to know whether he was in funds upon arrival at Marseilles, a point having a bearing on his apparent change of attitude seeing that he left Istanbul totally penniless," Allen wrote. "It would be most particularly interesting, from the point of view of this office's investigations, to know the name of Mr. Wingo's traveling companion, the owner of the three trunks in question, since, knowing this name, it might be possible to discover locally something regarding the activities of the individual bearing it."

An investigator followed up on Allen's suggestion and wrote that Plennie "appeared to be without any resources whatever; and about an hour afterwards he was in the American consulate asking for some monetary assistance, or, if they could find him a ship on which he could work his passage home to the United States." The investigator said the consulate gave him no pecuniary assistance, but did get him on the steamship *Exeter* as a worker. During his three-day stay in France, the investigator wrote, Wingo stayed at Hotel Trieste, "a dirty sort of hostelry, where people may sleep for a few francs a night. Official enquiry there reveals that Wingo, who seemed to be living on charity, had no friends or visitors during his stay." The investigator also tried to trace "Wingo's travelling companion, the owner of the trunks, through the ship's manifest," and found only three suspicious names of guests in first-class cabins: Strugo, Turkish; Rumann, Polish; and Szmidt, Turkish. At a minimum, there had been no arrest on the docks, and no official sign of Al anywhere.

Contrary to the investigator's report, Plennie would write in his book that upon arrival in France he took a room in the YMCA near the consulate, and, "I took to enjoying myself, eating at outdoor cafés. Nobody knew who I was, and I had no spirit to announce it." And he would suggest that he had the money to afford a good room and good food for a solid week in France before catching a free ride home on the passenger ship *Exeter*.

"It was due to poor Al," Plennie would write, almost like a wink, "that I had the money."

27.

LONE STAR

Early in 1932, a black cloud ten thousand feet from ground to ceiling appeared outside Amarillo, Texas, a moving mountain, and people in it said it felt like a blizzard with an edge of sandpaper. A month later, the economy found its bottom after shrinking 27 percent from its peak in 1929. In the spring, Adolf Hitler embarked on a postelection flying tour, and the masses stood waiting for seven hours in Donauwörth in southern Bavaria for the Führer. "What now?" Joseph Goebbels wrote in his diary. "Something has to happen. We have to gain power. Otherwise we will triumph ourselves to death." A month later, a delivery truck driver pulled off the road in rural New Jersey to relieve himself in a grove of trees and found Charles and Anne Lindbergh's baby. A week later, a group of unemployed veterans from Portland, Oregon, riding the rails to Washington, were rounded up by the National Guard in St. Louis and shipped out of state on trucks. The incident received attention in the press, and thousands of other veterans joined the march on Washington of the Bonus Expeditionary Force. Their encampment in Washington would swell to eleven thousand by the end of the following month. Two weeks later, President Hoover signed into law the largest peacetime tax increase in history, expecting it to raise $1 billion. Two weeks after that, Henry Ford was published in *Literary Digest*, writing, "I do not believe in routine charity. I think it is a shameful thing that any man should have to stoop to take it, or give it." Two weeks later, having passed the Statue of Liberty on the *Exeter*, having hitchhiked into Middle America, Plennie Wingo dropped a hastily written letter, replete with misspellings, in the mail to his kin in Abilene.

Canton, Ohio

June 25, 1932

Dear Mother and all,

I am sure you will all be supprised to know I am in the good old U.S.A. again.

I arrived in New York City June 15. I sure have had a wonderful trip since I left Constantinople. The Itallion friend took me with him to Marceille, France. We sailed on a large French steemer. It was the Sphinx, one of the greatest pleasures I have ever had. There was nothing to good for me by my friend. I will never forget him.

I took a passenger boat of the American export lines from Marceille to N.Y. I hitchhiked to Canton...I met a good fellow in New Haven, Conn., he was a chef cook on a large diner when I met him and I was just 36 miles from Canton and this fellow come along in a new sport roadster Ford and I flagged him and he recognized me and stopped.

He is on his way to California. He is going to stop a few days in Chicago and then on the Cal, so I will get to visit with Aunt Marie again. I am going on with him to Cal, so I can finish my trip from there to Fort Worth.

I am going to try to make some real money on the rest of my trip. I come back over some of the road that I walked over last year and I was recognized by several people. Dad, you must be careful with that truck and not get hurt for the roads are dangerous now. I am sure glad you didn't get hurt the other day in that wreck. Mother, I know I should have wrote you from N.Y. but I had in mind to come straight home and supprise you. How is everyone? I hope all are well.

This fellow I am with now is a real good fellow and seems like I have known him a long time allready, he's so friendly. Aunt Nola and all sure like him. If I can I am going to try to get him to come by home. I know you all will like him, too.

Well, we are getting ready to go to town so I will close for this time. Lots of love to all and I hope I will be able to see you soon. The Lord has been with me all the way through and I am so happy to get back.

—Plennie

He visited his aunt again in Chicago, and in Los Angeles he took in the Summer Olympics and palled around more with his new friend Charles Carlson, splitting gas and a hotel room, and failing to mention in later writings where he got the money to pay for them.

* * *

He looked over the railing of the Santa Monica Pier and out at the infinite blue before him, and dropped a pebble into the Pacific Ocean. The date was August 13, 1932, and 1,450 miles spooled out between him and that healthy purse in Fort Worth and whatever else life might hold. He had gained a certain maturity that comes to those who leave their hometowns to face the world. He looked different. The portraits of Plennie that ran in the California newspapers like the *Los Angeles Times* and the *San Diego Union* portrayed a thinner, more serious man, one who had broken a few promises, shed the goofy smile of last year, and stood now with a confidence. He bore the expression of a man running for office rather than walking backward across the desert. He finally looked a little around the eyes like the Okie migrants on the dusty shoulders of the California byways, like the first and last of a kind.

The backing was old hat now, and he made good time toward San Diego, thinking he'd drop down south and take Highway 80 east to Abilene, then Fort Worth. The evidence of his change surfaced in Anaheim, when he stopped at a filling station to get a drink and a crowd gathered around him. Some bought cards and others asked questions and he didn't mind the money or attention. A bullish police officer interrupted the scene.

"You will have to get on out of town," the cop said. "We don't allow your kind to stop here." Then he turned to the crowd. "Break it up!" he shouted. "Scatter!"

The old Plennie might've slunk away apologetically, happy to stay out of trouble. But a year on the road had planted a seed of rebellion, or obstinacy, or something. Plennie told the cop he knew his rights, and this was not a foreign country.

"Since when is it against the law for a man to walk backwards through any town?" he asked. He said he would leave when he was good and ready. "If that don't suit you, let's see what you can do about it." The crowd around them had grown in the sixty seconds since the cop had approached. Someone booed. More people joined in, shouting at the officer now. He appeared for a moment to consider his options and, finding but one, he walked toward his vehicle, climbed in, and sped away from the group of people at the filling station, who were cheering and clapping on the back a thin, ragged-eyed dirt-trooper.

* * *

The late-August desert was brutal, and he suffered the 120-degree heat, especially at night, as he tried to sleep on the roadside or in stuffy hotel rooms. He brought along a feather pillow, blanket, and Thermos, preparations for the trek through the desolation. He enjoyed meeting strangers in the small towns but hated to see so many on the edge of life, living among the shuttered bank buildings and dusty main streets and towns that seemed ready to blow off the maps. He dropped into Mexico for a drink a time or two, and he slept a handful of nights under the Southwestern stars.

On the outskirts of Phoenix he was overtaken by a lawman.

"It's against the law to walk backwards within the city limits," the man said. "You are under arrest."

The thing that frightened Plennie this time around was the officer's direct certitude. He was abrupt and surprisingly violent when he shoved Plennie into the car. When they arrived at the jail, atop the courthouse, the deputy let on that there was one other prisoner, a tough criminal named Ruth Judd. Plennie knew the name. The whole country knew about the Trunk Murders, as the papers called them. Winnie Ruth Judd stood accused of shooting her two friends, cutting one into pieces, and packing both into trunks before traveling with the friend-bearing luggage from Phoenix to Los Angeles. It was, perhaps, the most sensational murder story of 1931, involving infidelity, drug addiction, and sex perversion.

"I'm going to put you in the cell next to her," the officer said, clutching Plennie's arm, "and you two can get acquainted."

Plennie found his voice at the last minute and asked to place a phone call, which the cop considered. "I suppose there would be no harm," he said. He escorted Plennie back downstairs, and there stood his old friend Jim Thurmond, who used to own a café in Abilene, and the Phoenix police chief W. C. LeFebvre, and Oren

Arnold, a writer for the local newspaper, all of them bent over laughing.

*   *   *

A writer in Phoenix did a bang-up job on a lengthy story, complete with illustrations and factual errors, which ran in Sunday feature sections in many newspapers, including the *Washington Post*. "Now he is about to claim that fat purse of money," the reporter wrote.

> *The photographs taken of him must run into the thousands, he says. The questions asked him surely run to a million.*
>
> *The one question asked him more than any other—the one which he has heard from little children, from octogenarians, from Mayors and Governors, from Portuguese and Viennese, from Swiss and Spanish, Turk and German, from everybody everywhere, is, "What are you doing it for?"*
>
> *And even Plennie Wingo himself is a little hazy on the answer!*
>
> *That is, his reason doesn't sound convincing. Because, simply, there is no very definite reason other than the haphazard promise of a purse when he returns to Fort Worth and the fact that he faced unemployment anyway.*
>
> *The real reason probably is, Plennie admits, that he wanted to do some adventuring. And this idea, silly as it sounds, presented an inexpensive way to go about it.*
>
> *But having done it once, Plennie can face old age and senility with a wealth of memories and a thick notebook filled with important autographs, seals, photos and clippings.*

None of the stories out west mentioned his family, or his divorce, or the shambles of the life to which he was about to return.

Of course, none of them knew what he carried in his pocket, either. And he wasn't going to tell.

While he was killing time in Istanbul, he got to thinking about the woman he'd met in Baxter Springs, Kansas, the one whose brute of a husband was interested in murdering him. Irene was her name, and she was a beauty. Anyway, he had promised that night in the spring of 1931 to send a postcard, and so he did, fitting as much as he could about his adventure into the space provided and telling her that he might start his walk again in Los Angeles or San Francisco, but that he'd be checking his mail in New York City if she wanted to write back. So when he got to New York, he went to the post office after his mail and was utterly surprised to find that she had written, and it was a long letter, and he kept it.

* * *

He wrote to his mother on September 15, 1932, from Globe, Arizona, to congratulate her on opening a vegetable stand, and to say that he was in the mountains, 335 miles from El Paso, Texas, and would be home soon. He wrote that he had killed a rattlesnake as long as his cane, with seven rattles, like he had done when he was just a boy, and that he was unafraid.

* * *

West Texas is too big a place for everybody to know everybody, but small enough that everybody knows somebody who knows somebody else. Once he hit the border, he had friends or family in practically every town. He stayed with Frank Kane in El Paso, had a drink across the border in Juárez, Mexico, at the Cantina La Luna Azul, and slept sitting up in a phone booth somewhere east of there on account of the pack of coyotes closing in. He bumped into his old pal Ben Oden, who operated a cantaloupe truck, at the Western Union in Pecos. His aunt Hattie put him up in Big Spring, where he bought a new suit to look nice and convinced the head man at a department store to give him a new pair of shoes in exchange for his old ones and the stories attached. He left his twelfth pair of brogans in the department store window in Big Spring and wore his thirteenth toward Abilene.

Far fewer people lined the streets for Plennie than for Colonel Lindbergh, but he arrived as the high school was letting out for the day, and that felt like an excited crowd.

Vivian had graduated the year before, and Plennie had missed it, but he saw three of her friends. He recognized them from Vivian's birthday party, the kids who were talking about how everything under the sun had been accomplished, how there were no more records to break.

"We never thought you would do it," one of them said.

One of Plennie's brothers showed up too, and clapped his back a bunch. Della and Vivian came to greet him, and invited him home if he needed a place to stay. Vivian had been working as a hostess in a hotel coffee shop, and Della was working part-time as a private nurse at a hospital. They were doing okay.

The writer for the *Abilene Morning Reporter-News* pointed out that although Mr. and Mrs. Wingo were divorced since last January, they were on speaking terms. "Friendly," Plennie called it.

The reporter asked the usual questions. Plennie said he felt great physically, and that he'd dropped from 166 pounds to 130. He was still hoping to make Fort Worth in ten days to collect. Why had he done it? He still didn't have a sharp answer, but it was getting better.

"I just had a notion to see the world in a manner never before used," Plennie said. "My friends kidded me about it, and that made me all the more determined to carry out my plan. A few times I would get a bit discouraged, but never at any time did I lose my determination to stick it out. I wore out twelve pairs of shoes, most of them half-soled several times, and now I am wearing the thirteenth pair. I walked backward about seven thousand miles, saw most of America and Europe, added, I believe, ten years to my life, managed to eat every day, met thousands of interesting people, saw many wonderful sights—and have nothing to regret."

The reporter pointed out that a "wealthy Italian, taking a shine to the determined young Texan, paid his passage first-class from Istanbul to Marseilles and put him up at the finest hotel in that French port for a full week."

Ceretle, or whoever he was, was a phantom now, and who knows what was in those trunks?

Plennie tried to assess his journey, physical and emotional, but it was hard to squeeze all he had seen and done into a quote. The reporter scrambled to keep up as he spoke.

"People ask me what I expect to get out of it," Plennie said. "Well, I did something everybody said I couldn't do—or at least I demonstrated that it could be done. That's some satisfaction. I expect to write a book of my experiences and there should be some monetary reward in that. I paid my expenses by selling postcards, acting as a sandwich man to advertise various business houses, and otherwise earned money.

"I hope the Fort Worth people will reward me in some way, for I put in some good advertising for Fort Worth. And for Abilene, too," he said. "But whether I realize any material benefit, I'll always have the satisfaction of doing something nobody else ever did."

* * *

There was never any promise of a purse in Fort Worth. He had lied about that.

He felt like it would help people understand why he was doing something abnormal, because that question—why?—drives us all, and even those of us who aren't walking backward need a satisfying answer. Plennie perfected his response later in life, developing a quip that made no sense and was perfectly understandable.

"With the whole world going backwards," he would say, "maybe the only way to see it was to turn around."

He arrived in Fort Worth on October 24, 1932, after one year, six months, nine days, four hours, and twelve minutes. He'd backpedaled more than five thousand miles.

A. C. Farmer, the first man to sign his book, was still at the Western Union.

"That's amazing," Farmer said when he saw Plennie.

He walked down to the chamber of commerce and there sat Charles Cotten, still on the job, surprised to see Plennie back, ashamed that he had nothing to offer.

"We have tried every which way to figure out some means of rewarding you," Cotten said, "but I am sorry to say there is nothing we can do."

Plennie understood. Besides, what recourse did he have?

He was glad to finish, glad to be back in Texas. He had four dollar bills in his pocket, a poor man's fortune. He could have, that very month, on the terrible downhill slope of what had been the most expensive orgy in history, bought four healthy sheep.

Mathematically, he had started with nothing, and therefore had nothing to lose, and he had traveled for more than a year and a half through nine countries, slept in nice hotels, met interesting people, and never missed a meal. And he had made four dollars.

You could do worse.

EPILOGUE

My first guest, now listen to this. His name is Plennie Wingo. P-L-E-N-N-I-E W-I-N-G-O," Johnny Carson said. It was late July of 1976, on a television program called *The Tonight Show Starring Johnny Carson*. "And Mr. Wingo once set a record for walking across the United States, Europe, and part of Asia. Now, the remarkable thing about it was that it was an eight-thousand-mile trek. He did it walking backwards. That's true."

There was mild giggling. Someone in the audience whistled.

"Now, that happened forty-five years ago, and Plennie, I understand, is now eighty-one years of age, and is in training to walk across the United States, backwards," Carson said. "I thought you might like to meet this man, and find out why. Would you please welcome, Plennie Wingo."

An elderly Plennie walked backward onto the stage a little awkwardly, toward the audience first, then swerving back toward Carson, who stood to greet him. Plennie was wearing a sharp crimson suit and a spotless felt cowboy hat. On his face he wore glasses with small round mirrors protruding from the brackets. He was eighty-one years old and still trying to squeeze money out of his stunt.

"Get a close-up of that, Bob, the glasses here," Carson said. "He's got little rearview mirrors on each, on each . . . Well, Plennie, we've talked about you a lot this week."

"Have you?" Plennie smiled.

"Yeah, I find it fascinating," Carson said. "Now that looks easy to do, walking backwards. Is it easy to do?"

"Well, it wasn't to start with," Plennie said. "It wouldn't be easy to anyone who hasn't practiced it."

"Yeah?" Carson was feeling his guest out, searching for comfort and timing in the exchange. "Why...When did you get this idea? It was forty-five years ago?"

"Yes, forty-five years ago," Plennie said.

* * *

Where does a man pick up when his journey ends?

Plennie was not welcome at home in Abilene. The divorce was not just a judgment but a lifestyle. So he moved to Archer City, Texas, and took a job as cook at a little café, the old routine. Within a few years, Vivian joined him and went to work there too, which seemed natural because as a baby her father would put her to sleep in a bassinet under the counter of his own café in Abilene. In the late 1930s, Della moved to Archer City as well, and the patches on their relationship held pretty good. They even got remarried.

Somewhere around that time the family developed a new nickname for Plennie. They began calling him Blackie, and his descendants would come to understand that it was a reference to him being the wayward black sheep among his siblings. He was the unusual one, prone to take strong drink, and there were persistent rumors about gambling jags and financial problems. But Texans tend to mind their own business, and Plennie was grown enough to make his own bad decisions.

Plennie and Della opened another café soon after, at Kadane Corner, west of Wichita Falls. But in 1941, just before world war broke out again, the patches wore thin and they divorced again and abandoned their café and all its promise.

That's when Plennie disappeared. No one heard from him for several years, which was odd because theirs was a family of correspondents, and they routinely circulated a progressive letter, passing updates from one household to the next by the US Mail.

Plennie resurfaced in the fall of 1943, when his sister's doorbell rang in Arcadia, California. "I answered the door and to my amazement Blackie was standing on our doorstep, looking for all the world as though he sure needed love from our family," wrote his sister, Dee Wingo Miles, much later. "He worked and stayed in Los Angeles for several months and visited us often."

In the fall of 1945, he returned to Texas and went to work in another café, this one in a little town called Olney, and it was there he fell in love with a young, plump waitress. The waitress would often repeat their love story, how Plennie had invited her outside the café one night to behold the beauty of a rare star hovering so near to the Texas moon, surrounded by some kind of supernatural circle. The newspaper reported the next day that it wasn't a star, but Venus, and it was sixteen million miles from the moon, as it was every twenty-two months. Nonetheless, after a short romance, three days after Valentine's Day in 1946, Plennie Wingo, who was fifty-one, married Juanita Billingsley, who was just eighteen and nearly twice his size.

The two then began to bounce around the country, finding employment periodically in the hospitality business. They had more ups and downs than the average couple, but they were determined to make it. They took want ads in newspapers, declaring they were a husband-wife kitchen team, willing to travel. They took over a concession stand in California. They worked and lived as house parents at the Kappa Sigma fraternity at UCLA until 1959, when a young pledge choked on a piece of raw liver during a hazing ritual and the fraternity was shut down. They then ran the kitchen at a boys' ranch in the Santa Susana Mountains near San Fernando, California. They helped open three casino restaurants in Las Vegas.

Plennie Wingo and his wife, Juanita Billingsley Wingo, in Salt Lake City, Utah. Undated. (Courtesy of Pat Lefors Dawson)

Juanita and Plennie Wingo at the Nugget, a concession stand they operated in Southern California. Undated. (Courtesy of Pat Lefors Dawson)

Through it all, for decades, Plennie searched for ways to profit off his exploits of 1931 and 1932. He often carried his old journal with the newspaper clippings and autographs to show those who had not seen it, and he routinely brought his adventure up in conversation, to such a degree that it became an annoyance, something to be endured by those who loved him.

Plennie Wingo working on his manuscript at home in 1962. Around the World Backwards *was published in 1966. (Courtesy of Pat Lefors Dawson)*

Much of the time Plennie dealt silently with the burden of having never completed a book. It has been said that there are but two kinds of plots in great literature: a man leaves home, and a man returns. He had done both, backward. But writing a readable manuscript proved a more formidable challenge than the backwalking. He would at times sit at a typewriter with his coffee nearby and hunt and peck until he tired. Juanita captured a photograph of him writing once, and he bears the dull look of an armadillo caught in headlights. "Blackie Wingo 1962," she wrote in blue pen along the edge of the frame. "Write his Book 1962."

By 1966, he had finished a manuscript and somehow managed to get *Around the World Backwards* published by a house called Carlton Press in New York. The book was clothbound and more than two hundred pages, with photos and chapter titles such as "I Startle a Mule" and "I Walk Backward on a Skyscraper." Those who loved him overlooked the mistakes. Few outside of his family bought copies, and there is no evidence he made any profit to speak of. What is known is that he was soon searching for another publisher.

* * *

Johnny Carson: "What gave you the idea to walk backwards around Europe?"

Plennie Wingo: "Well..."

Carson: "Or around any place?"

Plennie: "At that time, my daughter was hosting a party for her classmates in high school, and we lived in a rather nice house. It used to be a banker's home. And we had a big front room and a fireplace, and the kids was playing in the game room, so they came in to the, three or four boys came into the in the room where I was, the front room, and I was reading the paper, and they said...they got to talking about the hard times. It was hard times. One boy said, 'I'd like to do some kind of a stunt. Maybe make a lot of, get a lot of publicity and make a lot of money.' He said, 'You know, everything's been done.' He says, 'Lindbergh flew across the ocean and every flagpole was full of sitters.'"

Carson: "Yeah. People won't remember that. They used to sit on flagpoles for months."

Plennie: "Then he says, 'There's that fellow that pushed the peanut up Pikes Peak with his nose, and...'"

Carson: "So there wasn't much left?"

Plennie: "They just said, 'Well, everything's been done, I guess.' I laid my paper down and I said—I didn't know I was going to say what I did—I said, 'Well, boys, everything hasn't been done.' They challenged me to tell them what it was. I said, 'Well, I don't believe I've ever seen anybody walk around the world backwards.'"

Carson: "Those were simpler days."

* * *

In June of 1932, a US cavalry division with naked sabers charged the twenty thousand war veterans and their families camped on the Anacostia flats, across the Potomac from Congress. Convinced the veterans demanding their bonus pay were communists, General Douglas MacArthur violated the president's orders and sent troops into the encampment with tear gas. Two babies were killed and a seven-year-old boy was bayoneted through the leg while trying to save his pet rabbit. It was a vicious attack by the American military on American citizens.

Bonnie Parker and Clyde Barrow were murdered in a police ambush in Bienville Parish, Louisiana, in May 1934. He was twenty-five, she was twenty-three. Some twenty thousand people showed up at her funeral. He was buried under a granite marker bearing a four-word epitaph he had selected: GONE BUT NOT FORGOTTEN.

After his conviction for tax fraud in 1931, Al Capone served eight years in prison and then all but retired, shunning the spotlight that had followed him for a decade. He was living in a mansion in Florida when he died from cardiac arrest in 1947.

With two *TIME* magazine covers under his belt, Jimmy Walker resigned as mayor of New York in September 1932, as the walls of scandal were closing in. He lay low in Europe until criminal charges against him evaporated. Then he moved back to America and took over Majestic Records and died of a brain hemorrhage in 1946.

Herbert Hoover lost the presidential election of 1932 in a landslide to New York governor Franklin D. Roosevelt and began to seek historical vindication, which, to a certain degree he would find, though his legacy would never recover from the Depression.

Oklahoma governor Alfalfa Bill Murray, who for a brief moment held the 1932 Democratic presidential nomination, retired in 1935 to a small farm with no electricity or running water. By then his mental and physical health were fading and he would never hold public office again. He hung around the capital during his son's term as governor in the 1950s, trying to sell copies of his memoirs, but few people recognized the skinny, bent old man carrying a bag of books, as one historian noted. At the time of his death in 1956, he was a shambling, unkempt figure occupying a dingy room in Tishomingo, sharing a bathroom down a long hallway with the same poor Okies he had once tried to help.

The Indians refused to vanish, despite attempts to brainwash tens of thousands of Indian children in boot-camp boarding schools in the first decades of the twentieth century, and despite the continuing theft of land they'd been promised. By the time Plennie finished his walk, some 90 million acres of the original 138 million acres protected for Indians by treaties was held in white hands. The pace of theft was such that in three generations the tribes would be landless. The Indian Reorganization Act of 1934 stopped the seizing of "surplus" land, and Indians eventually gained the right to sue the federal government for past wrongs. Though the wrongs would continue as corporations and the federal government violated their sacred grounds in efforts to squeeze money from the earth, Indians also got the right to build casinos on their land, and several of the Oklahoma towns through which Plennie walked were revived economically by slot machines and table games. Seventy-three years after Plennie crossed the toll bridge over the Red River, the Chickasaw Nation, which had been cheated in the War Between the States, would open the WinStar Casino, and it would quickly grow to become the largest in the country. It would take from white Oklahomans and Texans many millions of dollars.

Not far away, at the site of the Muncey-Jamison massacre in Plano, Texas, the state erected a marker where the settlers had been "savagely slain" during the final Indian raid in the county. Now the property is a suburb that hosts a hot-air balloon festival and treetop zip lines, and the wooden piling marking the spot of the murder was used by a homeowner, unaware of its significance, in the building of a playhouse for his children.

* * *

Carson: "Let's go walk. I want to see, I want to see that. Can you come over here, Plennie, and show us the walk you use? What happens when you are on a highway and people pass by? Don't they ever stop and wonder what you are doing?"

Plennie: "Oh, yes, they do. That's where I'm supporting myself. People stopping and see what I'm doing and buy a postcard."

Carson: "Oh, you sell them a little postcard to kind of sponsor the walk?"

Plennie: "Yeah. Supporting myself by selling postcards."

Carson: "Oh, I'll take one. How much are they? See, he got his first card already."

Plennie: "That's a dollar."

Carson: "Okay, I'll take one. I want to be the first sponsor of the trip, Plennie."

Plennie: "Well, thank you. And this here is the kind of pictures I sold when I was walking across the United States and Europe for twenty-five cents. But that was harder to dig up than a dollar is now."

* * *

In March 1933, Franklin D. Roosevelt stood at the threshold of the greatest opportunity any new American peacetime president had faced. "He will be thought of as something of a miracle worker," the *New York Times* prophetically editorialized on the morning of his inauguration. The first thing he did was turn left, then harder still.

He employed in his first one hundred days in office a philosophy of try it and see if it works. On the heels of fearing fear itself, Roosevelt focused on conservation of national land, developing public power, putting people to work and paying them for it, and protecting the money they were able to save. And for the first time, the federal government got into the business of caring for the poor, elderly, and ill, laying the groundwork for Social Security, unemployment programs, and government health care. Beyond that, systems were put in place to regulate business, protect workers' rights, and establish a minimum wage.

The Depression seemed to validate the claims that scores of intellectuals had made over the years, that an unregulated economy built on greedy competition between egotistical men destroyed healthy society. But the arguments about freedom and regulation, individualism and concentration would persist.

In any event, by December 1933, Americans could raise a glass to the hope for their new future because Prohibition was dead and they were free to enjoy a cocktail again.

* * *

Carson: "If you've just joined us, the gentleman sitting to my right is Plennie Wingo and he's going to do something you won't believe. We had a gentleman last week who did weird things. He balanced things on his nose, and you are going to walk from San Francisco backwards to the Santa Monica Pier. When do you start?"

Plennie: "Last day of this month. Ten o'clock in the morning."

Carson: "Do you wear any particular type of gear?"

Plennie: "I'll go just like I am dressed now."

Carson: "Suit and tie?"

Plennie: "Yeah."

Carson: "You really dress up, don't you?"

Plennie: "Yes I do."

* * *

Just after 6 a.m. on June 18, 1942, a German submarine fired torpedoes and hit a ship called the *Seattle Spirit* on the port side, flooding it and killing one officer. Fifty-one survivors—crewmen and passengers—were rescued. One sailor died of shock and exposure after jumping into the water. The *Seattle Spirit* sank at ten-thirty that evening.

Adolf Hitler rose swiftly and in March of 1936, in violation of treaties, ordered German soldiers into Rhineland, the demilitarized buffer zone between Germany and France. Nobody lifted a finger. America had entered a period of pacifism and isolationism. As Hitler advanced abuses and aggression, much of America sat still. Macho Ernest Hemingway thought we should stay home. The poet E. E. Cummings wrote that "death's clever enormous voice" hides in "a fragility of poppies." Even Colonel Lindbergh emerged as an isolationist star. After lying low in Europe for a few years to escape the intrusive press and to deal with the grief and trauma of his son's death, Lindbergh emerged in support of the Nazis as a bulwark against communism. He even accepted the Service Cross of the German Eagle at a government dinner in Berlin and criticized Jews in the press and government, blaming them if war came.

Of course, war came. Roosevelt rejected Lindbergh's attempt to join the army after the Japanese bombed Pearl Harbor. "If I die tomorrow," the president told his advisor, "remember Lindbergh is a Nazi." The rejection stayed with Lindbergh, but when he died in Hawaii in 1974, President Gerald Ford overlooked his sins and said the courage of his Atlantic flight would never be forgotten and he would be remembered as one of America's all-time great heroes.

Adolf Hitler brought no small amount of ruination to his homeland. The cities Plennie visited in 1931 were obliterated. The war's first firestorm came to Hamburg on June 24, 1943, and her people were turned to ash. American and British planes dropped 8,344 tons of explosives on 580 factories, and 50,000 people were killed. Beautiful Dresden got 2,660 tons and lost between 40,000 and 50,000 people. Hitler was buried around April of 1945 in the rubble of his ambition.

* * *

Carson: "What would you do if you were out there walking all the way from San Francisco, and some other guy came by you going the other way? You think that could be a possibility?"

Plennie: "You mean walking backwards?"

Carson: "Yeah. Now that you've announced you're going to do this, you might have people walking up..."

Plennie: "I might be meeting a lot of them."

* * *

Plennie Wingo as depicted in the newspaper strip Ripley's
Believe It or Not! *(Courtesy of Pat Lefors Dawson)*

Plennie's stunt was memorialized in the syndicated newspaper strip *Ripley's Believe It Or Not!* His name was added to the *Guinness Book of World Records* for the longest backward walk at 8,000 miles. An assortment of backward records have been set since, including the largest backward walk (1,107 participants), longest distance cycling backward on a unicycle (68 miles), and fastest time to walk twenty meters with feet facing backward (19.59 seconds).

In the mid-1980s, a Bemidji, Minnesota, man named Marvin Staples set out to claim the backward distance record. "This is supposed to be a free country and I'm just doing what I want to do," he told a reporter, having logged 300 miles on a pedometer. "I got tired of people telling me, 'You have to do things this way.' I want to do it my way." No evidence could be found to suggest he got close to the record distance. In May 2003, *The Hindu*, a reputable newspaper in India, chronicled the story of D. Muniyappan, a young man who was trying to break Plennie's record. He walked 11,934 kilometers, or 7,415 miles, just shy of Plennie's mark. But he, too, faded from the public record.

Plennie's record for distance remains.

* * *

Carson: "I tell you, you're a remarkable man. Eighty-one years old. To even attempt something like this. But it keeps you young. Keeps you in good spirits."

Plennie: "That's what I'm doing it for. Longevity."

* * *

He was looking for a sponsor, still, forty-five years later. The *Ripley's Believe It Or Not!* Museum in San Francisco had called a few months before to inquire as to whether Plennie had any relatives who might be capable of making a 400-mile backward walk across California to celebrate America's 200th birthday, and to promote the museum to remarkable feats. Plennie offered himself up, but he never heard back, not until after he talked his way onto *The Tonight Show*, which paid him $372 for his appearance, the most money he had made in forty-five years of trying.

He took the museum's $500 and proudly pinned a *Ripley's* button on his lapel and started backward. Juanita met him along the way with clean clothes and sandwiches. He sold postcards for a dollar. He spent the night with a preacher and his wife, the president of a soup company, and with a hippie in the back of a

Volkswagen van, the symbolic Americana trifecta of religion, business, and resistance.

Plennie Wingo walked 400 miles backward across California in 1976 and ended at Ripley's Believe It or Not! *museum. (Courtesy of Pat Lefors Dawson)*

Several newspaper stories publicized his trek, and he arrived at the Santa Monica Pier to find that the museum had brought out a life-size wax version of the backward-walking champion. There, too, was Leena Deeter Bare, who could write backward and upside down with both hands simultaneously, and George Dillman, who could break 1,200 pounds of ice with a karate chop, and Allen Lauer, who, when he was three, was the world's youngest motorcycle rider. Vivian flew in from Texas, along with some other family members. They had a nice time. Plennie was proud again.

Time slipped by. Della died in 1978. Vivian, too, a few months later, by her own hand, according to family.

Plennie made money and lost money, and was regarded by friends as a lovable eccentric. He found a new publisher, Eakin Press of Austin, Texas, and launched his own tour when his book, essentially the same as the first with a different cover, was released in 1982. He put promotional stickers on his brown camper van and drove around Texas, visiting newspapers that had long been friendly to him. When a sister died in 1988, Plennie attended her services at the church. As soon as the funeral wrapped up, he set up a card table to sell his books.

In his last public effort to monetize the walk, Plennie contacted a reporter for the Associated Press in August 1991. He was ninety-six years old, living in Wichita Falls, Texas, and his medical bills were mounting. He happened to be broke. He wanted to leave something behind to help Juanita, who had loved him and stuck with him for forty-five years.

"I've been wondering how I could ever get any money out of walking backwards around the world," he told the reporter.

He said he expected to live just three or four more years. Not because he felt bad, but because he had recently come to face the brave and simple truth that death catches up to every man, even if he tries to rewind. He had reached his peak early, in the first act of life, and spent much of the rest of his time trying to capitalize on his climactic achievement, hoping to find the financial vein with a thousand needle pricks. What had been his crowning moment was but an annoying triviality to others, and now he could see nothing before him that he wished to accomplish and little behind that he wanted to recall. He could only hope that his last gasp of salesmanship would afford him a few more painless sunsets.

"I would be willing to sell the rights to use my feet after I die," he told the reporter soberly, "to anyone that would want them."

The story ran in newspapers across the country, under playful headlines. Plennie L. Wingo was again an oddity, even as the end appeared in his little mirrors. The man who walked backward was selling his feet to afford to live. There were no takers.

In the end, time was a forward march. He was glad he had his book, which gave him a sustaining sense of satisfaction. He was his story, a thread in the tapestry of his era, and his book, at least, would survive in the dusty bins of a handful of Texas libraries.

He died at home on October 2, 1993, and they buried him outside Wichita Falls, a stone's throw from a two-lane Texas highway that sliced through the smoke bush and buffalo grass and mesquite trees, and ran south through Archer City and Olney, and down toward Abilene.

Plennie Wingo in August 1965. (Courtesy of Pat Lefors Dawson)

ACKNOWLEDGMENTS

I'd like to thank the following friends for their help in shaping this book through conversation, interpretation, and inspiration: Michael Kruse, Thomas Lake, Tony Rehagen, David von Drehle, Tom Junod, Justin Heckert, Bill Duryea, Lane DeGregory, Laura Reiley, Leonora LaPeter, Charles McNair, Brooke Jarvis, Bronwen Dickey, Michael Hall, Corey Johnson, Chris Jones, Matthew Shaer, Josh Sharpe, Amy Wallace, Denise Wills, Elizabeth Lake, John Lake, Robert Lake, Liddy Lake, Hank Stuever, Mark Johnson, Kim Cross, Mike Wilson, Dieter Miller, Kelley and Tom French, Glenn Smith, Kathryn Miles, Brian Mockenhaupt, Michael Graff, Michael Mooney, Eva Holland, Tommy Tomlinson, Alix Felsing, Scott Lambert, Demian Miller, Brendan Meyer, Cary Aspinwall, Charlie Scudder, and especially Lorraine Monteagut.

I'm grateful to the Wingo family, specifically Pat Lefors Dawson, who preserved important pieces of the past and opened her home to a complete stranger.

Tremendous thanks to Tracy Behar and Ian Straus at Little, Brown, and to my agent, Jane Dystel, the best there is.

As always, sincere thanks to my mother, Donna, who patiently listens, and to my children, my faithful critics and companions, Asher, Morissey, and Bey.

BIBLIOGRAPHY

Adams, James T. *The Epic of America*. New York: Little, Brown, 1931.

Adonis, Joe, and Jim Jones. *American Villains*, Vol. 1. Ipswich, MA: Salem Press, Inc., 2008.

Agee, James, and Walker Evans. *Let Us Now Praise Famous Men*. Boston: Houghton Mifflin Company, 1988.

Allen, Frederick L. *Only Yesterday: An Informal History of the 1920's*. New York: Harper & Row, 1931.

Allen, Henry. *What It Felt Like: Living in the American Century*. New York: Pantheon Books, 2000.

Ariely, Dan. *The Upside of Irrationality: The Unexpected Benefits of Defying Logic at Work and at Home*. New York: Harper, 2011.

Baron, Robert C., and Samuel Scinta. *20th Century America: Key Events in History*. Golden, CO: Fulcrum, 1996.

Burg, David F. *The Great Depression: An Eyewitness History*. New York: Facts On File, 1996.

Cullen, Jim. *The American Dream: A Short History of an Idea That Shaped a Nation*. New York: Oxford University Press, 2004.

Custer, George A. *My Life on the Plains or, Personal Experiences with Indians*. Norman: University of Oklahoma Press, 1962.

Dorman, Robert L. *It Happened in Oklahoma: Remarkable Events That Shaped History*. Guilford, CT: Globe Pequot Press, 2006.

Douglas, William A. S. *Racketeers of Europe: A Political Travelogue*. Mechanicsburg, PA: Stackpole Books, 2013.

Egan, Timothy. *The Worst Hard Time: The Untold Story of Those Who Survived the Great American Dust Bowl*. New York: Houghton Mifflin Co., 2006.

Eichengreen, Barry J. *Hall of Mirrors: The Great Depression, the Great Recession, and the Uses-and Misuses-of History*. New York: Oxford University Press, 2016.

Ellis, Edward R. *Diary of the Century: Tales from America's Greatest Diarist*. New York: Kodansha, 1995.

Evans, Harold, et al. *The American Century*. New York: Knopf, 1998.

Ferber, Edna. *Cimarron*. New York: Grosset and Dunlap, 1929.

Fulton, Robert E. *One Man Caravan*. Center Conway, NH: White Horse Press, 1996.

Galbraith, John K., and James K. Galbraith. *The Great Crash 1929*. New York: Houghton Mifflin Harcourt Publishing Company, 2009.

Gladwell, Malcolm. *Outliers: The Story of Success*. Little, Brown and Company, 2008.

Green, Harvey. *The Uncertainty of Everyday Life, 1915–1945*. Fayetteville, AR: University of Arkansas Press, 2000.

Greene, Graham. *Stamboul Train*. London: Penguin, 1963.

Hall, Thomas E., and J. David Ferguson. *The Great Depression: An International Disaster of Perverse Economic Policies*. Ann Arbor: University of Michigan Press, 2001.

Henry, Lyell D. *The Jefferson Highway: Blazing the Way from Winnipeg to New Orleans*. Iowa City: University of Iowa Press, 2016.

Himsl, Sharon M. *1920–1940: The Twentieth Century*. New York: Greenhaven Press, 2004.

Jeansonne, Glen, and David Luhrssen. *Herbert Hoover: A Life*. New York: New American Library, 2016.

Kennedy, David M. *Freedom from Fear: The American People in Depression and War, 1929–1945*. New York: Oxford University Press, 1999.

Kennedy, William. *An Albany Trio: Three Novels from the Albany Cycle*. New York: Penguin Books, 1996.

Koch, Michael. *The Kimes Gang*. Bloomington, IN: AuthorHouse, 2005.

Large, David C. *Between Two Fires: Europe's Path in the 1930s*. Norton, 1991.

Lewis, Sinclair. *Babbitt*. New York: Penguin Classics, 2012.

Lyman, Robert H. *The World Almanac and Book of Facts for 1931*. New York: The New York World, 1931.

Lyman, Robert H. *The World Almanac and Book of Facts for 1932*. New York: New York World-Telegram, 1932.

Mappen, Marc. *Prohibition Gangsters: The Rise and Fall of a Bad Generation*. New Brunswick, NJ: Rutgers University Press, 2017.

McElvaine, Robert S. *The Great Depression: America, 1929–1941*. New York: Three Rivers Press, 1993.

Munching, Philip Van. *Beer Blast: The Inside Story of the Brewing Industry's Bizarre Battles for Your Money*. Collingdale, PA: Diane Publishing Company, 1997.

Plavchan, Ronald J. *A History of Anheuser-Busch, 1852–1933*. New York: Arno Press, 1976.

Raper, Arthur F. *The Tragedy of Lynching*. New York: New American Library, 1969.

Steinbeck, John. *Cannery Row*. New York: Bantam Books, 1954.

Steinbeck, John. *The Grapes of Wrath*. New York: Viking Press, 1939.

Steinbeck, John. *The Pearl*. New York: Bantam Books, 1956.

Volker, Ulrich, and Jefferson Chase. *Hitler: Ascent, 1889–1939*. New York: Knopf, 2016.

Williams, Rusty. *Red River Bridge War*. College Station: Texas A&M University Press, 2016.

Wingo, Plennie L. *Around the World Backwards*. Austin, TX: Eakin Press, 1982.

INDEX

Note: Italic page numbers refer to illustrations.

ABOUT THE AUTHOR

BEN MONTGOMERY is a former reporter for the *Tampa Bay Times* and founder of the narrative journalism website Gangrey.com. In 2010, he was a finalist for the Pulitzer Prize in local reporting and won the Dart Award and Casey Medal for a series called "For Their Own Good," about abuse at Florida's oldest reform school. Montgomery lives in Tampa with his three children. He is the author of *Grandma Gatewood's Walk*.